# Auroville

*"A map of the world that does not include Utopia is not worth even glancing at, for it leaves out the one country at which Humanity is always landing. And when Humanity lands there, it looks out, and seeing a better country, sets sail. Progress is the realisation of Utopias."*

**Oscar Wilde** in *"The Soul of Man under Socialism"*
Penguin London 1954

# Auroville

*Its Struggle in the Quest for a Spiritual Utopia*

*A New Perspective*

Joseph Vrinte

MLBD PUBLICATIONS

**Motilal Banarsidass Publications**

**MOTILAL BANARSIDASS**
**PUBLICATIONS**
4741/23, Ansari Road, Daryaganj, New Delhi - 110002 (India)
Email: mlbd@mlbd.com | sales@mlbd.com
exports@mlbd.com | publications@mlbd.com
Website: www.mlbd.com



**Auroville**
***by***
**Joseph Vrinte**

*First Edition Published in 2025*



Published in India by Motilal Banarsidass Publications

ISBN : 978-93-49939-94-3 (HB)

Printed and bound in India

## Dedicated

*To all the achievements and failures of those pioneers, who dedicated their lives to building Auroville from its inauguration onward with unconditional faith in Mother's Dream, they remain the motivating force to investigate Auroville's present struggles on its journey toward a new man, a new society, and a new city.*

# PREFACE

This book aims to provide, as much as possible, a deeper understanding and a broader perspective on complex issues related to the current crisis through an objective analysis from a sympathetic viewpoint without hiding unwelcome evidence that contradicts the prevailing turmoil in Auroville. The questions postulated in this work are less derived from a preoccupation with a speculative theory, but they are more related to the chaotic reality of Auroville's community at present. These questions are, therefore, as much as possible, pertaining to facts rather than the author's one-sided interpretations of events. He endeavours to present these questions in an accessible way without offering clear-cut answers.

Mother's task is supposed to be difficult, and these difficulties need to be discussed candidly to make the task less complicated. The author aims to encourage the reader to reflect upon the development of various social and psycho-spiritual issues in the community's social organisation. His concern resists proof, as these questions offer only suggestive evidence to be examined; they are not meant to guide him in bringing his ideas to the forefront but rather to be investigated and open to new insights. As a participant-observer practitioner in the Auroville experiment, this study aims to provide an analytical reflection on the project's actualised potentialities, as well as the various movements that fell short of its goals.

Questions, as elaborated in this work, are not to be solved as an intellectual puzzle where the citizens remain mere onlookers; they need to be approached with a culture of dialogue that enables each of them to respect the engagement of the views of all the citizens to build consensus in planning and creating a spiritual society. To avoid a controversy does not end the controversy; avoiding new knowledge means submission to some fixed belief, where the devotee lacks the courage to examine new lights.

The author tries to be as honest as possible. However, honesty and pleasing people do not always go together. The community is divided into uncontrolled bubbles of the citizens' truths, habits, and beliefs. Are the various opposing groups destroying the spark of engagement in sincere critical thinking when they do not stimulate the art of debate and dialogue? Are responsible Auroville leaders avoiding matters related to the difficulties encountered by citizens on their journey as co-travellers, building a bridge between the personal and collective structures for a new world?

The author does not endeavour to disguise complicated and ticklish issues in a beautiful style; his critical, constructive questions are related to practical interests and foster a meaningful dialogue among citizens. It is not his intention to make unfavourable comments about Mother's spiritual insights; he only aims to offer a critical, loyal evaluation as a window frame to those who seek more clarity without remaining closed in their cocoon.

In his questions regarding Mother's vision and other spiritual issues associated with her establishment of Auroville as a new city of the future, he attempts to raise awareness about various obstacles and pitfalls in the practice of Integral Yoga, as well as the possibility of its disastrous consequences for its practitioners. Some of these questions may lead to controversy within the community when related to the understanding of the challenges regarding the process of psychic transformation during and after the psychic experiment. He tries to understand the gap between the idealism of Auroville's different groups of perceptions related to the development of the future city and the so-called justification of the reality of the government's outside intervention; the latter may achieve their goal within a short time without necessary introspection or course direction and critique, but such approach may contradict the long-time impacts of Mother's stated spiritual ideals in promoting a new consciousness in a new society for the world. The author provides an analysis of the positive and negative characteristics associated with the concept of growth and progress within the Auroville project. Negative characteristics will not be comprehended if they are merely seen as unavoidable aspects of the products, the flip side of growth and progress. He aims to shed light on various dimensions of the current situation within the Auroville community, employing a blend of objective and subjective approaches through philosophical, psychological, and social analysis, complemented by a critical evaluation.

To avoid distortions, this evaluation needs to be placed in perspective regarding his other writings, and this repetition of some of the same ideas in a different context is in itself advantageous for the reader, as it offers a better understanding of the complexity of Auroville's present crisis. He aims to develop an understanding of the root causes of the present crisis, the first step toward enabling the citizens to communicate with each other. Hopefully, this book will contribute to the growing interest in Auroville's current chaotic situation.

Although the crisis is unavoidably complex, the author has attempted to make this work accessible to all those interested in more in-depth research and a different perspective on the crisis, thereby exposing and refuting false dilemmas.

**Auroville June 2025**

Email; josephvrinte@yahoo.co.in
Web-side josephvrinte.org

# CONTENTS

## *CHAPTER ONE*

# UTOPIA

The longing for a paradise on earth is as old as humanity. Throughout the ages, a long series of Utopians and idealists tried to realise this need. It isn't easy to define the utopian venture precisely. Still, the central theme broadly centres on an activity that seems to make the world a better place in a world that needs necessary improvement. The term comes from the Greek 'eu-topos', meaning good place and 'ou-topos', meaning no place. This different or new world map encourages our imagination regarding progress and prosperity. Its concept is attributed to Sir Thomas More (1478-535), who described Utopia as an ideal, perfect place. At the core of utopian ventures lies the realisation of enhancing human potential through collective ownership, residence in communal property, and work for the community. The idea of utopia existed long before Thomas More. More only invented the word utopia, and later, new words were added to describe the different types of utopias.

Changes in utopia after Thomas More are linked to the evolving phases or stages of modernity and post-modernity. In More's Utopia, all natural needs are satisfied, and there is no need to increase the members' wealth; for them, a good life implies the cultivation of mind and spirit. After Thomas More, science was introduced to Utopia, and although it sought to harness the resources of modern science and technology, science itself was never Utopia's ultimate goal. The members used science to serve some ethical or social ideal. However, science contradicted the finality of utopian perfection, which was constantly rejected by the aimless march of science. The scientific utopia gave rise to Huxley's and Orwell's dystopias, in which scientific research in the new world is strictly controlled.

Utopia addresses the central dilemmas of complex modern society, embodying the conflicting pulls of contradictory needs for order and freedom, while the utopian members endeavour to overcome these contradictions. Rather than offering solutions or ready-made answers, utopias function more as guideposts that inspire citizens to change themselves and society.

Utopians have a long history, dating back to Plato's "Republic", where he describes the first Western utopian system. All utopians share the belief that an ideal society exists, and that humanity is somehow meant to live in utopia. The basic premise of utopianism assumes that the present organisation of the social system needs a total revision. Utopians do not endeavour to root out the shortcomings of society one by one; they propose a complete radical overhaul and universal reform to remove the suffering of humanity as a whole. In their utopian vision, the pioneers interpreted their utopian venture as a referendum on human nature; are the various aspects of their character inherent, such as innate goodness, or are they the result of a disorganised society where man is perfectible through education, experience, culture, morality, etc.? Utopianism is always born in discontent regarding the current state of affairs in society, but it also assumes humanity to be a species of optimism where man, in an ideal reinventing society, may be able to remake the world into a paradise through human ingenuity by building a working prototype of a perfect society.

Only in America there are thousands of utopian communities whose citizens endeavour to create heaven on earth in a new world through a shared effort in a community. Utopians share a common faith in the goodness of human nature and the possibility of a more perfect individual and society. The member's lifelong commitment not only focuses on collective sharing, but their lives are also based on sacrifice, labour, and surrender to the uncertain adventure of creating a new, truly caring society —a real heaven or earth, though the various utopias may differ regarding their vision of heaven. Utopia, as an urgent and meaningful activity, projects human beings both back into the past and forward into the future. Although there is a need for individuals to subordinate their desires and goals for the overall good of the community, these goals and desires should not be neglected but respected. However, Utopia as a vision of an ideal future can be rather hostile to human individuality, and in the regulation of a model state, its social experiments in reform may be accompanied by an authoritarian leadership that builds its utopia on abstract conceptions.

Writing about utopia in all its manifestations is a complex and often contradictory endeavour. Utopia is a process aiming towards transformation, and without a fixed blueprint for a new society, it employs an open-ended and self-critical approach, along with programmatic realisation, as necessary steps toward an effective and enduring transformed utopian society. The utopian impulse for a better life and a more peaceful society is not restricted to Western culture; its realisation is universal in character. People from Plato's "Republic" and Thomas More's "Utopia" to the recent projects of Auroville have been aiming toward the realisation of an ideal alternative society without indulging in wishful thinking. In moments of crisis, when dominant ideologies are no longer able to answer the needs of the day, people emphasise that a better ideal society could be realised as an experiment in a real-life utopian community. Most utopias pose questions and suggest actions to improve the present situation; they envision a transformed everyday life, encompassing concerns about economic, political, social, cultural, religious, and spiritual matters.

## What is Utopia

This introduction about utopia is far from comprehensive in its coverage, but to investigate the present-day difficulties in Auroville as a spiritual utopia, it may be helpful to give a limited exploration of the concept of utopia in general. It attempts to offer some of the utopia's different characteristics and point out some of the various types of utopias that propose future change.

Man, in his imaginative description of social evolution, believes in a utopia as a complete future model state where all citizens will be equal, free, good, cultured, and affluent. However, legitimate in fairy tales, these assumptions are out of place as the destined outcome of a natural evolution of society. Any march in the renovation of society is a change in the character, ideas, aspirations, and feelings of disciplined individuals who create that society, who can discriminate the possible and practicable from the impossible.

It isn't easy to give a single definition that captures the essence of the utopian tradition. It is often described in terms of equality, harmony, peace, freedom, and paradise, and is linked to brotherhood, communal work, and social progress. The word "utopia" often carries a negative connotation, associated with impractical dreams or a dictatorial leader who seeks to control a utopian community in pursuit of his vision of perfection. However, utopia is taken more seriously as a social, cultural, and idealistic tradition that implies high technology, although technological means are no longer taken for granted as the sole means to shape the future. Utopia is often perceived as being unable to achieve the necessary change in a self-determining society, but such an attitude overlooks the thousands of alternative settlements worldwide where people have built and continue to build a better society. All utopian thinking embodies elements of fantasy, aiming for a better life and a better world, which expresses the possibility of developing a more ideal social order and enables its citizens to become better individuals. The word "Utopia" implies an allegedly perfect society, although the concept of perfection varies from person to person and from one society to another. In a genuine utopia, perfection encompasses a radical change in social conditions and is qualitatively different from a non-utopia. Perfection remains an empty word unless it is given specific content. The utopian citizens do not seek changes in some limited realms but seek change everywhere in the basic structure of society, where the welfare of all its citizens is the central concern and not a means of escape from the world, i.e., to make the real world a better place.

In the history of Utopia, Gregory Claes and L. Tower Sargent, in "The Utopian Reader", acknowledge four stages which are based on equality, sociability, and sustainability. Starting with Thomas More's 'Utopia', they move to the 2nd stage during the late 18th century, when Christianity was gradually replaced by a human agency that believed in human perfectibility. Here, utopians are more concerned with promoting citizenship rather than sainthood and salvation. Nevertheless, there is confusion about a perfect society. Utopia relates more to perfectibility as a process of indefinite improvement rather than as an end. The 3rd stage in the late 19th century was characterised by science, technology, and industry, including Marx's anti-capitalist utopian revolution. The fourth historical change began in the late 20th century and early 21st century, when the ultimate victory of capitalism over consumerism and Fukuyama's "end of history" seemed to be overshadowed by an environmental catastrophe. They maintain that, at present, there are political theorists, sociologists, psychologists, philosophers, theologians, and scientists who all have their own definitions of utopia; however, it seems they lack a common grand cause, which confuses the field.

In "The Utopian Reader," they distinguish between utopia as a literary genre and utopia as a general category. They describe Utopia as "a literary genre, utopia refers to works that describe an imaginary society in some detail. Utopian thought is construed more widely. However, it is not restricted to fiction and includes visionary millenarians and apocalyptic as well as constitutional writings united by their willingness to envision a dramatically different form of society as either a social ideal type or its negative inversion. Not all forms of imaginative literature and social and political thought, however, should be called utopian."[1] In utopian literature, they distinguish between two fundamental utopian traditions, "utopias of sensual gratification and utopias of human contrivance. Those traditions represent alternate ways of expressing the utopian impulse—that need to dream of a better life, even when we are reasonably content."[2] "Utopias and the changes they undergo both help bring about and are reflections of a paradigm shift in the way a culture views itself. Sometimes it is possible to identify precisely the role of a utopia or a group of utopias in this process, but all such shifts take place unevenly, and, therefore, different utopias at any time and place may reflect various stages in the paradigm shift. Including reactions against it."[3]

Utopia, according to Lewis Mumfort attempts to actualise a more harmonious, ideal society that has taken a variety of forms ranging from the purely philosophical, religious, spiritual, ecological, social and political to their reconstructive and revolutionary aspects of society, which includes a new set of habits, values, a different net of relationships and institutions, and an alteration of the physical and psychological characteristics of people. It is necessary to distinguish the utopias of intellect, which present a theoretical blueprint for a perfect society, and concrete attempts to actualise utopian social theories through communalistic experiments. Philosophical utopias, in addressing social problems, tend towards solutions through mechanistic plans, which require an authoritarian social structure for enforcing a hierarchical, static society. The reconstructive utopias of the people are transformative in their approach and use a more organic structure to create a new social order, emphasising the process of participants' determination to adopt a new set of habits and values.

Russell Jacobi offers his reader a meaningful distinction between two currents of utopian thought: The blueprint tradition and the iconoclastic tradition. "The blueprint utopian maps out the future in inches and minutes, they have detailed what the future will look like, the blue printers, the largest group- gave precise instructions. [ Thomas More, BF Skinner] ...The iconoclastic utopians declined to give their precise measurements...they were protesters and breakers of images."[4] The future for the iconoclastic utopians could only be approached through hints and reflections rather than through measurements, whereas the blueprint utopians' proposals can be studied, embraced, or rejected.

The blueprint utopians focus on large and distant goals and ideals, they appear rather repressive and show an inevitable authoritarianism. The iconoclastic utopians aim at social reform, and they do not visualise details and renounce images of the future. The future cannot be envisioned, and it needs to be approached with an open heart, passion and spirit. R. Jacobi concludes that the place of utopia for the incredible riches and paralysing poverty in the present world is "for both the prosperous and the destitute, utopian ideas are as dead as doornails. They are irrelevant for the affluent and immaterial for the hungry - and dangerous for many intellectuals, to boot. To the desperate, utopian dreams seem meaningless; to the successful they lack urgency or import; to the thinking classes, they lead to a murderous totalitarianism."[5]

The blueprint utopist, in his holistic approach, aims at modelling the whole of society by a definite plan, but this may end in totalitarian intuition without any forms of democracy. The iconoclastic utopia is utopian in its commitment to a different and better future, but unlike the blueprinters, they abstained from depicting it and were more involved in a mystical longing for the future. The notion of a perfect whole, the perfectibility of mankind, seems incoherent and unattainable for iconoclasts. Those who work with a blueprint for a perfect social structure and have as their goal the creation of a new man and a new world often turn this into a system which is not the true spirit of the community and will collapse. We will likely encounter such a situation later on when the Auroville project becomes involved, where government officials gradually erode the community's spirit. For Jacobi, the history of utopian communities often ends in a history of failure; however, out of defeat emerge challenging ideas and new movements, which radically alter people and perceptions.

E.M Cioran describes his different society as "a society incapable of generating – and of dedicating itself to a utopia is threatened with sclerosis and collapse. Wisdom-fascinated by nothing-recommends an existing, a *given* happiness, which man rejects, and by this very rejection becomes a historical animal, that is, a devotee of *imagined* happiness" [6] He continues in a more pessimistic critical way, "the delirium of the poor is the generator of events, the source of history: a throng of histories who want another world, here and now. It is they who aspire for utopias; it is for them that utopias are written. But *utopia*, let us remember, means *nowhere*. And where would these cities be that evil never touches, in which labour is blessed, and that is never feared? There one is constrained to a felicity of geometric idylls of adjusted ecstasies of a thousand disgusting wonders necessarily offered by the spectacle of a *perfect* world, a fabricated world"[7]

William McCord describes four types of the more important, permanent and universalistic utopian enterprises of our time. First, the secular utopias were "a simpler, more just, more communal life where man's natural goodness will blossom". Second, the religious utopias, where the utopians 'attempt to create a genuinely religious social order that reflects their vision of God's wishes or the supernatural realm". Third, the political utopias who" are impressed with the political, technical and economic possibilities of the modern world, and envisage a more just and abundant life. Fourth, the capitalist utopians who have produced paradises for the rich and who have thought to build societies that they hoped to fulfil their vision of human potential".[8]

McCord defines the quest for utopia as "a search for a more perfect society encompassing many aspects of life. The utopians need not assume the absolute perfection of mankind, but they are not mere reformers aiming at the improvement of just one sector of human behaviour, economic, social, religious, cultural or political. They seek to create institutions that embrace and inform and improve the whole person".[9]

In the "Individual and Utopia", Clint Jones and Cameron Ellis elaborate in various articles, "what an individual does or contributes to a utopian project, but also how the utopian project impacts, changes, or challenges the individual, as it stymies or supports individual growth. Taking seriously the prospects and problematics of the individual and utopia requires that the individual as a spiritual, emotional, mental, physical and social being be opened up to inquiry both prior to and at the intersections of utopia... What is the status of the individual under the social structures and rituals of an already established utopia in preparation for it and in the practice of maintaining it? Could it be otherwise, or is the individual fated to remain a danger? A menace. A threat. A perpetual worry in utopia?"[10]

"The individual and Utopia" focuses on the individual experiences of utopia beyond the limited scope of describing utopia as a purely social, communal, globalised project. Is there a need for the individual to pursue their personal goals at the cost of the overall good of the community? What is required of individuals to sustain a utopian community in a utopian setting? Do they have to abandon selfish personal desires for the good of the utopian community, and does utopian communal fulfilment degrade the fulfilments of individuals who may attempt to change the community from the inside rather than obeying the ideas based on a single leader? Any deviation might shift the balance of the conceptual framework of utopia and, out of fear, impel the inhabitants to pursue and sustain communitarian practices to avoid unexpected consequences.

E.Hamsot offers a meaningful distinction between two distinct literary utopian traditions, classical and modern utopian thought. They both seek to accomplish different purposes; the modern ones attempt to incorporate change into the ideal society, with a congruence between utopia and reality, aiming to alter the social arrangements. They offer a critique of existing culture in the direction of pragmatic thoughts, and their proposed change is closely related to the present problems. Both utopias focus their attention primarily on the process of change, leading society in the direction of their proposed utopia, but only indirectly upon changes in the character of the individuals living in utopia. Classical utopias aim primarily at changing the individual and only secondarily at societal arrangements. For classical utopias, the static, non-developmental character of perfection does not pose a problem because the classical utopian ideal does not directly depend on a particular form of social organisation. Classical utopians, as valuable thought experiments, maintain that the phenomenal world is the expression of a noumenal reality; they are representative of the phenomenal world and point beyond it. Change is viewed as a transition from a potential to an actual, permanent state of being, rather than a temporal occurrence. Plato's "Republic" and More's "Utopia" are categorised as classical utopian thoughts.

The modern utopia, in its idealism, is more concerned with a set of arrangements in the utopian social organisation; its social ideal is not transcendent, and in its call for change, it offers criticism regarding the existing society and prepares the way for such change. They view change as a temporal process and desirable for the attainment of utopia. Challenges will persist in utopia, and humanity will continue to evolve in response to those challenges. Through utopian institutions and proper social arrangements, utopia will be achieved. G. Wells's "A Modern Utopia," as well as Orwell's "1984" and Huxley's "Brave New World," are examples of modern utopian thought.

Ruth Levitas introduced the utopian individual, along with his various characters, into the scope of utopian studies. In exploring the existing definitions of utopia, she considers three different aspects—form, function, or content — separately, which may have descriptive, analytic, or normative elements. However, these narrow definitions are all undesirable for her. Her new definition incorporates a wide range of the three terms, and although she acknowledges that such a definition leaves the boundaries of Utopia vague, it is less problematic than more restrictive definitions. Definitions in terms of content tend to be evaluative and normative, and if utopia is defined in terms of form, it describes a good society or an ideal commonwealth. In terms of function, her new definition raises questions related to some goals. Her utopia "entails not just the creation of a better society, but the assertion of a radical change of values."[11] This transformation is an essential element of a utopian vision. For Levitas, "Any general definition needs to accommodate the fact that utopian scholarship does encompass a wide variety of approaches and questions, and this multi-dimensional approach is itself fruitful. One of the reasons people work with different definitions of utopia is because they are asking different questions."[12] An agreed-upon definition needs to be inclusive, and the present absence of consensus results in a lack of peaceful coexistence of different definitions due to their competing claims of primacy. Levitas explores how form, function, and content interact and are conditioned by the social context of utopia. Distinctions should still be made between the different kinds of utopias based on form, function, and content; however, the study of utopia should incorporate all of these elements.

Narrow views of what constitutes utopia limit the fields of study, leading to mistaken judgments and failing to encompass a wide variety of different questions. "The problem of limiting utopia to the 'possible world' is that it conflates the categories of hope and desire. It limits utopia to the question 'what may I hope' and refuses the question 'what may I dream'? It implies also that the function of utopia is necessary that of change- a means of grasping and effecting the hoped-for future."[13] She concludes that "there is no consensus within utopian studies about the meaning of the term utopia and therefore no agreement about the object of analysis... We have a range of definitions related to a range of different questions, all of which are problematic as general definitions of utopia."[14] Though the term' Utopia' suggests to most people that this is an impossible dream of the good life or an escapist fantasy, for Levitas, Utopia is not a dream to be enjoyed but a vision to be pursued, detailing how we would live and what kind of world we would live in. This world may be imaginary, yet it encompasses a range of perspectives, from religious and secular to literary and political, diverse in form, content, and location. She challenges the notion of a fixed ideal conception of perfection but emphasises that the impulse is driven by desire, one that is socially constructed and not innate. Contemporary utopian studies employ the term utopia in a more expansive sense, encompassing practice, concept, and theme, with a broader application as described in Thomas More's Utopia.

In the current era of individualism, marked by a withdrawal of commitment to the common good, there appears to be a growing devotion to selfish interests that dominates 21st-century life. The members of an intentional community rely on shared values, where other members nurture individual growth, all are equally responsible for one another, and everyone is treated with equal respect. In an intentional community, members share a collective activity within a shared physical space to undertake a collective endeavour for a common purpose. The member's lifelong commitments do not only focus on collective sharing but also build upon sacrifice, labour, and surrender to the uncertain adventure of creating a new, truly caring city—a real heaven on earth, even though the various utopias differ regarding their vision of heaven.

A community, unlike a cult, is not led by a charismatic guru, where discipline is established by consensus and not blind obedience. In a decision-making device, consensus is not sufficient as it implies that something needs to be done, so the issue is often postponed; only unanimity is acceptable. A generalisation about communes is almost impossible and beyond definition; it involves people who choose to live together, but no single characteristic marks all communes. In his research, T. Miller discovered that in some communes, the authority of charismatic leaders was the basis of all structure, and for "communes without charismatic leaders, the great majority found it difficult to figure out how to structure things. Many communes striving to function without leaders use consensus government and endless, often daily, meetings, often expanding far too much energy on the process... It became a real obstacle to progress... On the other hand, at some places, consensus did work."[15]

T. Miller defines communitarianism not in terms of form but more in terms of motivation. He is aware that others define communes in other ways. In his historical research, he has found no entirely satisfactory system of categorisation of communities, but he does distinguish between religious and secular communities, and further subcategorisation becomes too difficult for him. However, he offers us various features that an intentional community must have: a sense of common purpose, some form of self-denial in favour of the good of the group geographic proximity, personal interaction, economic sharing, real existence, and critical mass. An intentional community should include at least five individuals.[16]

For Tom Moylan, utopian writing in its many manifestations is complex and contradictory. He describes a critical utopia as "Utopia is, at heart, rooted in the unfulfilled needs and wants of specific classes, groups and individuals in their unique historical context, it opposes the affirmative culture maintained by the dominant ideology. Utopia negates the contradictions in a social system by forging visions of what is not yet realised, either in theory or in practice." [17] He presents his utopia in a more critical light, where each of the new utopias in society is shown with its faults, problems, exploration, and domination in a better place. "Here is echoed the historic failure to achieve perfection, a false goal in the first place of the revolutionary societies from the USA to the more recent flawed alternatives experienced in the Soviet Union. People's Republic of China, Vietnam, Cuba and Nicaragua."[18] Utopia does not only represent an alternative to life in the dominant society. It also endeavours to realise unique aspirations, ideals and dreams from idealists, practitioners and intellectuals who provide new ideas and propose alternative directions.

Rosabeth Kanter gives a meaningful description of a modern utopia in the USA during and after the hippie period, and could be useful when, later on, the inauguration of Auroville will be discussed. She described utopia as," Utopia is the imaginary society in which humankind's deepest yearnings, noblest dreams, and highest aspirations come to fulfilment, where all physical, social, and spiritual forces work together, in harmony, to permit the attainment of everything people find necessary and desirable. In the imagined utopia, people work and live together closely and cooperatively, in a social order that is self-created and self-chosen rather than externally imposed, yet one that also operates according to a higher order of natural and spiritual laws. Utopia is held together by commitment rather than coercion. In a utopia, what people want to do is the same as what they have to do; the interests of the individuals are congruent with the interests of the group; and personal growth and freedom entail responsibility for others. Underlying the vision of utopia is the assumption that harmony, cooperation, and mutuality of interests are natural to human existence, rather than conflict, competition and exploitation, which arise only in imperfect societies. By providing material and psychological safety and security, the utopian social order eliminates the need for divisive competition or self-serving actions, which elevate some people to the disadvantage of others; it ensures instead the flowering of mutual responsibility and trust, to the advantage of all. Utopia, then, represents an ideal of the good, to contrast with the evils and ills of existing societies. The idea of utopia suggests a refuge from the troubles of this world as well as a hope for a better one."[19] For Kanter, the human organisation in utopia involves complex problems of social organisation where decisions are made according to everyone's wishes. The organisational issues include regular group meetings with member participation in decision-making, the process of selecting new members, the degree of autonomy, the community's values, and the commitment of its citizens to the community's work.

For Kanter, "the ideal of social unity has led to the transformation of numerous communes and utopian communities. These are voluntary, value-based, communal social orders. Because members choose to join and choose to remain, conformity within the community is based on commitment to the individual's desire to obey its rules, rather than on force or coercion. Members are controlled by the entire membership or by individuals they respect within the community rather than by the outside agents of political forces. A commune seeks self-determination, often making its laws and refusing to obey some of those set by the larger society.... It intentionally implements a set of values having been planned to bring about the attainment of certain ideals, and its operating decisions are made in terms of those values. Its primary end is an existence that matches the ideals. All other goals are secondary and related to ends involving harmony, brotherhood, mutual support, and value expression. These ideals give rise to the key communal arrangement, the sharing of resources and finances."[20]

Maintaining a sense of group solidarity is as important as meeting specific goals. It is the individual's commitment that links self-interest to social requirements, i.e., it forms the connection between individual interests and collective interests. According to Kanter, " The group builds commitment to the extent that it cuts off other possible objects of commitment, becomes an integrated unity tying together all aspects of life within its borders, develops its uniqueness and specialness, and becomes capable, by itself, of continuing the person's gratification....The person making a moral commitment to his community should see himself as carrying out the dictates of a higher system, which orders and gives meaning to his life. He internalises community standards and values and accepts their control because they provide him with something transcendent. This commitment requires, first, that the person reformulate and evaluate his identity in terms of meeting the ideals set by the community."[21]

## Term Community

The Webster's Encyclopaedic Dictionary defines community as 'a social group of any size whose members reside in a specific locality, share government and have a common cultural and historical heritage... or a social group sharing common characteristics or interests and perceived or perceiving itself as distinct in some respect from the largest society within which it exists." For Suzan Brown "community is also a term used in the abstract to denote connection with others-a sharing sometimes of evanescent qualities, as in *a community of like minds* or a *community of spirit.* Such meaning broadens understanding and encompasses connections that are not limited."[22] She maintains that the purpose of intentional communities is "voluntarily founded to achieve a specific goal for a specific group of people bent on solving a specific set of cultural and social problems. The goals of intentional communities vary as much as the people who found them, and they represent the views of small numbers of people. However, the small numbers can reach such a critical mass that the founding of intentional communities becomes a solution to the problem of an increasing interest." [23] She disagrees with those who often call an intentional community a utopian community because the ideals of the intentional community are not realised as separate from society; on the contrary, in the realisation of their ideals, they interact with the larger society. Intentional communities differ from society in general because they are intentional, communal, participatory and usually have an identifiable beginning and end. Its members actively strive for a shared identity. Participants are authentic, where standard social distinctions are abandoned, and in their new identities, they live together happily. In equality, they are bound together by strong, emotional, brotherly love.

Lucy Sargisson interprets Utopias as "that lie at the heart of politics, society and everyday life. They tell us about people's dreams and desires. They stem from discontent, yet they gesture towards different and better ways of living. Intentional communities, groups of people who have chosen to live and sometimes work together for a common purpose beyond relationship or family, are, in some sense, concrete utopias. There are physical, observable spaces in which people try to create a context in which their everyday lives are closer to their utopia."[24] Though intentional communities may not be utopian in the way that the word utopia is used, there are close connections between utopianism and such communities. Intentional communities are putting their vision into communal practice by withdrawing from the larger society or demonstrating to the broader society that their utopia can be put into practice. Laman Tower Sargent defines intentional community as "a group of five or more adults and their children, if any, who come from more than one nuclear family and who have chosen to live together to enhance their shared values or for some other mutually agreed upon purpose"[25] She called utopianism "social dreaming", and she distinguishes three faces of utopianism as- the literary utopia, utopian practice, and utopian social theory. She defines the literary utopia as "the non-existent society described in considerable detail and normally located in time and space. In standard usage, utopia is used both as defined here and as an equivalent for utopia, or a non-existent society described in considerable detail and normally located in time and space that the author intended a contemporaneous reader to view as considerably better than the society in which that reader lived." [26]. Utopian practice encompasses intentional communities, utopian experiments, and practical utopias. "All utopian practice is about the actual rather than the fictional transformation of the everyday." [27] Utopian social theory includes "utopia as a method of analysis; the relationship between utopia and ideology;...the ways in which utopianism has been used to explain social change; the role of utopianism in religion...colonialism and post-colonialism and the debates between globalisers and anti-globalizers."[28]

As a model for a better human future and a community's successful model, it may attract others to the usefulness of the utopia. The traditional community demonstrates that living a better life is possible and essential for the improvement of the human condition; however, if misused, utopianism can be rather potentially dangerous when misused by others to gain power, prestige, and money for themselves. She concludes that "Utopia is a tragic vision of a life of hope, but one that is always realised and always fails. We can hope, fail and hope again. We can live with repeated failure and still improve the societies we build."[29]

## Technological Utopia

Technology has brought about significant progress; we now know and can do many things, which we translate into ingenious solutions. Modern technological capabilities have undeniably transformed our lives in unforeseeable ways, and as a result, they will alleviate human suffering. Technological development assumes an image of humanity where man is entirely self-determined, where life is fully controlled and optimised, and where nature is being subjugated. It attempts to realise what is technically possible. If this does not change, then technology will determine what kind of man and our children will be. Once new techniques get a grip on man, it will determine their thoughts, experiences, and feelings, and they will change existing power relations. The numerous utopias that followed Thomas More's "Utopia", which have guided humanity towards the rise of modernity, almost always depicted societies in which both nature and society are presented as completely controllable and malleable. It seems there is a future ahead in which safety, security, and technology could be realised. In today's techno-society, modern humans are in many ways linked to technology; there is no longer a distinction between society and technology, which means that human change cannot be separated from technological change. This does not mean that modern technology can solve all kinds of social problems, but when it is based on a recognition that technology has a decisive influence on our norms, values and behaviour, then natural scientists and technologists become creators of cultures standing next to artists. These new technological developments and scientific explorations hold great social promise, provided they are adequately framed within society.

The modern utopian state seeks order, unity, and integrity, aiming to create a population that is easy to control amid a chaotic and constantly changing social reality. The input of technocratic knowledge endeavours to create a new society based on fundamental changes which occur in almost all fields of society. The technological utopia aims at an ideal society where the design and detailed blueprint become an object of the engineer, a thing of nature. The dynamic machine, with its complexities and interdependencies, can give rise to unpredictable social movements. In this mechanistic worldview, the mechanic of the computer is no longer the instrument of the creator but becomes the creator itself; in other words, the computer becomes human; having become a universal model to explain not only human functioning but also how the world functions. In the future, it might finally become Superman and control men and the world. All imperfections are solved in the human machine, which ultimately promises a healing cure for all kinds of social misery. As the rapid process of artificially directed intelligence enhancement is unstoppable, humanity may be nearing the end of Darwinian evolution if, in the post-human future, machines transcend human limits. In the near future, as evolution accelerates with advances in genetics, artificial intelligence, digital communication, and quantum computing, such extended frontiers of humanity's knowledge may operate far faster than natural selection. Ultimately, machines may render the physical body redundant, and humans may become incorporeal, creating a self-evident next phase in human evolution: cyborgs, which are human beings linked to machines. It may seem like a narrative from a science-fiction story, but we must acknowledge that most of us are already cyborgs - creatures linked to other devices that cannot survive a day without technology. Technology has entered man's inner life and is pressed into the service of values that transcend it; without this, the new man may misuse his godlike powers in the service of his greed and domination. Resulting in more suffering. When the emerging post-human technology replicates itself and takes over, where man is no longer in control of its evolution, does this mean that our essential human potential for self-transcendence will be lost in the technical-machine man?

Technology can find a solution for a problem without addressing the deeper causes, and as such, it may divert people's attention to the most fundamental problem: the problem of growth in a limited system. There exists a mixed vision regarding growth, does it need a process beyond growth or a process of de-growth? Does growth, with its obsession with technology, have its limits, and does it require a new paradigm shift where boundaries are no longer crossed and human life is no longer endangered? Where post-growth followers are concerned with models that prioritise the goals of sustainability and social well-being over growth, degrowth followers are more concerned with shrinking production and consumption as the primary means to sustainability. Growth can be a positive force and a driver of change, allowing investments in renewable energy. However, there is also some scepticism about technological development, which may prevent inevitable damage to the planet.

According to Nicholas Carr, "Utopia is creepy—or at least it looks creepy. That's probably because utopia requires its residents to behave like robots, never displaying or ever feeling fear or anger or despair or bitterness or any of those other messy emotions that plague our fallen world"[30]. He assumes that the hierarchy of innovation runs in parallel with A. Maslow's hierarchy of needs, who focuses on the gratification of basic needs. The more comfortable you are, the more time you spend thinking about yourself until the need for self-actualisation arises. In the hierarchy of innovation, once the material needs are met, one's needs are directed towards technologies of the self, such as cosmetic surgery,

Viagra, or Facebook. Inventors who focus on technologies of self are already physically comfortable and require more powerful tools to modify their internal state. At the top level of the innovation hierarchy, there is no need to alter the shape of the physical world or society; instead, the focus is on changing moods and reshaping the invisible self. However, unlike Maslow's self-actualisation, which ultimately leads to a healthy individual, in the innovation hierarchy, the pursuit of self-actualisation often turns into mere self-indulgence, where inventions have less transformative effects. In Maslow's instant gratification of basic needs, the consumption need is forced on man through manipulation of needs for a vested interest to keep production going rather than stimulating transcendental elements in the higher needs, which form a distinct dimension of reality. This neglect overlooks alternatives and fails to distinguish between two dimensions that converge, namely the ontological tension between potentiality and actuality, i.e., what is and what could be. In this sense, technology and science become the servants of a society focused on profit and efficiency. It is almost impossible to predict in advance where the limits of the changes that technology may bring about in our future humanity lie.

In modern times, the belief in the feasibility and benefits of natural science and technology is being questioned by a range of unpredictable events. Natural disasters still threaten humanity, but more threatening are the technologically related apocalyptic scenarios of the world's demise. i.e. atomic energy, environmental problems, and biotechnology. It is no longer nature that is experienced as a threat, but more the collapse of the ideas of feasibility and technological controllability that frightens man. This is best described in the great anti-utopias of the last century, in which fear reigns in a world that is completely controlled and fixed, as seen in "A Brave New World" and "Nineteen Eighty-Four". As representatives of modern Utopia, Huxley and Orwell, in their anti-utopia, reacted largely against certain socialist practices and technological developments of the 20th century. "Brave New World" and "Nineteen Eighty-Four" are chilling visions where utopia runs amok into dystopia. In an unprecedented kind of change within, the near future humanity may become malleable through the development and effects of genetic modification and cyborg technologies. Questions may arise regarding the intrinsic limits and impact of 21st-century sciences, bio-cybernetics, and artificial intelligence on their long-term prospects, as their misuse looms as an increasing danger to humanity. Only when technology is developed appropriately and deployed wisely through innovations that do not exploit natural resources and conserve energy can the dystopian downsides be avoided. Long-term planning, accompanied by lifestyle changes, is necessary to ensure the welfare of future generations is not jeopardised. Many contemporaries have criticised rampant technological development, but new developments need not be automatically judged by using past criteria. Each new initiative in technological development brings its own forms of life, along with associated norms and values.

Despite all technological claims, some fundamental truths about complex human nature may not be fully grasped without the support of social science and ethics. A futuristic techno-scientific world requires a broader social discussion in which new technologies are viewed as new cultural life forms of humanity, offering prospects for social acceptance. In the context of human concern about technological development, continuous critical reflection has become a pressing need in today's crisis. Although it offers humanity numerous benefits for further evolution, it is not premature to address various ethical questions and challenge scientists' limited grasp of reality. Krishan Kumar meaningfully expresses this as follows: "Utopia confronts reality not with a measured assessment of the possibilities of change, but with the demands for change... In its guise as a utopia, by the very force of its imaginative presentation, it energises reality.... To some, this has always appeared as an abandonment rather than an illusion and wish-fulfilment, as well as an irresponsible fantasy in the face of the real world. But there are different ways of grasping reality." [31]

## Ecotopia

In the sixties, a new Utopia was constituted: an ecological utopia, a society organised according to environmental principles that offers the best possible life for its citizens. The organisation opposed large-scale technology, and in its specific ecological concern, it emphasised the dehumanising effects on work and life, natural resources, and environmental destruction. Its members are not anti-technology, moving back to pre-industrial ways of life. However, ecologists have never developed a formal ecological utopia. According to Krishan Kumar, "Ecotopia has so far resisted the temptation to turn into a primitivist utopia of a Rousseaunist kind. It has looked to a post-industrial future, not to a pre-industrial past. However, its strength lies in the social and moral sphere rather than in the economic and technological spheres, despite its concerns with 'alternative' technology. This is fully in tune with the classic utopian tradition inaugurated by More. ... we see how the terms of utopia and anti-utopia can pass into each other, the material abundance of the modern utopia being transferred, in this instance, to anti-utopia, and the moral protest of the modern anti-utopia being embodied in the austere ecological utopia." [32] Ecotopia rejects dependence on many 1960s visions related to economic growth and large-scale industrial technology. He claims that anti-utopias continue to attract a considerable following in our time, but they remain relevant in their particular targets, such as totalitarian power, features of the contemporary environment, artificial intelligence, robotisation, and climate change; they all address specific audiences. "Utopia, where it still exists, is now addressed to specific groups and constituencies, as a special mode of communication among them, and the vehicle of a largely internal debate about ultimate goals"[33] Kumar claims that "present-day anti-utopias have communicated little idea of a dominant trend or central principle in contemporary developments; nor have they been able to impose a compelling sense of a march into a nightmare future...and as utopia loses its vitality, so too does anti-utopia." [34]

He asks whether there is today no place for utopia as the ideal place that is nowhere or not yet. Kumar meaningfully answers this question in relation to Thoreau's building castles in the air, where the work need not have been lost and where the foundations have to be put under them. He concludes, "If you have built castles in the air, said Thoreau, your work would not have been lost.... we have come to concentrate on the foundations to the exclusion of the castles which are the only reason for existence? So hard-headed and 'realist' have we become, so anxious not to be thought 'utopian' that we worry away at the earthworks and ground plans without lifting up our eyes to the structures rising up from them. We have all become converts to piecemeal 'engineering' without bothering ourselves too much with the final shape of the structure, which we are so busy piecing together. The result is a wilderness without meaning or purpose." [35]

## Conclusion

There are many studies about Utopia-man's dream of a better world from political, economic, scientific, social and spiritual/religious points of view. Utopias, as a dream of the future, are written out of hope and despair, and are interpretations of the existing order, related to programs of social change, and founded on a sense of solidarity, discipline, and loyalty to its citizens in day-to-day life. Utopianism is connected with thought processes which structure knowledge with a wilful desire for change. It projects an ideal society by imagining what might be in the future but does not exist at the moment; it involves presenting utopian ideas not as purely imaginary aspects of reality but as realistic and attainable aspects of possible utopian futures. In the preceding centuries, utopias were more closely tied to a society defined by human interaction and a greater sense of unity and belonging. In the 21st century, utopias are a complex organisation and a realisable form of enhanced equality and sociability, which must also be wedded to sustainability. Without this integration, sustainability would lead to unlimited material abundance, which is incompatible with the utopian vision.

Critics have criticised utopia as being unrealistic, impossible states of fantasy inhabited by escaping or non-existent human beings. They are sceptical of the dreamer's scheme in the perfect lands, which exists only in the imaginative mind of the founder or author. However, the citizens of utopias project their ideal into action and offer humanity flashes of perfection in the future, along with means to improve their lives. In the end, utopias always 'fail' in the sense that the perfect place has not yet been realised on earth, and this inherently subjective concept may not come into existence any time soon. Any utopia responds to the context of the problems in its specific historical movement and old issues, and these old problems relate to an evolving society, which evolves alongside them and where the corresponding old vision changes as well. To reject the old world in the expectation that a new one is ready, a utopia as a dream, which excludes everything else, could be rated as dangerous. Is only a total revolution able to establish such a society as a mere concrete social reform, or would pursuing social improvement and emancipation only keep the system alive longer or improve the system rather than the collapse of the system?

Others view the revival of utopia as a powerful means of individual and social change, where humanity needs to move beyond the limits of its everyday reality to confront the challenges of planetary survival. Such a vision must be grounded in history and demonstrably practical, with empirical verifiability, rather than mere dreaming or wishful thinking. The utopian promise includes a future in which people can, in an efficient way, shape their lives with freedom and happiness. However, utopias that cling to holism with a blueprint for another and better world often ignore the fact that reality is ultimately unruly and frequently causes distractions. Misfortunes need to be surmounted and demand more input and effort from the utopian citizens to reach the goal and uphold their faith in a new future. What could be a purposeful resolution among utopians to move beyond the pitfalls of utopia? Would utopians learn to be more coherent, more penetrating, more intelligent with a taste of evidence, more ideological and less cynical, a bit of both? In a burst of the sentimentalism of an embittered group of people, utopia can comfortably become an escape from the finite futility of man's imagination to an eternal hope of divine stability. The images of hope could be as extravagant as the expectations.

In pressing to transform society, the wheels of change are in constant movement, where new questions will always follow old causes and conclusions. It may need incorruptible saints whose souls sense a divine reformation to find a divine liberation of man in an imaginary paradise. Perhaps we need a re-evaluation of utopia, in which the values of the traditional, modern, and postmodern worldviews are integrated with the ideals of the future. Though there are many adverse reactions against numerous utopias due to their idealistic, never-realised objectives, various utopias offered answers to social, cultural, economic, and political problems that were related to reality and functioned as a source of inspiration for these movements. At present, utopian studies is a relatively new field in academic research, and its disciplinary character draws on history, philosophy, sociology, psychology, politics, literature, and religion. This diversity of subject matter and approach may lead to deliberation and confusion. In outside academic circles, Utopia is often characterised as unrealistic and equated with totalitarianism.

## Notes

1.) L. T. Sargent/Gregory Claes, *The Utopian Reade*r, p 1

2.) Ibid., p 2

3.) Ibid., p 3

4.) Russell Jacobi, *Picture Imperfect*, p XIV

5.) Ibid., p1

6.) E.M Cioran, *History and Utopia,* p.81

7.) Ibid., p 82,83

8.) William McCord, *Voyages to Utopia*, p 20

9.) Ibid., p 21

10.) Clint Jones/Cameron Ellis, *The Individual and Utopia,* p 2

11.) Ruth Levitas, *The Concept of Utopia*, p 124

12.) Ibid., p 179

13.) Ibid., p 190

14.) Ibid., p 178

15.) Timothy Miller, *The Sixties Communes*, p 168-169

16.) Ibid., p XXII

17.) Tom Moylan, *Demand the Impossible*, p 1

18.) Ibid., p 43

19.) Rosabeth Kanter, *Commitment and Community*, p 3

20.) Ibid., p 2

21.) Ibid., p 71-72

22.) Suzan Brown, *Intentional Community,* p3

23.) Ibid., p 5

24.) Lucy Sargisson/L.T. Sargent, *Living Utopia*, p 3

25.) Ibid., p 5

26.) Ibid., p 6

27.) Ibid., p 7

28.) Ibid., p 7

29.) Ibid., p 127

30.) Nicholas Carr, *Utopia is creepy,* p 108

31.) Krishan Kumar, *Utopia and Anti-Utopia in Modern Times*, p 107

32.) Ibid., p 414-415

33.) Ibid., p 420

34.) Ibid., p 422

35.) Ibid., p423.

*CHAPTER TWO*

# PERFECTION

Before discussing Sri Aurobindo's ideals of perfection, it will be helpful to outline the aim of Integral Yoga, distinguishing it from other yoga systems and thereby placing his concept of perfection within a broader context. The very essence of Integral Yoga is the transformation of the entire individual being into a higher spiritual consciousness and a larger divine existence through the union of human consciousness with the Divine, achieved by identifying the separate individuality with the true universal or transcendent Self. This means getting into a consciousness in which one is no longer limited by the ego, but is in union with the Supreme Self, one's true being and the real truth of existence. This union of the individual's instrumental being and soul must be expressed by a change of one's imperfect nature into the very likeness of the Divine Nature. A spiritual shift in consciousness is necessary for the liberation of the soul and its union with the Divine. In Sri Aurobindo's words, "The object of Yoga is to raise the human being from the consciousness of the ordinary mind to the consciousness of the Spirit and using the circumstances of mind, life and body as self-figuring determinations of the Spirit."[1] Here, yoga does not mean union itself but the process by which the union is to be achieved. In this way, yoga comes to mean a perfect method of bringing about union with the Divine.

Integral Yoga is Sri Aurobindo's name for his synthesis of Yoga methods. It encompasses the essence and many processes of other Yoga systems, but its uniqueness lies in the underlying aim of its comprehensiveness: a total and integral transformation of consciousness and nature, bringing the fullness of the Divine into human life. It complements all one-sided approaches by integrating the entire being of man through a synthesis of Karma, Jnana and Bhakti Yoga. According to Sri Aurobindo, "The triple way takes for its chosen instruments the three main powers of the mental soul-life of the human being. Knowledge selects the reason and the mental vision, and it makes them by purification, concentration and a certain discipline of a God-directed seeking its means for the greatest knowledge and the greatest vision of all, God-knowledge and God-vision. It aims to see, know and be the Divine. Works, action selects for its instrument the will of the doer of works; it makes life an offering of sacrifice to the Godhead and by purification, concentration and a certain discipline of subjection to the divine Will a means for contact and increasing unity of the soul of man with the divine Master of the universe. Devotion selects the emotional and aesthetic powers of the soul. Turning them all Godward in a perfect purity, intensity, infinite passion of seeking makes them a means of God- possession in one or many relations of unity with the Divine Being. All aim in their own way at a union of the human soul with the supreme Spirit."[2]

Action is the first power of life, the starting point of the initiation to the Divine, works fulfil themselves in knowledge, and knowledge is not complete without works, and love is the crown of knowledge as love without knowledge is passionate but blind and often dangerous, a stumbling block; love leading to perfect knowledge brings infinite and absolute union. In the integral view of things, "these three paths are one. Divine Love should normally lead to the perfect knowledge of the Beloved by perfect intimacy, thus becoming a path of Knowledge, and to the divine service, thus becoming a path of Works. So also, should perfect Knowledge lead to perfect Love and Joy and a full acceptance of the works of That which is known; dedicated Works to the entire love of the Master of the Sacrifice and the deepest knowledge of His ways and His being. It is in this triple path that we come most readily to the absolute knowledge, love and the service of the One in all beings and its entire manifestation."[3] The perfection of Integral Yoga comes to each man when he is able to follow his own path of Yoga, pursuing the development of his own nature in its upsurging towards that which transcends nature. The practice is not based on a fixed system which has to be followed as a routine.

This triple way of work, knowledge, and love becomes the keynote of Integral Yoga, but it has to be extended into a yoga of spiritual self-perfection. It is a complete lifting of the whole nature of man into its power of a divine essential condition of Integral Yoga, and each of the three ways, if it is pursued with a certain largeness, then it can take into itself the powers of the others and lead to their fulfilment. It is sufficient to start with one of them till a point is reached when it meets parallel lines of advance and melts into them by its own widening. The possibility of starting with the three lines together should be postponed till the conditions of the yoga of self-perfection are ready. It is for this reason that his synthesis of yoga cannot be arrived at by a simple combination of the various systems of yoga or a successive practice of the different systems. Sri Aurobindo's integral method favours the harmony of our inner being and outer activities in the divine consummation of both, and in its aim, it exceeds the limited Yogas in its unique goal of the divine transformation of man and the world.

For Sri Aurobindo, perfection is related to reality, which is both an internal being and an eternal becoming. The perfection of the world is the manifestation of the supermind at all levels of material and spiritual reality. The world is a movement of the involuted Divine in evolution to higher levels of consciousness and manifestation. Other forms of human perfection have failed in the end because they omit the true nature of the Divine Becoming. With the Mother's emphasis on the experiential and practical aspects of Integral Yoga and Auroville as a living laboratory, Integral Yoga becomes a means to this perfection. Through the practice of Integral Yoga with the variety of paths as a necessary means, the individual is able to promote a Divine evolution toward true perfection, the creation of a new world and the attempt toward a collective realisation.

In the words of Sri Aurobindo, "the principle of this yoga is not perfection of the human nature as it is but a psychic and spiritual transformation of all the parts of the being through the action of an inner consciousness and then of a higher consciousness which works on them, throws out their old movements or changes them into the image of its own and so transmutes lower into higher nature. It is not so much the perfection of the intellect as a transcendence of it, a transformation of the mind, the substitution of a larger, greater principle of knowledge, and so will be the rest of the being. This is a slow and difficult process; the road is long and it is hard to establish even the necessary basis. The old existing nature resists and obstructs, and difficulties rise one after another and repeatedly till they are overcome."[4] His Integral Yoga demands a total dedication of life to the aspiration for the discovery of the Divine Truth and to enter into a complete dedication to the spiritual life. The aim of Integral Yoga is not only to free oneself from the bondage of human nature but also to achieve perfect control over it, with the intention of transforming, spiritualising, and divinising it. It aims to bring down the higher levels of consciousness on earth, stabilise them, and create a new race where the principles of the higher levels of consciousness govern the outer and inner individual and collective life.

While the object of ordinary yoga is liberation and the union of the individual soul with the Divine, Integral Yoga adds participation with the Divine in the fulfilment of the spiritual purpose of its manifestation in humanity and cosmic Nature. It aims to manifest a higher consciousness upon the earth and not to escape from the earth into some supreme Absolute. "The individual yoga then turns from its separateness and becomes part of the collective Yoga of the divine Nature in the human race." [5]

## Imperfection

If a Divine perfection of the human being is the aim of Integral Yoga, a distinction has to be made between human and divine perfection. The individual's perception of an unsatisfactory world marked by suffering, evil, and inadequacy is often the starting point of the spiritual urge. However, this imperfect condition of what is manifested to the individual is not the essence of the manifested world and "the imperfection, the evil, the suffering may be a besetting circumstance, but not the very essence of birth in Nature. And if so, the highest wisdom will lie not in escape, but in the urge towards a victory here, in a discovery of the spiritual gate to perfection which will be at the same time an opening for the entire descent of the Divine

Light Knowledge, Power Beatitude."[6] For Sri Aurobindo our present imperfect status offers man an opportunity for the achievement of a higher, wider and greater purpose that shall be divine and perfect, not only by the secret spirit within it but also in its most outward form of existence. According to Sri Aurobindo, "A perfected human world cannot be created by men or composed of men who are themselves imperfect. Even if all our actions are scrupulously regulated by education or law or social or political machinery, what will be achieved is a regulated pattern of minds, a fabricated pattern of lives, a cultivated pattern of conduct; but a conformity of this kind cannot change, cannot recreate the man within, it cannot carve or cut out a perfect soul or a perfect thinking man or a perfect or growing living being. But knowledge, thought, action- whether religious, ethical, political, social, economic, utilitarian or hedonistic, whether a mental, vital or physical form or constitution of existence,- cannot be the essence or object of life; they are only activities of the powers of being or the powers of its becoming, dynamic symbols of itself, creations of the embodied Spirit, its means of discovering or formulating what it seeks to be."[7]

Imperfection is relative in its nature and not absolute, like Truth, Good and Beauty, which are the inherent aspects of eternal self-existence. Sri Aurobindo does not want to limit the description of the individual's and the world's undivine perfection solely to moral evil or suffering, on the contrary, he wants the sadhak to consider the general principle of imperfection, i.e., the principle of division, attachment to this experience of division and ignorance which form contradictions of the divine elements. However, imperfection is only a first condition and opportunity for the achievement of a greater perfection in the manifestation of the hidden divinity, and "our present nature can only be transitional, our imperfect status a starting-point and opportunity for the achievement of another, higher, wider and greater that shall be divine and perfect not only by the secret spirit within it but in its manifest and most outward form of existence."[8] As such, imperfection becomes a necessary term for the manifestation of the divine nature. The soul's dissatisfaction with imperfection and its divine aspiration for the elimination of all imperfections from one's nature is a law of the being but also a law against which the sadhak revolts

All these imperfections are only the first condition of a greater perfection, and the revolt of men's consciousness against them is a necessary valuation to face, endure, reject and transform them. Perfection, in the sense that it is used in Integral Yoga, means a growth out of the lower undivine into a higher divine nature. For Sri Aurobindo, "a perfection has to be aimed at which amounts to the elevation of the mental into the full spiritual and the supramental nature. Therefore, this integral Yoga of knowledge, love and works has to be extended into a Yoga of spiritual and gnostic self-perfection... The mental being has to enlarge itself into the oneness of the Divine before the Divine will perfect in the soul of the individual its gnostic outflowering. That is the reason why the triple way of knowledge, works and love becomes the key-note of the whole Yoga....At the same time, each of the three ways at its height, if it is pursued with a certain largeness, can take into itself the powers of the others and lead to their fulfilment" [9].

For Sri Aurobindo "Purna [perfection] Yoga means 1) that instead of approaching the Divine through the mind alone (Jnana) or the heart alone ( Bhakti) or through will and works alone (Karma Yoga ), one seeks the Divine with all the parts and powers of the consciousness and the being, uniting these three ways and many others in a single Yoga (way of union with the Divine) and receives the Divine in His presence, consciousness, force, light and bliss in all the consciousness and the being 2). That one seeks not only the realisation of the Divine in the soul and self, but also in the whole nature, (that means the transformation of this lower human into the divine spiritual nature.) 3). That one seeks the Divine not only beyond life (by the cessation of birth) but for life, so that life also may become a realisation of the Divine and the manifestation of the Divine Nature."[10] "This Yoga-siddhi, the perfection that comes from the practice of Yoga, can be best attained by the combined working of four great instruments. There is, first, the knowledge of the truth, principles, power, and processors that govern the realisation.... Next comes the force of our personal effort [a watchful introspection and a constant practice and vigilant will of self-modification and self-transformation] .... and the direct influence of the Teacher. Last comes the instrumentality of Time."[11] These external instruments aim to awaken the sadhak's soul to the Divine within. When the normal instruments are perfected, then they are no longer disturbed by undue interference from each other, and when this perfection rises in its capacity for action, then the instruments will be ready for transformation in which they will discover a luminous spiritual truth of the whole perfect nature.

According to Sri Aurobindo. "The normal instruments thus perfected will act each in its own kind, without undue interference from each other... This perfection must rise constantly in its capacity for action, the energy and force of its working, and a certain greatness of scope of the total nature. They will then be ready for the transformation into their own supramental action in which they will find a more absolute, unified and luminous spiritual truth of the whole perfected nature. The means of this perfection of the instruments.... the principal conditions are will, self-watching and self-knowledge and constant practice, abhyasa, of self-modification and transformation.... the mental being must open the way by a clear and watchful introspection. ..a vigilant and insistent will of self-modification and self-transformation... and an unfailing practice which will constantly reject all defects and perversion and replace it by a right and enhanced working."[12] So, no perfection can be attained without radically dealing with the complex nexus of mental, vital, and physical beings. To achieve a higher utility, this nexus needs to be partly broken up, exceeded, and transformed into a larger harmony of action.

## Self-perfection

Sri Aurobindo describes sadhana as "the practice by which perfection, Siddhi, is attained."[13] He defines yoga as "a methodised effort towards self-perfection by the expression of the potentialities latent in the being and a union of the individual with the universal and transcendence. Existence we see partially expressed in man and the Cosmos. But all life, when we look behind its appearances, is a vast yoga of Nature attempting to realise her perfection in an ever-increasing expression of her potentialities and to unite herself with her own divine reality."[14] As a discipline of self-perfection, sadhana is a liberation from human bondage, it is the unravelling of the knot of Life's difficulty. When the self is purified and liberated into its self-existent being, then spiritual perfection becomes possible. "A spiritual self-perfection can only mean a growing into oneness with the nature of the divine being and therefore will be the aim, effort, and method of our seeking after this perfection...for the integral Yoga perfection will mean the divine spirit and a divine nature which will admit of a divine relation and action in the world; it will mean also in its entirety a divinising of the whole nature, a rejection of all its wrong knots of being and action, but no rejection of any part of our being, or any field of our action....The approach to perfection must be therefore a large and complex movement and its results and workings will have an infinite and varied scope."[15] In Sri Aurobindo's Yoga of self-perfection, "intellectual, volitional, ethical, emotional, aesthetic and physical training and improvement are all so much to the good, but they are only in the end a constant movement in a circle without any last delivering and illumining aim, unless they arise at a point when they can open themselves to the power and presence of the Spirit and admit its direct workings. This direct working effects a conversion of the whole being, which is the indispensable condition of our real perfection. To grow into the truth and power of the Spirit and by the direct action of that power to be made a fit channel of its self-expression -a living of man in the Divine, and the divine living of the Spirit in humanity,- will therefore be the principal and the whole object of an integral Yoga of self-perfection...So long as there is only an intellectual, ethical and other self-training for the now normal purposes of life which does not travel beyond the ordinary circle of working of mind, life and body, we are still only in the obscure and yet unillumined preparatory Yoga of Nature; we are still in pursuit of only an ordinary human perfection...By personal effort, a precursory change, a preliminary conversion can be effected.... That is as far man can go by his unaided or indirectly aided effort, because that is an effort of mind and mind cannot climb beyond itself permanently."[16]

Sri Aurobindo describes mundane perfection as something outward, social, involving a more rational approach to our fellow humans and environment, or more as an inner, subjective ideal—a raising of intelligence, will, and reason, a nobler, richer aesthetic, and a better-governed vital and physical being. "A change of education and social institutions is the outward means adopted, or an inner self-training and development is preferred as the true instrumentation. Or the two aims may be clearly united, the perfection of the inner individual, the perfection of the outer living."[17]

The aim of human perfection includes self-mastery and a mastery over the surroundings, but as long as man is subjected to the attacks and slavery of his lower nature, his passions, desires and attachments, judgements and egoism, he can't be a self-ruler. To surmount his lower self is the condition of self-rule. Human perfection is pursued along aesthetic, ethical, religious, philosophical, scientific, and technological lines, and its aim includes self-mastery. The Mother describes the ideal of moral perfection as "There are thousands of moral perfections. Everyone has its own ideal of moral perfection. What is usually called moral perfection is to have all the qualities that are considered moral: to have no defects, never to make a mistake, never to err, to be always what one conceives to be the best, to have all the virtues- that is, to realise the highest mental conception: to take all the qualities- there are many, aren't there?-all the virtues, all that man has conceived to be the most beautiful, most noble, most true, and to live that integrally, to let all one's actions be guided by that, all the movements, all the reactions, all the feelings, all... That is living a moral ideal of perfection. It is the summit of man's mental evolution. Not many people do it... but still, there have been some and there still are. This is what men usually take for the spiritual life. When they meet a man of this type they say, 'Oh! He is a great spiritual being', He may be a great saint, he may be a great sage, but he is *not* a spiritual being. And yet it is already very good and very difficult to realise this. And there comes a time in the inner evolution when it is very necessary to try to realise it. It is obviously infinitely higher than to be still guided by all one's impulses and ignorant outer reactions. It is to be already in a way the master of one's nature. It is even a stage through which one has to pass, for it is the stage when one begins to be master of one's ego, when one is ready to let it fall away-it is still there but sufficiently weakened to be nearing its end. This is the last stage before crossing over to the other side, and certainly, if anyone imagines that you can go over to the other side without passing through this stage, he would risk making a great mistake, and of taking for perfect freedom a perfect weakness concerning his lower nature. It is almost impossible to pass from the mental being-even the most perfect and most remarkable-to the true spiritual life without having realised this ideal of moral perfection for a certain period, however brief it may be. Many people try to take a short-cut and want to assert their inner freedom before having overcome all the weaknesses of the outer nature; they are in great danger of deluding themselves. The true spiritual life, complete freedom, is something much higher than the highest moral realisations, but one must take care that this so-called freedom is not an indulgence and a contempt for all rules." [18]

The object of Integral Yoga is more integral and comprehensive; it embraces all these tendencies of a significant impulse of self-perfection and harmonises them into a higher-than-mundane principle. There is something in man's nature which goes beyond this first terrestrial nature of humanity; however, Sri Aurobindo is also aware that "Almost all men normally devote the major part of their energy to the life on earth, to the terrestrial needs, interests, desires, ideals of the individual and the race. It could not be otherwise.... the pursuit of high individual and large collective ideals which start from the idea of an attainable human perfection are imposed upon us by the very character of our terrestrial being: they are part of its law, its natural impulse and rule, its condition of growth, and without these things man could not attain to his full manhood. Any view of our being which neglects, unduly belittles or intolerantly condemns them is, therefore, unfit to be the general and complete rule of human living. Nature takes good care that the race shall not neglect these aims which are a necessary part of her evolution."[19]

## Summary

Sri Aurobindo is quite frank when he writes. "Man in himself is hardly better than an ambitious nothing. He is a narrowness that reaches towards ungrasped wideness, a littleness straining towards grandeurs which are beyond him, a dwarf enamoured of the heights...This imperfect being with his hampered, confused, ill-ordered and mostly ineffective consciousness cannot be the end and highest height in the mysterious upward search of Nature.... Something there is in us yet unexpressed that has to be delivered by an enveloping illumination from above.... Man's greatness is not in what he is but in what he makes possible. His glory is that he is the closed place and secret workshop of a living labour in which supermanhood is made ready by a divine Craftsman."[20]

For Sri Aurobindo, the object and purpose of his yoga is self-perfection. "Perfection has to be worked out, harmony has to be accomplished. Imperfection, limitation, death, grief. ignorance, matter, are only the first terms of the formula-unintelligible till we have worked out the wider terms and reinterpreted the formulary; they are the initial discords of the musician's tuning. Out of imperfection we have to construct perfection, out of limitation to discover infinity, out of death to find immortality. Out of grief to recover divine bliss, out of ignorance to rescue divine self-knowledge, out of matter to reveal Spirit. To work out this end for ourselves and humanity is the object of our yogic practice.... Only that which aims at possessing the fullness of God is purna Yoga; the sadhaka of the Divine Perfection is the purna Yogin. Our aim must be to be perfect as God in His being and bliss is perfect, pure as He is pure, blissful as He is blissful, and, when we are ourselves siddha in the purna Yoga, to bring all mankind to the same divine perfection.... whatever our immediate success, our unvarying aim must be to perform the whole journey and not lie down content in any wayside stage or imperfect resting place."[21]

The Mother describes Sri Aurobindo's higher and lower perfection as, "The lower perfection is to be able to make the human being in his present form and in his body, in his relation with all terrestrial things, do the utmost he can. This is the case of all great men of genius: artistic genius, literary genius, genius in organisation, the great rulers, those who have carried physical capacities to their maximum perfection, human development to the limits of its possibilities. The higher perfection is the spiritual perfection, integral union with the Divine, identification with the Divine, and freedom from all the limitations of the lower world. That is spiritual perfection, the perfection that comes from yoga—quite independent of the body and the physical world—which, in ancient times, meant first rejecting the body and the physical life to have a relation only with the higher world, and finally with the Divine. That is the higher perfection."[22]

Integral Yoga aims at the divine perfection, where the Divine becomes the direct guide of the sadhana and effects the entire spiritual conversion of the being. Human perfection aims at being a genius, the human development to the limits of its possibilities, i.e., all human qualities carried to their utmost limits. However, this leaves the human consciousness fundamentally unchanged, and for Sri Aurobindo, it is only by a transformation in man's present nature that it can be developed into an integral union with the Divine, transcending the human state.

The working of mind, life, and body and the unillumined Nature in ordinary human perfection are the means for the fulfilment of the divine principle within the individual and in the world, and they find their last perfection only by opening themselves to the power and presence of the Spirit and admitting its direct workings. Sri Aurobindo rejects nothing essential in the mundane aim, but he enlarges it and finds a truer meaning that is now hidden from it, transfiguring it from earthly human life to an ideal divine life. Human perfection will not disappear; the higher perfection will transform it. Whatever perfection has already been attained is included in the new and greater perfection, but with the larger vision of a spiritual consciousness and with new forms and powers. It proceeds by a personal effort followed by a divine influence, like a divine Grace, which is not a mysterious flow from above, but the all-pervading act of a divine presence within, as the power of the highest Self of our being entering into the soul and live in its law and possess it as the whole power of our spiritual nature. The entire object of an Integral Yoga of self-perfection is "to grow into the truth and power of the Spirit and by their direct action of that power to be made a fit channel of its self-expression- a living of man in the Divine and the divine living in the Spirit of humanity."[23]

In a divine life, individual perfection is the first essential condition for a perfected life on earth, followed by a preoccupation with the perfection of the individual's spiritual relationship with all around them, and finally, a new, perfected collective life in the natural world. According to Sri Aurobindo, "The nature of man and things is at present a discord, a harmony that has gone out of time. The whole heart and action and mind of man must be changed, but from within, not from without, not by political and social institutions, not even by creeds and philosophies, but by the realisation of God in ourselves and the world and a remoulding of life by that realisation. This can only be effected by Purna Yoga (the yoga of perfection), a yoga devoted to the fulfilment of the divine humanity in ourselves and others."[24]

Integral Yoga's ultimate aim is a total perfection in a divine life, the life of the Spirit fulfilled here on earth in the conditions of the material universe, a union of the spiritual summit and the material base. A supreme perfection is possible only through the transformation of our lower nature, as an instrument of right action, lifting it beyond its present narrow potentiality. But the perfection sought in integral Yoga is not to be one with the highest spiritual power and one with her universal action, but to possess and realise the fullness of the Shakti in our individual being and nature. To reach this integral self-perfection, "we have to become aware of the divine Shakti, draw her to us and call her in to fill the whole system and take up the charge of all our activities. There will then be no separate personal will or individual energy trying to conduct our actions, no sense of a little personal self as the doer, nor will it be the lower energy of the three gunas, the mental, vital and physical nature,... and as the crown of this process, transform all the lower energies into energies of her supramental nature and raise us into our being of gnosis."[25]

Sri Aurobindo's perfection envisioned the evolution of the individual, society, and the larger environment in terms of the Absolute, based on the truth of his spiritual realisations and intuitive knowledge, which transcended the limits of the mind and physical senses. The means for such perfection is his Integral Yoga through a personal acceleration of the evolutionary process. Each individual strives for personal perfection, encompassing both physical and psychological refinement. For the Mother, the divine Force at work provides individuals with internal motivation and leads each individual to self-perfection. Those who have attained this perfection, the Supramental consciousness or gnostic beings, will collaborate with others and prepare a spiritual community that will affect the world. In her writings, the Mother most likely referred to the Ashram as a field for the future gnostic beings, but it seems she related the development of the new life in the city of Auroville more to the growth of the inmost psychic being.

## A Human and Divine Perfection; A Dialogue

There has always been the quest for progressing toward a more perfect society. The pursuit of human perfection, encompassing technological, scientific, ethical, religious, and spiritual advancements, is essential to humanity. The individual and collective man have forever tried to perfect himself and society, and this quest for a perfect society includes the perfection of his fellow human beings. Mankind's striving for a gradual societal perfection through social change aims at human progress and makes the world a better place in which to live harmoniously. Humanists believe that a perfect society can be achieved only through the will and actions of humanity, and progress toward humanity's perfection requires the greatest human efforts and full responsibility. Human progress needs no dependence upon any external power, and where human nature is purified, man's dignity acquires the nature of the sacred. Liberty, equality, and fraternity are the highest ethical ideals that humanity has yet to reach in order to fulfil a perfect society. Striving for the perfection of mankind is not a static individual affair but a never-ending, infinite progress by an infinite number of steps to advance toward a more perfect state, and hence, no end of progress will ever be reached on the journey to an ideal society. Is the involvement in various kinds of human virtues, such as love of one's work, brotherly and sisterly love, art, technological achievements, though not perfect, and participating in such activities, not essential in determining the quality of the future society? What are the essential prerequisites for attaining perfection? Does it need the exercise of one's free will and one's own effort, or the infusion of the divine Grace, or a combination of the two, or maybe by the intervention of one's fellow man, like the spiritual teacher? If the ideal of perfection for mankind is identified with moral or practical perfection, then man's task is not metaphysical but moral perfection. Human perfection in such cases is the harmonious realisation of the guru's ideal.

A non-metaphysical absolute human perfection, when cut off from the roots of the infinite divine Grace, what can be achieved in transforming man's finite virtues without being dependent on the unpredictable ways of the Divine? A morality manifested in men's deeds and in their relations with their fellowman, i.e., not as a spiritual experiment but in the daily practice of morality without a mere submission to the divine Will or a blind faith and passive waiting for Grace? Is there such a thing as a future perfect divine man? By bringing about moral improvement, does there exist something as 'a perfecting man', the possibility of an endless progressive improvement?

The humanitarian, altruistic approach promotes the secular ideal as an end in itself, a moral perfection of the human being, and a happier and more united society and race based on mundane principles.

Although temporary, they are necessary as an evolutionary attempt to grow and as a preparatory stage for their time until a higher spiritual standard can replace them. They are imperfect and evolutive attempts to grow toward the supramental working whereby the sadhak moves towards the surrender of his individual to the divine Will. In Mother's Yoga, the mental and moral ideals do not satisfy the demands of the soul, which aims at the development of the human into the divine true soul, the sublimation of human love into the divine love, i.e., the elevation of the mental to its spiritual plane. Only in the spiritual divine Being, where the mind's ideal formulas dissolve into the vastness of the supramental realities, can the conflicts between the members of our race be reconciled. To arrive at such a proposed destination, a transition period is needed where the citizens have to create their collective path for a justifiable change with collective support to keep each other in good balance.

In human perfection and the perfection of life of the race, there is a profusion of rudimentary, unsatisfying solutions when a man looks at ethical and social relations with another man in solving his problems. However, in human perfection, all great men of genius have carried human development to the limit of its possibilities. In their skill, they carried all kinds of human qualities to their utmost limits, independent of any spiritual claims. They supplied the human race with intellectual, psychological and social optimism, but for the Mother, no rationalised and mechanical constructions can harmonise present-day complexities. Mental ideas and formulations are not able to forecast in detail the essential inherent unity of a divine life. The search for human perfection through the scientific mechanism of human life ignores the psychic elements in our nature. Nature has also implemented in the race an intuition that there is something in the being which goes beyond human perfection.

In spiritual perfection, the geniuses realise a higher spiritual force in which they are not the originators or creators of their own creations, and they function only as instruments. By making this instrument as perfect as possible, it becomes, through the intervention of the Supramental force, an immediate pure instrument for the expression of the Spirit. The perfect scientist is the real genius who has mastered his instrument to produce works that express human possibilities combined with the supramental force, which makes such a scientist an integral divine being on earth. One does not need to be a mature genius to undertake this path, but one first needs to develop a certain level of emotional stability, mature self-awareness, and physical well-being, along with a longing to transcend ordinary life. In the early stages of practising the Yoga of Perfection, practitioners strive to understand and recognise the patterns of their emotions without acting out their negative impulses, trust their own higher self, and maintain their highest known moral standards. The goal of this yoga of perfection is integration, self-transformation, and bringing down the supramental in everyday human life. The practice of this yoga may, therefore, not be for all.

The Mother assumed that in a perfect society, mere intellectual belief in human unity is doomed to fail, as underlying the ideal of human unity is a divine reality, a perfect society where individuals manifest their psychic consciousness, celebrating all the diversity of creation through human unity. In such a society, social problems are not solved by some skillfully devised machinery or crushed out of the social mould, but by the encouragement and growth of the psychic being. In an ideal society, the citizens are conscious of their psychic being, and they organise themselves spontaneously without fixed rules and social laws. The idea of the construction of a spiritual city on earth is a human fabrication, the divine imagined in the image of man, and in this sense, Mother's utopian longing has to be ultimately directed toward a real divine city beyond the earthly surrogate. On the journey itself, she emphasised that it is not only essential "what" the citizens are doing but also "how" they are doing it, i.e., the endeavour to be a morally good person with goodwill for human unity; one who pursues virtues such as sincerity, humility, honesty and empathy, and use these virtues in daily life. It is more the pursuit than the achievement.

The Mother's integral perfection may sound a little too mystic, or an arbitrary fantasy of a divine supramental consciousness, and man's impulse towards spiritual perfection, when looked at in a realistic way of thinking, might seem more like daydreaming that cannot be realised. There appears to be a contradiction between the factual and the ideal in human life, but for the Mother, these opposites become an occasion for a harmonious synthesis to be achieved in the course of future evolution. To leave humanity, as imperfect as it is today, is to limit its divine possibilities, and that's why men have to bring a broader meaning into their lives and manifest in it much more than we secretly are. Mother's perfect and ideal man is superman, and in the beginning, the status of supermanhood will be realised only by a few persons, whereafter it will be open to the whole human race. There are now prospects for a further evolutionary emergence in which Nature's higher workings would resolve the opposition between human imperfections and spiritual perfections. The Mother comments on this evolutionary intention as, "There is an ascending evolution in nature which goes from the stone to the plant, from the plant to the animal, from the animal to man. Because man is, for the moment, the last rung at the summit of the ascending evolution, he considers himself as the final stage in this ascension and believes there can be nothing on earth superior to him. In this, he is mistaken. In his physical nature he is yet almost wholly an animal, a thinking and speaking animal, but still an animal in his material habits and instincts. Undoubtedly, nature cannot be satisfied with such an imperfect result; she endeavours to bring out a being who will be to man what man is to the animal, a being who will remain a man in its external form, and yet whose consciousness will rise far above the mental and its slavery to ignorance." [26] If men could draw down the power of the Divine supramental consciousness into the material world, individual perfection, the perfect ability of the race, of society, and complete mastery of the forces of Nature could see at long last a prospect of total achievement. The summits are attainable at first only by a few exceptional pioneers, far from the threat of the race.

## Critical Analysis

In its utopian vision of human fulfilment in a perfect society, life is characterised by imperfection, complexities, unpredictability, and a certain degree of randomness in real human life and attempts to deny these tragic dimensions of life and transcend these limitations, the utopist might create disillusionment that even may create new forms of suffering. Conflicts, as enduring features of human life, are a fundamental dynamic of unpredictable human existence.

The relentless drive toward the attainment of a perfect society might lead to the suppression of imperfections, which may result in new forms of conflicts when encountered by the resistance to achieving a better world. Lyman Tower Sargent maintains that it is difficult to equate the utopian with the perfect, as in English, perfection suggests something completed, unchangeable, and therefore it looks rather foolish to equate utopia with the perfect since nothing human is complete, finished, or unchangeable. "Very few actual utopias make any pretence of perfection...Most utopias are better at depicting change from current conditions to the utopia than the change within the utopia, and some deliberately restrict change within the utopia on the assumption that something good should not be changed without careful consideration." [27]

In Utopia as a work of progress, perfection may never be attained, however, it may be possible to work towards it and improve Utopia. How much history does humanity need to shape the future? Do we need another utopia, or should we be wiser after all the failed utopias and try to find some happiness and peace in imperfection? In response to our deeper quest, is it not better to accept initially our imperfections and limitations and ultimately also look for answers and solutions more on the psycho-social level and not merely from the spiritual level, with a kind of secret longing to a lost sacredness, or a feeling of respect and wonder towards the unknown? The question of the perfectibility of modern society is a concern shared by all of us with goodwill, regardless of our secular, religious, or spiritual background.

According to A. Braunthal, "There is no reason to nourish illusions about the prospects for perfecting society. The contending forces in human nature and social structures-fraternal v. s aggressive, conservative v. s progressive-have always imposed limits on social progress and will continue to do so... But while it is important to be aware of these limiting factors [political, economic and ecological limitations] they tend to be countered by so many favourable trends that the pessimism about the prospects of society, which has lately become so widespread, can be challenged effectively. If progress toward a more perfect society appears attainable, does modern humanisation, both religious and secular, fulfil any function in this scheme of societal development? The answer is that humanism is inseparable from this scheme.... Humanists are people who consider progress in the direction of perfecting society to be in their personal interest and they act and fight accordingly...The perfect society does not seem to lie within reach! Indeed, the question appears to be eternal...humanists are convinced that higher degrees of societal perfection can be achieved and that the tendencies toward perfection do exist, however fragile their roots"[28]

According to Krishan Kumar, "the notion of perfectibility will, of course, be interpreted in different ways by different people at different times. But what unites utopians and gives to utopian theory its distinctive emphasis is the assumption that there is nothing in man, nature or society that cannot be so ordered as to bring about a more or less permanent state of material plenty, social harmony and individual fulfilment. There are no fundamental barriers or obstacles to man's earthly perfection... Men can, in short, become gods (if not god)" [29]

Is Mother's Auroville an experimental perfection-seeking spiritual utopia, where perfection is an end state in a predesigned world, or is it more related to utopian aspiration towards perfectibility as a process? As such, utopian Auroville cannot be described as a perfect state, but its creation can be described in terms of new forms of life that rely on today's proven methods. The form of this process cannot be anticipated or prescribed; it develops alongside progressively heightened levels of consciousness within the collective organisation, i.e., it develops in tandem with its future members. Where "the process" becomes the central issue of concern for citizens, their ideal society is no longer static and perfect, and it is no longer a perfection of the Mother's final, complete ideal. If citizens want their city to become more dynamic, perhaps the Aurovilians could gradually adopt their creative process and idea of progress, shifting towards change and possibility, even though they seek the prospect of living in a complete future utopia. In this way, the utopian mode of thought becomes an exercise in exploring the possibilities that lie laterally in reality. Suppose the disciples evoke Mother's ideological vision with a nostalgic attitude that emphasises a future perfect utopian society, could it be that they are losing sight of a breakthrough in the free expression of an open-ended utopian city?

To explain this important issue differently, is utopia the earthly representation of a timeless realm of truth, a perfect or perfected society that eliminates the imperfections of existing societies, or is the culminating point of utopian perfection a product of an evolutionary sequence whose future phases are difficult to predict? Progress is not just the law of human nature and human society, and utopia needs to inspire human action rather than mere scholarly contemplation. Mother's utopian experiment needs to be a way beyond theorising her dream, beyond the limits of academic conceivability. Her future spiritual utopia serves as a bridge between a subjective experiment of the psychic being and a new social order; however, it is necessary that the desire to transcend the dream of perfection needs to be supplemented by the living reality. Mother's utopian vision of a perfect future society and the utopian practice by her disciples in the community are different things. They share their ideal of perfection, but the success of the practical utopians on their way to accomplish their ideal is not measured by how far they match up to the ideal of Mother's dream, but how far in their spiritual practice do they develop the possibility of their own spiritual life with the Mother's guidelines on the way. Although the pursuit of perfection persists to this day, its attainability remains a subject of debate.

Auroville functions as a spiritual experiment in conscious evolution, and any form of future organisation will emerge from this process. The outcome of this process, a heightened level of Auroville's collective consciousness, cannot be anticipated. Its development cannot be predetermined as a fixed state; instead, it evolves according to the new consciousness of its citizens for collective change. Perfection in Auroville's utopian development must be flexible, progressive, experimental and responsive to spiritual evolution, but how will it ever be attained? As a work in progress, it is possible to work towards improving its spiritual utopian character through the citizens' practice of Mother's teachings. Does Auroville, in its attempt to create a perfect society, echo the historic failure to achieve such perfection? Aurovilians are not perfect disciples, and they carry within themselves their imperfect human nature, being aware, each in their own way, of what is going on in their society and what needs to be changed. Mother's social-spiritual transformation does not simply require a radical vision for building the city, but it also necessitates a radical practice within an overall movement to change the world. The Mother did not aim at a static, reified object of a passively perfect society, nor the authoritarian guidance of a blueprint, but rather the emancipating and participatory nature of her dream, without the tendency to lapse into a rigid system.

The Mother offered her disciples a multifaceted utopian practice, and she is hardly concerned with the fixed structure of social institutions, but more with a vision of the possibilities for a better future and the activism needed to reach them. Life in Auroville is still far from perfect, and it seems that there is a tendency to reduce alternative visions to a closed and perfect system. A spiritual utopian society might not be able to perfect the present human situation out of existence. Any utopian future will have to fight for its existence and will always continue to face the complexity of life with its problems and contradictions. The complexity of the present situation in Auroville may require diverse actions of opposition, as a single approach approved by some of its citizens may be merely an ineffective invitation to an authoritarian approach. One of the main problems at the moment is the danger of the centralisation of power and the reduction of the ideals of Mother's dream into a dogmatic ideology that inhibits certain activities. Auroville's future is not fixed, and nobody is certain about the future, as it is subject to regressive behaviour within its own population and continuous attacks by forces seeking to control the project. Her dream could be crushed by those who are subordinate to this centralised power. This requires not only a collective radical vision but also a few strong individuals with a radical practice.

In a perfect society where all kinds of individual and social problems have been resolved, and everything runs smoothly, we may ask ourselves what we are doing any longer in such a place where there is no deep sense of one's destiny. We may go mad at new vistas of reality, but nobody knows because nobody has been there yet. Sri Aurobindo foresaw a race of perfected individuals belonging to a gnostic society, a society that would act not as a mechanical but as a spiritual unity. This first requires a few individuals to open themselves to a higher level of consciousness, as any attempt to transform human society begins with a few spiritually developed individuals. According to Sri Aurobindo, "The individual is indeed the key of the evolutionary movement; for it is the individual who finds himself, who becomes conscious of Reality. The movement of the collectivity is a larger subconscious mass movement, it has to formulate and express itself through the individuals to become conscious: its general mass consciousness is always less evolved than the consciousness of its most developed individuals."[30]

In the complete supramental transformation, the divine being and the new race will be as much beyond humanity as humanity is beyond the animal. In the divine being and the divine life, "It is, then, this spiritual fulfilment of the urge to individual perfection and an inner completeness of being that we mean first when we speak of a divine life. It is the first essential condition of a perfected life on earth... The perfection of the spiritual and pragmatic relation of the individual with all around him is our second preoccupation ...But there still remains the third desideratum, a new world, a change in the total life of humanity or, at the least, a new perfected collective life in the earth-nature."[31]

These three aspects of the perfection of the individual, social and phenomenal reality are the integral parts of his goal, and the practice of his Integral Yoga is the necessary means for the individual to promote the Divine evolution toward true perfection. The Mother does refer to ethical perfection; it may help, and there may be a change, but it is not a transmutation of the surface outer reality into an inner and higher spiritual reality. The Mother's spiritual humanity, as a blending of spirituality and materiality, is the only hope for the future, although she never articulated her preference for humanity because humanism, in its focus on the welfare of man, does not accept any form of attainment of divinity.

Sri Aurobindo has not attempted to predict how this world will evolve; however, he provided brief statements and specific expressions of possibilities, leaving the exact process to the Supramental development itself. In the author's "*Reflections upon psycho-spiritual obstacles in Integral Yoga*", when elaborating on the unpredictable aspects of evolution, he asks, "Are present-day developments and research by scientific investigators on future designer babies the resurrection of the soul and genetically engineered children from the laboratory the new humanity? "[32] It could be conceivable that there are a (great) number of Aurovilians who, with great persistence, might bring about profound changes in human evolution "by stamping these changes into body and brain through hereditary, of acquired transmission, evolve a superior race which would endure, and by the law of survival of the fittest eliminate the weaker kinds of humanity."[33]

A mythologised human version of a sterile, changeless perfectionism, a peaceful paradise, does it overlook one of the main aims of utopia, the empirical search for remedies and reform? It is not an unworldly utopian illusionism where the faith of its citizens in mere goodwill and ideal intentions is sufficient for a new society. Though utopian Auroville cannot be anticipated nor described as a perfect State, it indeed envisions newness. Participating in this newness requires a change of consciousness; it develops alongside the progressive heightened levels of consciousness of the collective citizens. Auroville, as an experimental intentional community, is it a perfection-seeking utopia, or is it more related to a utopian striving for or aspiration towards perfectibility rather than perfection itself? An absolute urge toward perfection could end in a kind of disease, as soon as it is used as a destructive attitude towards the imperfect.

## Notes

1.) Sri Aurobindo; *The Synthesis of Yoga*, p.754

2.) Ibid., p 584

3.) Ibid., p 35

4.) Sri Aurobindo; *Letters on Yoga,* p.848-849

5.) Sri Aurobindo; *The Synthesis of Yoga*, p.587

6.) Sri Aurobindo; *The Letters on Yoga*, p.24

7.) Sri Aurobindo; *The Life Divine,* p.1022

8.) Ibid., p 412

9.) Sri Aurobindo; *The Synthesis of Yoga*, p. 588

10.) Sri Aurobindo; *Letters on Yoga*, p.373

11.) Sri Aurobindo; *The Synthesis of Yoga,* p. 710

12.) Ibid., p. 710

13.) Ibid., p. 40

14.) Ibid., p. 2

15.) Ibid., p. 664

16.) Ibid., p. 592-593

17.) Ibid., p. 590

18.) The Mother; *Mother's Agenda*, Oct 1-1958

19.) Sri Aurobindo, *The Life Divine*, p. 674

20.) Sri Aurobindo; *Essays Human and Divine*, p.167-168

21.) Ibid., p.103-104

22.) The Mother; *The Mother's Agenda*, April 24, 1957

23.) Sri Aurobindo; *The Synthesis of* Yoga, p.592

24.) Sri Aurobindo; *Essays in Philosophy and Yoga*, p 73

25.) Sri Aurobindo; *The Synthesis of Yoga*, p 732

26.) The Mother; *CWM* Vol 12 p 16

27.) Lyman Tower Sargent; *Utopianism, A Short Histo*ry, p.104

28.) A. Braunthal; *Salvation and the Perfect Society*, p.532-533

29.) Krishan Kumar; *Utopianism*, p.29

30.) Sri Aurobindo; *The Life Divine*, p.1050

31.) Ibid., p.1031

32.) Joseph Vrinte; *Reflections upon Psycho-spiritual Obstacles on the journey to the Divine*, p.257

33.) Sri Aurobindo; *Man, Slave or Free*, p.20

## *CHAPTER THREE*

# CRISIS

At present, humanity, with all its technological advancements and progress, lives in uncertain times, marked by great global complexity and confusion, which hinders development and erodes humanity's capacity to manage human affairs related to justice, sustainability, and stability. Why does this all take place, for what purpose and to what end?

For Sri Aurobindo, "The present crisis of humanity is not a political, economic, social or cultural crisis, but at present mankind is undergoing an evolutionary crisis in which is concealed a choice of its destiny; for a stage has been reached in which the human mind has achieved in certain directions enormous development while in others it stands arrested and bewildered and can no longer find its way...Man has created a system of civilisation which has become too big for his limited mental capacity and understanding and his still more limited spiritual and moral capacity to utilise and manage, a too dangerous servant of his blundering ego and its appetites... he has created societies based on fixed ideas or fixed customs, a fixed cultural system or an organic life-system, each with its own order; the throwing of all these into the melting pot of a more and more intermingling life and a pouring in of ever new ideas and motives and facts and possibilities call for a new, a greater consciousness to meet and master the increasing potentialities of existence and harmonise them. Reason and Science can only help by standardising, by fixing everything into an artificially arranged and mechanised unity of material life. A greater whole-being, whole-knowledge, and whole-power are needed to weld all into a greater unity of whole-life. A life of unity, mutuality and harmony born of a deeper and wider truth of our being is the only truth of life that can successfully replace the imperfect mental constructions of the past, which were an accommodation of egos and interests grouped or dovetailed into each other to form a society...But because the burden which is being laid on mankind is too great for the present littleness of human personality and its petty mind and small-life instincts, because it cannot operate the needed change, the destiny of the race seems to be heading dangerously, as if impatiently and in spite of itself... into a prolonged confusion and perilous crisis and darkness of violent incertitude...For the problem is fundamental and in putting its evolutionary Nature in man is confronting herself with a critical choice which must one day be solved in the true sense if the race is to arrive or even to survive...A rational and scientific formula of the vitalistic and materialistic human being and his life, a search for a perfected economic society and democratic cultus of the average man are all that the modern mind presents us in this crisis as a light for its solution...Social machinery cannot form the soul and life-force into standardised shapes; it can at best coerce them, make soul and mind inert and stationery and regulate the life's outward action...a society governed or sanctioned by religion has not changed human life and society; It could not do so because, in governing society, it had to compromise with the lower parts of life and could not insist on the inner change of the whole being...A total spiritual direction given to the whole life and the whole nature can alone lift humanity beyond itself...It is only the full emergence of the soul, the full descent of the native light and power of the Spirit and the consequent replacement or transformation and uplifting of our insufficient mental and vital nature by a spiritual and supramental Supernature that can effect this evolutionary miracle... what is demanded by this change is not something altogether distant, alien to our existence and radically impossible; for what has to be developed is there in our being and not something outside it."[1]

The word crisis in Greek origin means "a point of elimination and separation, an instant when change, one way or the other, is impending." A crisis often disrupts the habitual and institutional patterns of behaviour and makes people more amenable to individual and social change. In a crisis, a struggle occurs during personal or social change, which is often necessary to form a new sense of self or a new society that emerges afterwards. Progress does not necessarily need to be a natural or assured result of change; it may require more human effort. One of the failures of modern societies is the lack of the individual's basic human needs for community identity. The merging of individual and societal needs contributes towards a feeling of belonging and a sense of unity where the collective begins to function as a whole. A crisis amid chaos and loss often has an inherent sense of purpose and can be experienced as a means to a paradise in which each of us is our brother's and sister's keeper, i.e., being free to live and act in a new, participatory way. The recovery of this purpose and the search for meaning are needed in today's crisis, which often challenges one's struggle against the current state of one's society. In practical utopias, as living utopian experiments, where members endeavour to realise a dream, they are often confronted with recurrent conflicts within the various groups of the community and how these conflicts are managed.

The nature, cause, and function of a conflict need serious analysis. A dispersed force of countless people making countless decisions, especially in a top-down management, may easily cause a significant crisis. During the crisis, a bureaucratic framework is one of the main obstacles, as the community needs innovations and improvisation, where things are done differently without a paternalistic approach to governance. It need not be mentioned that an evolving community is a dynamic process towards an expression of a better way of life and not an immediate realisation of perfection, and if the community wants to survive over time, it needs to find ways to manage its conflicts before it becomes an enduring unrestrained crisis which inhabits the achievement of its aim. A crisis needs to be managed properly as it threatens the stability of the community, but it may also be viewed as a valuable catalyst for change, even though it causes distress and disruption. Often, expertise in conflict mediation or comprehensive training in management can help prevent social disintegration, which may necessitate the re-evaluation of the power structure and interrelations within a community.

It seems that the crisis in Auroville brings back old memories of the conflicts with the Sri Aurobindo Society in the 1980s, which left irreparable damage to the community at that time and may still have some lingering effects. It caused serious infighting and destabilised the spiritual social foundation on which the Mother established the city. Through these conflicts, stemming from excessive outside interference, citizens should have by now strengthened their self-esteem and cultivated self- and mutual criticism, admitting their weaknesses, failures, and imperfections as a means to develop the ability to withstand future threats to their existence. It is a well-established fact that an outgroup threat enhances ingroup cohesion and intensifies the group's values. Fortunately, at that time, the Indian government intervened, and the city was able to survive. The citizens could gradually put their principles into practice again, according to Mother's teachings, and realise her vision of their psychic life.

Before the present crisis escalated, Aurovilians were already facing serious difficulties within the community, as had been the case under the preceding Secretaries of the Auroville Foundation. Mr. Bala Basker, who served two terms as a Secretary, did not think that things within Auroville were moving at the right pace and in the right direction, and he was not able to do much about it. He felt "that about 30% of the population here are doing very good work and another 30% are just here for themselves. But I feel that the other 40% who were in the middle are now drifting towards the negative side, becoming more concerned with their own problems than with the welfare of the community. And there is much more politics now. What makes it worse here, there is a dislike of rules and regulations, so decisions are taken based on personal likes and dislikes."[2]

The next Secretary of the Auroville Foundation expressed his concerns about the Auroville developments in a similar way. According to Mr. Mohan Verghese Chunkat, " Auroville seems to have splintered into different groups with different ideals, each with their own priorities; and there are many 'free' spirits who do not wish to have any rules. What all have in common is that none is ready to subsume their views and compromise with each other to reach a shared larger vision...Auroville must go back to its roots and do a lot of introspection on what Sri Aurobindo and the Mother said. This is very, very necessary, for unless you are able to harmonise different viewpoints, you cannot take decisions."[3]

Are Aurovilians facing complex problems in adapting to a changing environment? The original members, as they age, often suffer a deterioration of their communal ideals due to the practical needs of existence. Their idealism for realising Mother's ideals, which had formed the original basis for Auroville's existence, is gradually replaced by the scepticism of the later, younger generation who joined Auroville. It must address these changes, ranging from ignoring them to incorporating them for those who aim for limited consumption and those who seek wider availability of luxury goods. This often causes discontent. To include the products of external social change drastically undermines the communal base, shifting away from the old lifestyle and solidarity toward individualism, where personal fulfilment seems to be more important for the strength of the group. Now that the community has existed for more than 55 years, building the city as a product becomes increasingly important, and conducting business that conflicts with maintaining the community's feelings and commitment is often a challenge. The new city may attract a crowd of inhabitants who lack faith in Mother's vision and only join the community out of self-interest.

The eternal longing for a perfect and utopian world is often accompanied by dreams that collide with unpredictable reality. At present, Auroville, as an intentionally aspiring utopia that aims at perfection in its quest to build a new world, is in crisis. The project is again confronted with its own intrinsic faults arising from inherent tensions and contradictions. There seems to be a gap between their aspirations and their tangible accomplishments in partially realising Mother's dream. This has led to the gradual institutionalisation of the organisation, where the citizens are struggling to balance freedom and authority. Disputes over internal domestic progress and the realisation of Mother's foundational vision of the construction of the future city became explosive when a new Secretary took over in 2021. With a small group of devotees who supported her, she became responsible for enforcing a huge number of rules, rather than individual participation, where all group members together enforced their collective rules. A group of citizens have distorted the ideal of realising unity through diversity under the guidance of the Secretary, who is obsessed with building the city of 50,000 residents within a time limit as the ultimate goal. However, there are other citizens, who set out on another path, and though they also want to build the city they don't aim at erecting huge buildings and roads immediately, they are more in Auroville to look within, develop their full psycho-spiritual potential and evolve as a human species, free from evolvement of old institutions and conventional interference.

From the start of Auroville's inauguration, there was tension between those disciples who wanted to construct the city as soon as possible and those who emphasised a more gradual approach. Aurovilians have, over the last 55 years, been unable to reach a consensus on the design of the Town Plan (Galaxy Plan), with seeming polarities between pro-Galaxy and anti-Galaxy proponents, which actually need to be reconciled in a way that makes both viewpoints complementary. One of the old Aurovilians expressed these opposing views as, "Some say that the conflict in Auroville is between forces that want to build and forces that want to block the growth of the city, forces that want to block Auroville's physical manifestation. My take, rather, is that the opposition is coming from forces that want to block the development of the Auroville Spirit, to prevent the growth of the true Auroville consciousness. After all, what will be the use of building rapidly a city of concrete and glass? Will that then wait for some new, fresh generation of Aurovilians to come and inhabit it, to fill it with the true spirit? Both are needed now: the physical growth of the city and the growth too, and more urgently, the growth of the true consciousness of Auroville.... Auroville has to be the city the earth needs, ...the city with a Soul... with a living consciousness of unity. This is the challenge of today."[4]

It seems that most of the Aurovilians are not opposed to the Galaxy plan, but to what extent are its main elements modified in response to outside circumstances and changed reality on the ground, without destroying its integrity while working to build not only a city but building a city as an example for a better world? Planners need to consider the current reality and adjust plans accordingly to reflect changes in the situation. An ideal town plan requires a balance between full organic development and a detailed master plan, rather than a utopia.

This continuous struggle between contradictory tendencies within the Auroville community broke the fragile unity; on one side, the conservatists with their official faith in Mother's dream; on the other side, the radicals who have their own interpretation of Mother's views. Although the present crisis in Auroville is often described as a simplistic explanation between the Galaxy and the Forest, or the young and the old-timers, instead of stubborn resistance, Aurovilians should aim for a compromise and collaboration between the Galaxy and the Forest. Fortunately, some of the members remain loyal and dedicated to working out an agreement, and in their devotion, they try to find possible ways of congruence between Mother's original vision and Auroville's actual existence, creating a balance between order and freedom, and between involvement and autonomy. It is like starting to build the city by creating Aurovilians whose actions are required beyond theorising

Auroville as a utopia. This is not a matter of mere goodwill; there may be moments in the future when the continuation of Auroville's existence depends on them.

Could many of the proposed solutions have little results because they are based on a flawed diagnosis and an insufficient analysis of the present situation? Are only internal disagreements the cause of the inevitable problems of Auroville's life, or are there dilemmas arising from longevity itself? A diagnosis requires continuous, repeated research, self-criticism, and endless patience, and one must be aware of inconspicuous symptoms, as hidden causes may have profound consequences. The best diagnosis given at any time is often not a final diagnosis. It is easier to design a city than to predict the behaviour of people who are free to act, as human behaviour will most likely never be able to be predicted mathematically exactly. The present-day crisis compels citizens to re-evaluate the assumptions on which the community is founded. In times of crisis, there may be a few enlightened citizens who are able to share the rationale needed to explore the possibility of replacing some assumptions and creating a better community.

Is there a typical shift within the Auroville community where its leaders' authority turns into power? It may require a new group formation, one that is averse to traditional ideological formations and is fed up with the abuse of power by the current existing groups of people. At the beginning of Auroville's existence, a high degree of self-organisation and self-government existed, with authority based on community ethics. However, with the concentration of wealth, it became evident that a small group gradually gained more power.

Auroville's crisis may be necessary to break through outdated surface layers, which are an obstacle to the underlying potentialities that are hidden within and seek expression.

Auroville needs to continually adapt to the various changes within and outside the community, and if it ignores this fact, the community may become stagnant. This does not merely refer to outer expansion but is also closely related to fostering growth within. However limited, in times of crisis and the absence of true yogis, it may be more helpful to adhere to the more fundamental observance of sadhana related to the aims of old traditional yoga's, i.e., Yamas and Nyamas, the moral human do's and don'ts.

Are Aurovilians merely struggling to address various symptoms related to the crisis in order to avoid examining the more fundamental causes? As a matter of fact, could it be that one of the main causes of the present crisis is primarily related to the various difficulties associated with the spiritual practice of Mother's teachings on the journey of Auroville's experiment, where in the absence of Mother's direct guidance the devotees do not recognise and reconsider errors in their practice? One of the Auroville citizens experiences, "the present turmoil as resistance from those who oppose Mother's Auroville. But it is also possible that those who quote Mother's words in support of their present attempts to improve Auroville, whatever their best intentions, do not have sufficient wisdom and spiritual understanding (as well as, in certain cases, the practical competence) to apply them in an integral, harmonious way, and this has resulted in considerable collateral damage. Mother often emphasised that a drop of spiritual experience means more than thousands of words, and many of those early Aurovilians whom she personally chose were clearly not 'spiritual' in any conventional sense, suggesting that she chose them more for their openness to her Force than for their 'spirituality'. Perhaps even today, some of our less obviously 'spiritual' brothers and sisters are more in contact with that Force than those who so eloquently quote and write about our spiritual guides. In the same way that I think many of us—myself included—lack sufficient inner understanding to be able to select our spiritual leaders. I believe we lack the deep understanding of this complex, multilayered spiritual experiment that would allow us to judge who should or should not be in Auroville."[5]

While exploring these deeper causes, all citizens are faced with their backpacks, which contain their capacities and possibilities as well as their limitations and shortcomings. The external symptoms need to be transformed and challenged by our inner possibilities, and thereafter, our activities and developments need to be shifted from the inner consciousness to the outer environment. In other words, the collective experiment first involves the process of self-exploration at the individual's inward level, whereafter, the collective inner search in the soul of man can establish harmony in the complexity of various possible difficulties. What Auroville encounters today are mainly different kinds of symptoms that don't touch the root causes of the problems, which lie much deeper and need a breakdown of the collective ego shell. Are the upheavals in the various disturbing spheres in Auroville only symptomatic of a lack of spiritual development? For the Mother, the mental consciousness seems totally incapable of solving these problems and needs a higher power of consciousness. In Auroville's mundane matters, the Aurovilians do not seem to delve deeply enough into their psychic consciousness. As for the Mother, there is no material organisation capable of providing a solution to Auroville's problems. These problems will persist; they will only change the outer form and look. In case Mother's advice fails due to Auroville's inability to find a way out of the crisis, are Aurovilians able to reflect on themselves and their situation in a highly contemplative state and endeavour to heal some of the wounds?

The progressive differentiation between the interaction of Aurovilians causes the bonds that unite them to weaken, and the breach of doctrine and practice between the subgroups within the community may be another main cause of the crisis. However, when the issues that divide them are not made vital, the subgroups may be able to abandon some divisive issues of Mother's original ideological planning to re-establish the bonds amongst its citizens, rather than strict adherence to her belief versus greater spontaneity decision making, related to the permanently changed structure and new environment within Auroville. The outcome is unpredictable; the project may split apart or unite, but the nature of the conflict is a powerful speculative scene of human activity. It may be questioned if the outcomes of judicial interference resolve the conflicts; its effects may only place a superficial plug in a large hole. In this complicated conflict, should the inhabitants *initially* bring in some more rationality and plain human common sense, where the two rival groups allow to understand each other from their own perspectives, with an authentic identification of the suffering from both sides? Thereafter, it may be possible to analyse why this didn't happen when the conflict started. Each form of partiality causes blind spots; one takes sides involuntarily and adjusts reality according to one's own view. When confronted with facts that do not align with one's own views, they are often generalised and become less significant. In an attempt towards a process of connection with different views and opinions and overcoming partiality, there is no need to think about victory over and denial of the other. As mentioned before, it needs, first of all, some necessary introspection and self-reflection; critically look into the mirror and correct one's own mistakes, only then is an attempt to connect possible, i.e., all self-criticism precedes connection. As long as both parties are unable to reach a rational level, it may need to be enforced by a third party through practical measures that will clear up some of the major obstacles. Do Aurovilians need some time and an outside authority to remind them why they are in Auroville, as a motivating push to the next step of its realisation towards self-organisation? The Force may be present, and the citizens may remain collectively attuned to it, but her Force is unconventional, with its outcomes and consequences often unpredictable, as evidenced by its lack of efficient collective organisation in Auroville's journey toward self-governance.

Like humanity as a whole is facing an evolutionary crisis, is Auroville experiencing a similar evolutionary crisis? The present crisis may create some chaos, but seeming failures could be gateways to new opportunities, where inhabitants put greater emphasis today on manifesting their inner development rather than remaining stuck with their own external issues and outer reality. It may be time for Aurovilians to try something different, something that has not been done in the outside world. Do the citizens finally need to gradually replace their imperfect mental solutions of the past with a new, deeper, and wider consciousness that is much more capable of governing material solutions in a more beneficial way for Auroville's present-day crisis? This requires some necessary self-reflection and sincere individual effort, with a tendency to go inward and act accordingly. It is of no use to keep looking merely at the citizens' failures and force upon them all kinds of rules to deal with all their shortcomings. Mother's aim to create a spiritual society may be an ideal far away, but perhaps a transitional period is needed to find a realisable alternative in the form of renewed idealism to keep the polarisation under control. This renewed idealism could match with concrete and practical steps for the intermediate stage to propel the city forward through experimentation and research.

## Notes

1.) Sri Aurobindo, *The Life Divine,* p 1053-1058

2.) *Auroville Today,* August 2014

3.) *Auroville Today*, August 2019

4.) *Auroville Today*, November 2023

5.) *Auroville Today*, October 2023

## *CHAPTER FOUR*

# SOCIAL CHANGE

Throughout the course of spiritual development, man must realise his unity with other selves in the universe. Only the individual is able to think, but his thoughts cannot be adequately understood without a concrete setting of a social situation, which imposes uniformity of thought and experiences upon the members of the society. It is through the individual that its evolutionary self-unfolding reaches its acme, but if this aspect of the ideal is pursued in isolation, then man will fail to find a proper place in society where his needs cannot be fulfilled. In Mother's vision, we cannot decide beforehand the ideal type of collective life unless we know the true purpose of the individual's life. Man should be studied first as an individual, and only thereafter can we examine him through the changing features of his social life. Unless man knows the basic material and spiritual necessities of himself as an individual, we cannot say in which type of collective life he will be more perfect. Though the Mother will not deny that society shapes the individual, for her, the latter supervenes on society. From the individual, we must start, and once he realises himself and the inner significance of life's conditions, he becomes aware of the necessity of the society around him for his own perfection. Gradually, the human cycle develops through the progressive enlargement of the individual within society.

As described by Sri Aurobindo, "the growth of the individual is the indispensable means for the inner growth as distinguished from the outer force and expansion of the collective being. This indeed is the dual importance of the individual that it is through him that the cosmic Spirit organises its collective units...But the progress of the mind, the growth of the soul, even of the mind and the soul of the collectivity, depends on the individual, on his separate power to express and bring into being what is still unexpressed in the mass... The collectivity is a mass, a field of formation; the individual is a diviner truth, the form maker, the creator... In the crowd, the individual loses his inner direction and becomes a cell of the mass-body moved by the collective will or idea or the mass-impulse. He has to stand apart, affirm his separate reality in the whole, his own mind emerging from the common mentality, his own life distinguishing itself in the common life-uniformity, even as the body has developed something unique and recognisable in the common physicality. He has, even, in the end to retire into himself in order to find himself, and it is only when he has found himself that he can become spiritually one with all; if he tries to achieve that oneness in the mind, in the vital, in the physical and has not yet a sufficiently strong individuality, he may be overpowered by the mass-consciousness and lose his soul-fulfilment, his mind-fulfilment his life -fulfilment, become only a cell of the mass-body. The collective being may then become strong and dominant, but it is likely to lose its plasticity, its evolutionary movement."[1]

Despite mixing with society, man must maintain his individuality, just as his body is unique and recognisable in physicality. Nevertheless, there needs to be a proper and balanced relationship between the individual and society, where the individual, as a social being, must live in society and be of utility to it, while society is also supposed to serve the needs of all. Society has to offer each individual the right place, opportunities for growth, and the right frame of life in the world.

For the problems of the individual and the collective, Sri Aurobindo formulates an ideal law of social development that needs to be applied and described by him as, "The society has no right to crush or efface the individual for its own better development or self-satisfaction; the individual, so long at least as he chooses to live in the world, has no right to disregard for the sake of his own solitary satisfaction and development his fellow-beings and to live at war with them and seek a selfish isolated good."[2] "True, his life and growth are for the sake of the world, but he can help the world by his life and growth only in proportion as he can be more and more freely and widely his own real self....He has indeed the tendency of self-limitation and subjection to his environment and group, but he has also the equally necessary tendency of expansion and transcendence of environment and groupings...Thus the community stands as a mid-term and intermediary value between the individual and humanity and it exists not merely for itself, but for the one and the other and to help them to fulfil each other."[3] In other words, "The free development of individuals from within is the best condition for the growth and perfection of the community, so the free development of the community or nation from within is the best condition for the growth and perfection of mankind. Thus, the law for the individual is to perfect his individuality by free development from within, but to respect and to aid and be aided by the same free developments in others. His law is to harmonise his life with the life of the social aggregate and to pour himself out as a force for growth and perfection in humanity. The law for the community or nation is equally to perfect its corporate existence by a free development from within, aiding and taking full advantage of that of the individual, but to respect and to aid and be aided by the same free development of other communities and nations. Its law is to harmonise its life with that of the human aggregate and to pour itself out as a force for growth and perfection of humanity."[4]

Somewhere else, Sri Aurobindo describes this issue as more related to the object of Integral Yoga, he "regards the spirit in man not solely as an individual being travelling to a transcendent unity with the Divine, but as a universal being capable of oneness with the Divine in all souls and all Nature and we give this extended view its entire practical consequence. The human soul's individual liberation and enjoyment of union with the Divine in spiritual being, consciousness and delight must always be the first object of the Yoga; its free enjoyment of the cosmic unity of the Divine becomes a second object; but out of that a third appears, the effectuation of the meaning of the divine unity with all beings by a sympathy and participation in the spiritual purpose of the Divine in humanity. The individual Yoga then turns from its separateness and becomes a part of the collective Yoga of the divine Nature in the human race.... In other words, a perfection has to be aimed at, which amounts to the elevation of the mental into the full spiritual and supramental nature. Therefore this Integral Yoga of knowledge, love and works has to be extended into a Yoga of spiritual self-perfection."[5] These statements do not show that every man is truly individual or that no collectivism can be truly individual, but it can be said that if activities to attain a high degree of individuality is different for an individual, then it is easy to imagine that it is more difficult for the collective.

The laws and characteristic movements of surface life are easy to understand, but their practical applications do not take man far; they do not solve significant problems of existence. Sociology provides men with only a general account of the past and the external conditions under which communities have survived and, therefore, does not offer much help. However, social institutions and forces of custom and interest shape the lives of all men and cultural customs. When given the proper conditions, men's potentialities will be capable of building social order governed by the principle of equality, liberty and justice, expressed by Sri Aurobindo as," if the spiritual change is to be affected, it must unite two conditions which have to be simultaneously satisfied but are most challenging to bring together. There must be individuals who are able to see, develop, and re-create themselves in the image of the Spirit and communicate both their ideas and their power to the masses. And they must be at the same time a mass, a society, a communal mind or at the least the constituents of a group-body, the possibility of a group-soul which is capable of receiving and effectively assimilating, ready to follow and effectively arrive, not compelled by its own inherent deficiencies, its defect of preparation to stop on the way or fall back before the decisive change is made. Such a simultaneity has never yet happened... That the combination must happen someday is a certainty, but none can tell how many attempts will have to be made and how many sediments of spiritual experience will have to be accumulated in the subconscient mentality of the communal human being before the soil is ready" [6] This process works by striving, as well as through mutual assistance and unified effort. It employs two diverse forms of action, which seem contradictory but are always coexistent, competitive, and collaborative endeavours. From this dynamic character of life, the entire structure of human society has emerged, and the growth of human society depends on these motive forces, as without this life force, everything stagnates and moves toward disintegration.

The Mother, when referring to the collective self-assertion of the text above, explains that "this is exactly what Auroville is for" as the fulfilment of the second condition involves a psychic transformation, first in a certain number of individuals, as well as the formation of a group-soul towards the evolution of a new being and a new society. For the Mother, the ideal of human life is the preservation of individuality and the fulfilment of spiritual possibilities while actively participating in society's affairs. However, a society that lives by its institutions is akin to a machine, where life becomes a mechanical product and ceases to be a living, organic growth. As individualism and collectivism have equally deep-rooted human qualities, there is a strong possibility of a clash between the two tendencies. Humanity has used the ethical ideal of altruism as a solution, but for the Mother, the main aim of individual life is man's urge towards self-transcendence or the aspiration for the realisation of the divine, where the individual transcends his narrow self-interest.

In the words of the Mother, "For this formation to succeed, all human beings-even all living beings as well as their material environment-must be transformed. Otherwise things will remain as they are: an individual experience cannot change terrestrial life... not only an individual or a group of individuals or even all individuals, but life has to be transformed. Without such a transformation we shall continue to have the same misery, the same calamities and the same atrocities in the world. A few individuals will escape from it by their psychic development, but the general mass will remain in the same state of misery".[7] It needs a collective effort so that the supramental transformation can be realised in terms of an integral human perfection. Somewhere else she says "terrestrial transformation can be brought about by individual transformation, an inner development leading to the union with the Divine Presence and Social transformation, the establishment of an environment favourable to the flowering and growth of the individual. Since the environment reacts upon the individual and, on the other hand, the value of the environment depends upon the value of the individual, the two should proceed side by side. But for each individual there is also a twofold labour to be done, simultaneously, each side of it helping and completing the other; an inner development, a progressive union with the Divine light...An external action which everyone has to choose according to his capacities and personal preferences." [8]

## Social Laws

In human society, social laws are obeyed due to physical necessity or a sense of general interest, often under the pressure of environmental factors or a sense of duty. These social laws are a means by which the ego is subjected in order to learn discipline by subordination to a wider collective ego. They may express all the practical needs of society or be modified by an ideal law, which is binding on the developing individual in the shape of social duty, communal demand, or family obligations. For Sri Aurobindo, "The existence of a social law external to the individual is at different times a considerable advantage and disadvantage to the development of the divine in man. It is an advantage at first when men are crude and incapable of self-control and self-finding to discipline their rational and often violent movements and even to lose themselves sometimes in a larger and less personal egoism. It is a disadvantage to the adult spirit ready to transcend the human formula, because it is an external standard which seeks to impose itself on him from outside, and the condition of his perfection is that he shall grow from within and in an increasing freedom, not the suppression but by the transcendence of his perfected individuality, not any longer by a law imposed on him that trains and disciplines his members but by the soul from within breaking through all previous forms to progress with its light and transmute his members."[9]

Somewhere else, he writes, "Entering the path of works, while accepting the aim of integral Yoga, the social law as a term of progress is a means to which the ego is subjected so that it may learn discipline by subordination to a wider collective ego. This law may be quite empty of any moral content and may express only the needs or practical good of the society as each society conceives it...But the Sadhaka of the Karma Yoga will abandon this also to the Lord of works after he has made his surrender, his social impulses and judgements will, like his desires, only be used for their exhaustion, or enable him to identify his lower mental nature with humanity in general or with any grouping of humanity in its works and hopes and aspirations. But after that brief time is over, they will be withdrawn and a divine government will alone abide...If any social law is obeyed it will not be from physical necessity or the sense of personal or general interest or for expediency or because of the pressure of the environment or from any sense of duty, but solely for the sake of the Lord of works and because it is felt or known to be the divine Will that the social law or rule or relation as it stands can still be kept as a figure of the inner life and the minds of men must not be disturbed by its infringement."[10]

Man grows by his relations with others, and the social principle is perfectly justified as a field of relations which affords the individual his occasion for growth towards a greater perfection. However, "In our social building we labour to establish some approach to unity, mutuality, harmony, because without these things there can be no perfect social living, but what we built is a constructed unity, an association of interests and egos enforced by law and custom and imposing an artificial constructed order in which the interests of some prevail over the interests of others and only a half accepted half and forced, half natural half artificial accommodation keeps the social whole in being. Between community and community there is a still worse accommodation with a constant recurrence of the strife of collective ego. This is the best we can do and all our persistent re-adjustments of the social order can bring us nothing better than an imperfect structured life."[11] For Sri Aurobindo, "it is a spiritual, an inner freedom that can alone create a perfect human order... A deeper brotherhood, a yet unfound law of love is the only sure foundation possible for a perfect social evolution, no other can replace it."[12]

How to bring about the social transformation of a spiritual society towards human unity as a living sense and practice of human oneness in thought, feeling and life? Should it start without proper institutions or from within? A social transformation cannot be achieved all at once; exchanging morals with which we are familiar for a new spiritual valuation at some very remote period in the future may be a predominant power within us, but only a small dose will gradually impart a new nature in man. Greater social unity is only worth pursuing if it provides a means and a framework for a better and happier individual and collective life. A small ordinary democratic state as a modern utopia organises the social principles and processes that govern the collective secured by a fundamental equality of all, with the management of the whole social life and perfectly organised government and administration; this in one form or another mankind hopes to turn into a living reality and bring about some form of perfection in the collective human life. This central authority, with a growing uniformity in administration, social life, and culture, is the sole governing authority whose function is to represent the thought and will of the whole community, replacing a natural and organic development of society with a mechanically organised society. However, this form of a small collective life is always characterised by a tendency of its own defects, and its own impermanence or insufficient capacity for widespread material well-being tends to disappear. The mere formal, mechanical, administrative, political and economic union does not necessarily create a psycho-spiritual unity. Beyond external circumstances and necessities of which men are aware, there is always also an internal necessity in the being and nature which precedes the outward signals and gets itself realised. The inner factor for the outer frame may be created in its process of growth, but this change needs a transcendence of the ego principle without the destruction of man's individuality, i.e., the recognition of a soul in the humanity of which each man is incarnate.

For Sri Aurobindo, for long mental methods have always been a principle of selection and rejection, which "has taken the forms of a social or moral rule of life or an ethical ideal. But this is an empirical means which does not touch the root of the problem because it has no vision of the cause and the origin of the malady it attempts to cure; it deals with the symptoms, but deals with them perfunctorily, not knowing what function they serve in the purpose of Nature and what it is in the mind and life that supports them and keeps them in being"[13] Sri Aurobindo agrees, that mental control over our vital desires and instincts, our personal and social actions, and our dealing with others is indispensable. Yet, control is always imperfect, and that is not a lasting solution. Man always remains what he is: a mental ego with an imperfect command over his mental, vital, and physical nature. "A mental control can only be a control, not to cure; a mental teaching, rule, standard can only impose an artificial groove in which our action revolved mechanically or with difficulty and which imposes a curbed and limited formation on the course of our nature. A total change of consciousness, a radical change of nature is the only remedy and the sole issue."[14] For Sri Aurobindo, "The mental formation is a stage and not the goal of man's growth, the solutions they offer are a temporary help and guidance, a necessary means for a partial dealing with the root difficulty, the true solution can intervene only when by our spiritual growth we can become one self with other beings, know them as part of our self, deal with them as if they were our other selves; for then the division is healed....But even oneness with others is not enough by itself, if it is a oneness with their ignorance.... Our oneness with others must be fundamental, a oneness in the soul and spirit, and that can only come by our liberation into soul-awareness and self-knowledge. To be ourselves, liberated from ego and realise our true selves.... the discovery of the soul, the secret psychic entity, the divine elements in us."[15] Sri Aurobindo is clear about this when he writes, "the awakening to our inner realities, imposes itself as the prior necessity... we have to go into our inner being and learn to live in it and from it; the outer mind and life and body must become for us only an antechamber. All that we are on the outside is indeed conditioned by what is within us, occult, in our inner depths and recesses; it is thence that come the secret initiatives, the self-effective formations; our inspirations, our intuitions, our life-motives, our mind's preferences, our will's selections are actuated from there.... but the use we make of these emergent powers and these influences is conditioned, largely determined and, above all, very much limited by our outermost nature. It is then the knowledge of this inner initiating self, coupled with the accurate perception of the outer instrumental self and the part played by both of them in our building that we have to discover.[16]

The growth of the individual is essential for the inner development of society. The more an inner law replaces the outer law, the nearer man will be drawn to this true and natural perfection. In a perfect social state, man is able to live in harmony with his fellow humans through free agreement and cooperation. Somewhere else, Sri Aurobindo writes, "The normal society treats man essentially as a physical, vital and mental being. For the life, the mind, and the body are the three terms of existence with which it has some competence to deal. It develops a system of mental growth and efficiency, an intellectual aesthetic and a moral culture. It evolves the vital side of human life and creates an ever-growing system of economic efficiency and vital enjoyment, and this system becomes more and more rich, cumbrous and complex as civilisation develops... In the end, however, experience shows that society tends to die by its own development, a sure sign that there is some radical defect in its system, a certain proof that its idea of man and its method of development do not correspond to all the reality of the human being and to the aim of life which that reality imposes.... a cure is aimed at by carrying artificial remedies to their acme, by more and more Science, more and more mechanical devices, a more scientific organisation of life, which means that the engine shall replace life, the arbitrary logical reason substitute itself for complex Nature and man be saved by machinery.... the radical defect of all our systems is their deficient development of just that which society has most neglected, the spiritual element, the soul in man which is his true being."[17]

Sri Aurobindo refers here to 'a religion of humanity' which may be "either an intellectual and sentimental ideal, a living dogma with intellectual, psychological and practical effects, or else a spiritual aspiration and rule of living, partly the sign, partly the cause of a change of soul in humanity. The intellectual religion of humanity already exists to a certain extent, partly as a conscious creed in the minds of a few, partly as a potent shadow in the consciousness of the race."[18] The intellectual religion of humanity is characterised by the profound fundamental idea that mankind is the godhead to be worshipped by man and that human progress and life are the chief aims of the human spirit. All institutions of science, in which religion and ethics formally tolerated whatever it might do in their ideal rule, are a crime against the religion of humanity; man is sacred to man regardless of social advancement. This intellectual religion of humanity humanised society, provided hope, encouraged new ideas, self-development and human potentialities. However, to accomplish these noble ideas in the future, humanity is confronted with its principal individual and collective egoism, and the weakness of the intellectual idea is that it does not reach the core of human existence. Man's intellect and feelings are not only instruments of its lower and external form but also of the inner and higher man, i.e., servants of the ego or channels of the soul. The religion of humanity aims to re-create human society in the image of liberty, equality and fraternity. For Sri Aurobindo, none of these images has really been won despite all the progress that has been achieved, they remained outward and mechanical principles, and "though these aims are of great importance in their own field, they are not the central thing; they can only be secure when founded upon a change of the inner human nature and inner way of living; they are themselves of importance only as means for giving a greater scope and better field for man's development towards that change and, when it is once achieved as an outward expression of the larger inward life. Freedom, equality, brotherhood are three godheads of the soul; they cannot be really achieved through the external machinery of society or by man so long as he lives in the individual and the communal ego."[19]

The unity of the human race can only be made real if the intellectual religion of humanity spiritualises itself and becomes the inner law of human life. The hope of humanity lies in the growing number of men who will seek and develop this truth within themselves, leading humanity to its highest possible perfection. Once this spiritual religion of humanity becomes established in humanity, the quest for a spiritual society in a spiritual age will begin. It is clear that the more the inner law replaces the outer law, the nearer man will draw to his true and natural perfection. In a perfect social state, man is able to live in harmony with his fellow humans through free agreement and cooperation. The solution to creating a perfect human order and a perfect social evolution, characterised by inner freedom and deeper brotherhood, does not lie in the principle of reason, but in the soul of man. According to Sri Aurobindo, "no machinery invented by the reason can perfect either the individual or collective man; an inner change is needed in human nature, a change too difficult to be ever effected except by the few. This is not certain, but in any case, if this is not the solution, then there is no solution; if this is not the way, then there is no way for humankind. Then the terrestrial evolution must pass beyond man as it has passed beyond the animal and a greater race must come that will be capable of the spiritual change, a form of life must be born that is nearer to the divine."[20] The spiritual society will regard man as a soul incarnated for a divine fulfilment upon earth, not only in heaven beyond, but also using the life, mind, and body as mere ends in themselves, but as instruments of the soul, the imperfect instruments of an unfulfilled divine purpose. Accepting the truth of man's soul, it regards man too as a collective soul upon earth, for a divine fulfilment in its manifold relations and its many-sided activities. It will regard human society as a means of a complex manifestation of the Spirit.

Auroville's social transformation seeks to create an environment that fosters a higher and collective consciousness, a goal that, unlike other utopias, necessitates the transcendence of the ego, mastery over our desires, and detachment from material possessions. Progress in the implementation of Auroville's collective Yoga will flow naturally from within to without. By tuning to this higher consciousness, manifested by Mother's divine incarnation in the terrestrial atmosphere, Aurovilians are able to become Mother's instruments and continue to be her willing servitors, i.e., by relying on Mother's Force they become channels for this consciousness. Every individual must practice their own yoga, but they must also participate in collective yoga, and through the transformation of the social environment, both types of progress proceed side by side. As her instrument she will guide and support all those Aurovilians who sincerely aspire to do her work. According to the Mother, "The city will be built by what is invisible to you. The men who have to act as instruments will do so despite themselves. They are all puppets in the hands of larger Forces. Nothing depends on human beings—neither the planning, nor the execution- nothing!"[21]

For the Mother, the power of a higher consciousness is much more capable of ordering material things than any material power; it is the highest consciousness that is the best judge of the most material things. The Mother visualised Auroville as a collective evolutionary experiment in embodying a spiritualised society, one that could not be anticipated but instead would have to be progressively elaborated through experimentation and applied spirituality. In the Charter, it is written, to be a True Aurovilian, "one should organise one's life not according to outer and artificial rules, but according to an organised inner consciousness. The first necessity is the inner discovery to know what one truly is behind social, moral, cultural, racial and hereditary appearances. One lives in Auroville to be free from moral and social conventions; but this freedom must not be a new slavery to the ego, to its desires and ambitions." As a spiritual adventure, the Mother, in the movement of a divine life on earth, initially envisioned a community of approximately 50,000 citizens from diverse backgrounds and worldwide. The realisation of this project is bound to face innumerable practical difficulties and theoretical questions, and it depends very much on the inner consciousness of the citizens to battle divisive forces that come to the surface due to cultural, religious, racial, and language differences. The method of a contemporary properly arranged society depends primarily on the proper organisation. Auroville differs significantly from any other type of utopia. Freedom in Auroville relies not only on its organisation but also on the development of the inner being, where there is no conflict between order and freedom, an issue which is prominently featured in other utopias conceived over the millennia. Mother's utopia is a criticism of a society in which valuable human purposes are distorted rather than served by different social arrangements. It is not easy for her disciples to dismantle or abandon their old inherited social apparatus. Her acceptability needs a proper inner human development as a prerequisite for change within the experiential utopian spirit. In building the city, "Moral laws have only a relative value from the point of view of Truth; besides, they vary considerably according to the country, the climate and the period. Discussions are generally sterile and without productive value. If each individual makes a personal effort of perfect sincerity, uprightness and goodwill, the best condition for the work will be realised"[22] However, to be free from all moral and social conventions does not mean to sink below them into the blind satisfaction of desires, but to rise above them and replace moral rules by the obedience to the Divine. In this way, life is not organised according to external and artificial regulations but according to an organised divine Consciousness.

Does the Mother's vision pay sufficient attention to the various social causes in solving related, though relative social problems (poverty, racism, unemployment)? In the process of moving inward, the delight of self-realisation is the motive force of men's efforts to realise themselves in all their potentialities while passing through the ordeals of Integral Yoga. However, aiming endlessly at the psychic consciousness where the citizens are promised a new world in which they *finally* do not have to look at external social and ethical authorities, does it imply that the citizens interchange their self-realisation for the collective citizenship, as the psychic consciousness aiming at a self-perfecting life moves beyond and does not tolerate mental contradictions? If social virtues, though commendable, are no longer moral duties, then what are the results for society from this morality and the values of social empirical and statistical generalisations? Are human virtues only preserved for metaphysical reasons or more for positive social benefits? To what extent do citizens have to abandon the real world to enter Auroville's new world? Isn't it out of the first that the second is coming? *Initially*, without a utopian vision, social change may require first the concrete, workable development of existing abstract ideals, which can serve as a practical measuring rod to identify the root cause of existing social problems. Could it be premature to throw away all the old traditional social achievements before a completely new social order is established? By throwing away the defects of the old order, ideal virtues disappear with it. As social subjects, we may be more able to change the root cause of specific social arrangements that are sickening, rather than getting lost in the excesses of our spiritual experiments. According to Sri Aurobindo," the practical values given us by our senses and by the dualistic sense-mind must hold good in their field and be accepted as the standard for ordinary life-experience until a larger harmony is ready into which they can enter and transform themselves without losing hold of the realities which they represent. Enlarging the sense faculties without the knowledge that would give the old sense values their proper interpretation from the new standpoint might lead to severe disorders and incapacities, unfit for practical life, and the orderly and disciplined use of reason. Equally, an enlargement of our mental consciousness out of the experience of the egoistic dualities into an unregulated unity with some form of total consciousness might easily bring about a confusion and incapacity for the active life of humanity in the established order of the world's relativities." [23].

In their engagement with a new social way of life, citizens may escape working for social change in mainstream society. If one escapes to find out the roots of structural inequities and social reform, then his progressive spiritual values do not contribute anything to society. Are devotees who are merely wedded to Mother's spiritual ideology, on their way to watch a collective human unity in diversity, aware of their gradual detachment from the existing social reality, thereby disconnecting themselves from the social workable and practical aspects of human social issues and solutions? Is there a need to avoid seclusion and encourage more engagement with the outside world? For Sri Aurobindo, "the old order of things which depended on palliatives will not last much longer, for it was founded on circumstances and conditions which no longer exist. A new order is demanded by the new conditions and, so long as it is not created, there will be a transitional era of continued trouble or recurrent disorders, inevitable crises through which Nature will effect in her own violent way the working out of the necessity which she has evolved." [24] In the radical experiments of becoming more conscious in establishing a new man in a new society through the process of unlearning old patterns and relearning new ones, could it be that during a partial stage in this process, the transitional era, the constructive part of the old patterns which proved useful in present-day life need to be more integrated in the relearning of the new future patterns? Perhaps we need to re-enact the old system, which we know works well, to gain a clearer understanding of what is effective and what is not, and from this basis, work on more appropriate directions. Could it be that in their radical experiment to establish a new man in a new society, the constructive part of the old patterns that proved helpful in the present society is not sufficiently integrated into the new future society?

Why is it that nothing can be well done in the new approach to human affairs unless the old manners are first transcended? These well-tried external means should not be abandoned but used to serve in the realisation of a true and lasting human society. Although Mother's vision of social transformation takes place within Auroville's community, the contemporary accepted social significance of age-old traditions, customs, and habits, do they initially need to be observed separately from the administration of Mother's original vision, however important that vision might be ultimately? Some of these age-old traditions, which governed for many centuries, created stability and continuity in the world without historical parallel. What unites humankind is the common aspiration to human social values, which are, therefore, a reasonably practical and valuable guidance for social life. Men's capacity to learn from others inspires the development of their social skills, i.e., their interactions often foster solidarity, self-sacrifice, empathy, and fidelity — some of humanity's most innate qualities.

While building the city, the Mother guided the builders in their spiritual quest, emphasising the process of living within. However, did she pay sufficient attention to the social structures and institutions, which are essential aspects of social relations and a future virtuous world order? Individual and collective struggles for social change, as well as activities that focus on social change, can be useful for both personal and collective growth. Perhaps an inner transformation requires as much individual and collective struggle for a just social world order as it does mere 'living within the psyche'. Could this inner transformation be facilitated through the collective ethical struggle, where ethical practitioners contribute to the spiritual development of those individuals who participate in it? The relative term of practical life depends on social relations, and replacing such an attitude with an awakened inner perception of psychic consciousness does not address the question of social injustice within the community. Is psychic consciousness not immanent in ethical life? The Mother acknowledged that an ethical life has a primarily preparatory function before the sadhak detaches himself gradually from the moral man; only thereafter will ethics no longer affect the actions of the new integral man. Could it be that the transcendence of the ego first needs more ethical reflection towards a synthesis between ourselves and other people?

In elaborating on Mother's detail about the prophetic vision regarding the social life in a perfect society, was the validity of her ideal from the outset doomed to be a pure spiritual fantasy? Currently, a contradiction exists between the ethical and spiritual projection of the ideal and the critical analysis of reality. Her utopian vision appears helpless without a social base, as the ultimate destiny of the human race needs, first, a great or moral perfection. It appears that the construct of contemporary utopia needs, besides a spiritual ideal, also a realisable practical social experiment with appropriate social mechanisms connected with psychological procedures with an emphasis on change, novelty and infinite improvement as opposed to the need for a divine eternity, or a permanent state of divine perfection.

For Sri Aurobindo, "a spiritualised society would treat in its sociology the individual from the saint to the criminal, not as units of a social problem to be passed through some skilfully devised machinery and either flattened into the social mould or crushed out of it, but as souls suffering and entangled in a net and to be rescued, souls growing and to be encouraged to grow, souls grown and from whom help and power can be drawn by the lesser spirits who are not yet adult."[25] But is only the practice of a spiritual religion of humanity capable of bringing about a spiritual transformation that transforms every aspect of human life in the future and ceases to be a transcendental pursuit? Sri Aurobindo answers this question as follows, "The work or value of spirituality is not to solve human problems on the past or present mental basis, but to create a new foundation of our being and to our life and knowledge... at the same time the spiritual man has not stood back altogether from the life of humanity; for the sense of unity with all beings, the stress of a universal love and compassion, the will to spend the energy for the good of all creatures are central to the dynamic out-flowering of the spirit But the solution of the problem which spirituality offers is not a solution by external means, though these also have to be used, but by an inner change, a transformation of consciousness and nature....The most drastic changes made by these means change nothing; for the old ills exist in a new form....To discover the spiritual being in himself is the main business of the spiritual man and to help others towards the same evolution is his real service to the race; till that is done, an outward help can succour and alleviate, but nothing or very little more is possible."[26]

Mother's ideal city is a highly metaphysical and speculative design; she is not so much concerned with objective experimentation and outward observation, which is presentable to sense experience, but her design is more based on introspection, psychic insight and intuition. In her transcendental hypothesis, is she, at times, using some unexplainable mystification of plain facts? Does she take adequate notice of complex problems in reaching her ideal society or does she treat them in a rather uncritical manner? Are there several predictions of her original vision which have been falsified by subsequent development? In a collective social life granting unrestricted freedom to all citizens irrespective of their psycho-social weaknesses or defective character traits and destructive habits, how can we aspire for a sane spiritual society? The ideal has to be realised through action and not as a metaphysical fact to be passively accepted.

In their disciplined application of the sociological method, Aurovilians fashion their new tools of inquiry without relying on external or observable characteristics of social facts, while attending to their inner meanings. Is it possible to understand the spiritual practices of the citizens from the outside without becoming personally committed to the values given within the Mother's vision? Is it only through commitment and engagement with her dream that true insight into her future predictions can be attained? It likely requires a combination of theory and practice. Those who have direct experience of Mother's spiritual insights have a particular advantage in a process that is not immediately accessible to the external observer. However, spirituality is not merely a matter of experience; it encompasses a doctrine, and a doctrine may be an obstacle to experiencing it. The social scientist can undoubtedly contribute to the study of Mother's vision without the scholar being a devotee; sympathy with Auroville's community should not entail the adoption of her vision, which enables sociologists to view the subject objectively. Various social inadequacies cannot be fully and effectively eradicated; they can be reduced and tamed, their malevolent side controlled, but they cannot be wished away. This is why citizens still have a long way to go in creating a transformed spiritual society. Perhaps Auroville's experiment should ground its utopian promise more firmly in the context of empirical realities, bringing its utopian vision down to earth by intertwining Mother's vision with the particulars of empirical facts and the actual condition of human existence in the present day. The domains of the scholar and the believer are different, much like the realms of competence between the practitioner of Integral Yoga and the person who writes about Integral Yoga. However, the non-expert is open to new facts, accumulated techniques, methods of investigation, and sociological data in general. The practitioner tends to present sociological knowledge in highly abstract and speculative terms, which rarely produces concrete results.

New problems and challenges will emerge in Auroville, and its citizens will need to adapt to them. Are the citizens in their utopian reality able to respond to the challenges of modernisation in the contemporary world, and are they able to integrate their new innovative potentials and creativity into their psychic experiment, establishing valuable aspects in a better society that requires a transformation in the very nature of man and life? It is not easy for society to dismantle or abandon its inherited social utilities. To avoid dilemmas that render Auroville impractical and get lost in wishful thinking, its citizens may need to establish a congruence between reality and utopia, thereby changing the latter, to some extent, into the former. To ensure its survival, the community's inhabitants require faith in Mother's vision, without resisting all kinds of innovations from the outside world. However, where does the faith ladder end and the empirical one begin? Specific pragmatic questions need to specify where the community would like to go, how to get there, and who is responsible for the bureaucracy within the community, which threatens its autonomy and individual freedom.

In exploring new ways beyond social conventions, when Aurovilians isolate themselves from many of the realities of life in the present larger society, they remain highly dependent on the existence of that society. In the words of E. Hansot, "If utopia is to be achieved by the conscious effort of men, it cannot ignore the existence of non-utopian society. To do so would leave utopia open to the charge of egoism or narrow humanity...Modern utopias that are universal in scope thus avoid the charge of self-satisfied indifference in the presence of the less fortunate."[27] Instead of endlessly relating to the references from Mother's vision, modern utopian authors also offer a detailed explanation of how transformation occurs which allows the utopian founder to criticise in detail the defects of his society and to encourage his members to desire and plan for change.

D.P. Chattopadhyaya criticises Sri Aurobindo's sociology as "very abstract and very critical... his concepts are not testable by experience, which are unrelated to historical facts and empirical data."[28] He accuses Sri Aurobindo of "grand-theory construction and not of fact-fetish... Sri Aurobindo refers to facts only to illustrate his theories and laws, and not to establish them. One cannot fail to note that he is not a sterile inductivist. Certainly, he cannot be accused of excessive reliance on empirical data...His theory is purely speculative and not fair to facts...in other words, some facts may really prove very awkward and uncompromising" [29] He is aware of the position taken by some followers of Sri Aurobindo claiming that Sri Aurobindo's views on related matters are truths of fact and should not be regarded as theories. Personally speaking, he does not see how a particular view can claim immunity against rational criticism on the ground that it is based on the truth of facts. The question is whether the unknown is a matter of faith or assumption, but it seems that questionable assumptions are rationally preferable to unquestionable faith. In realising Mother's ideals, "one's commitment to an ideal and the difficulties involved in realising it should not lead one to pin one's faith in some metaphysical principle 'ensuring' the practical success of the ideal within an undefined time-frame. For the metaphysical faith, although the expression of a novel sentiment, is hardly of any practical consequence" [30]

According to Sri Aurobindo, "In the case of man, acting as an instrument of the Force the action is more complicated, because consciously or unconsciously man must receive, also he must be able to work out what the Force puts through him. He is a living complex instrument, not a simple machine. So if he has responsiveness, capacity, etc., he can work out the Force perfectly, if not, he does it imperfectly or frustrates it. That is why we speak of and insist on the perfection of the instrument. Otherwise, there would be no need for Sadhana or anything else... Naturally the best instrument even is imperfect and mistakes may be committed, but if the instrument is sufficiently open, the Force can set the thing to rights and the result still comes."[31] Sri Aurobindo refers to the spiritual yogic Force which has to work under the present world conditions where the Power does not work miraculously, but works by certain given means and under conditions, unlike the supramental Divine Force that works absolutely, because it creates its own conditions and can apply itself in any direction, always potentially all-powerful. His Divine Yoga Force does not act in an omnipotent ease regardless of the conditions; it all depends on the recipient and his receptivity, on the instrument, his faith and his conveying Power, and where there is resistance, there is no rapid effect. "The Divine knows best and one has to have trust in His wisdom and attune oneself with His will. Length of time is no proof of an ultimate incapacity to arrive-it is only a sign that there is something in oneself which has to be overcome and if there is a will to reach the Divine, it can be overcome"[32] In the search for perfection parts of a person can be highly evolved and in touch with the Divine psychic consciousness, but what about other parts which remain trapped in imperfection? The individual utopia also has a social dimension, and the sadhaks on their way to a perfect society, looking for a better world, are treated as mere instruments on the journey and would easily collapse in the complicated divide between their dreams and complex reality. Moreover, social change and social confusion, though confronting, offer at the same time unprecedented opportunities for new developments, when open inquiry of its members into sacred institutions and beliefs is not restricted.

The Mother offered the citizens a path to the final destination. It is a difficult path and a long way out of an imperfect society, and it is not a fast track on the paved side for the favoured few. On this journey, is it not better to adopt a more pragmatic attitude towards the permanently changing world that is often tormented by paradoxes? Our society undergoes exponential changes, which often give rise to various fears and spiritual uncertainties. A diversity of perspectives often leads to better and more creative decisions about significant questions related to Auroville's new developmental circumstances. These decisions should encourage citizens to take a united responsibility in developing a vision for Auroville's future. Sri Aurobindo offers support for this view when he writes, " the true scientist is always ready to reconsider old conclusions in the light of new facts, to give a candid consideration to every new idea or old idea revived if it deserves a hearing, no matter how contradictory it may be of previously ascertained experience or previously formed conclusion, is the sceptical temper, the temper of the enquirer, the true scientist" [33]

Mother's spiritual transformation requires not simply her radical metaphysical vision of a future place, but also a corresponding, if not more radical, practice to change one's outer consciousness. The utopian practice of consciousness-raising towards a new person and a new world gradually develops ways of dealing with the alienating effects of obstacles and ultimately transcends them. The Mother did not aim at a static, reified object of a passively perfect society, nor at the authoritarian guidance of a blueprint, but rather at the emancipating possibility of a dream without the tendency to lapse into a rigid system. Are some of her disciples within the bureaucratic system reducing alternative visions to closed, perfect systems that negate the utopian impulse that generates them?

What is the role of the psychic experiment in the collective struggle for creating a just and righteous social world order? The Mother is aware of the dangers inherent in technological developments; however, she maintains that only the creative higher or inner power of consciousness can resolve global social conflicts. Allegiance and identification in the modern world are profoundly based on social, cultural, and political relationships, and to maintain this, it needs the capacity to sustain internal diversity and constant renewal through consent. Are devotees who are wedded to Mother's spiritual ideology, on their way towards collective human unity, aware of their gradual detachment from social reality and disconnect themselves from the practical aspects of social issues, thereby ignoring social workable and practical solutions? Mother's metaphysical assumptions and faith in a transcendental spiritual ideal hardly take into consideration the practical aspects of complex social problems and the actions required to solve these problems critically.

How far is Mother's spiritual vision in today's world pragmatic and applicable for active participation in the struggle towards a better world order? Did the Mother offer her disciples a well-developed theory of social change when she guided them on their spiritual quest, focusing on inner psychic transformation rather than elaborating on the collective struggle toward social transformation? It seems that her emphasis on the spiritual dimension of social development ignores various aspects of social order and justice in secular societies. Mother's views on Auroville were highly metaphysical, and the rationale of social life and its development is founded on a spiritual basis. She does not elaborate extensively on the complex nature of social phenomena, and it may be easy to confuse her ambitions with the disciple's ability and achievements. Does Auroville, as a spiritual community, merely need the Mother as an example for social reform? Before it can produce divine citizens, it needs a whole succession of such divine people; otherwise, her vision will fritter away into a confused, lopsided utopia. These divine citizens are open to new knowledge, know how to deal with the latest facts, and how to cooperate with their fellow citizens. They are self-critical about their habits and behaviour because they are Aurovilians who want to save the city from excessive outside interference.

## Notes

1.) Sri Aurobindo; *The Life Divine*, p 692-695

2.) Sri Aurobindo; *The Human Cycle*, p 47

3.) Ibid., p 62

4.) Ibid., p 69-71

5.) Sri Aurobindo; *The Synthesis of Yoga*, p 587

6.) Sri Aurobindo; *The Human Cycle*, p 247

7.) The Mother; *Collective Works of The Mother*, Vol 15, p 316
8.) The Mother; *CWM Vol* 2, p 47
9.) Sri Aurobindo; *The Synthesis of Yoga*, p 183-184
10.) Ibid., p 199-200
11.) Sri Aurobindo; *The Life Divine*, p1035
12.) Sri Aurobindo; *The Human Cycle*, p 273
13.) Sri Aurobindo; *The Life Divine*, p 625
14.) Ibid., p 628
15.) Ibid., p 630
16.) Ibid., p 551
17.) Sri Aurobindo; *The Human Cycle*, p 222-224
18.) Ibid., p 564
19.) Ibid.,569
20.) Ibid., p 220
21.) The Mother; *CWM Vol* 13 September, 1969
22.) The Mother; *Mother's Agenda* p. 172
23.) Sri Aurobindo; *The Life Divine*, p 52-53
24.) Sri Aurobindo; *The Ideal of Human Unity*, p 234
25.) Sri Aurobindo; *The Human Cycle*, p 257.
26.) Sri Aurobindo; *The Life Divine*, p 883-885
27.) Elisabeth Hansot; *Perfection and Progress*, p 96
28.) D.P. Chattopadhyaya; *Sri Aurobindo and Karl Marx*, p 196
29.) Ibid., p 198
30.) Ibid., p258
31.) Sri Aurobindo; *Letters on Himself and the Ashram*, p.491
32.) Ibid., p 619
33.) Sri Aurobindo; *Essays Human and Divine*, p 23

*CHAPTER FIVE*

# THE MOTHER

## Introduction: Why the Need for the Mother

Mother's integral sadhana, as a progressive surrender of the ego to the incalculable yet always inevitable workings of the beyond ego, is not an easy sadhana. Difficulties in spiritual progress are common to all paths and seekers of Yoga, and none of her disciples can expect immediate, smooth progress. A mere restless dissatisfaction with the ups and downs of ordinary life is not sufficient preparation for Integral Yoga. One who does not have the courage to face life's difficulties patiently and firmly, he will never be able to go through the still more significant inner difficulties of the sadhana. The intricate and complex course of integral sadhana is only for those who accept seeking its aim through the true aid of faith and the guidance of the Guru. The call of the soul should not be confused or mixed with the development and satisfaction of the old external order of things or the surface orientation of the seeker's lower nature. The true essence of sacrifice at the beginning of the practice of sadhana demands an indispensable discipline. However, integral sadhana includes a discipline far more difficult than mere ethical and physical austerities, and the seeker must not enter this path only if he is sure of the psychic call. Not everyone can approach the Divine in a pure psychic way at once, and they need to be supported initially by mental and vital approaches. It is for this reason that the seeker ought not to plunge into this path without a fairly long period of preparation and purification. Not everyone is suited for the practice of Integral Yoga as it can be insistently demanding, "it is the way for heroes and strong souls, not for weaklings"[1]. Sri Aurobindo and the Mother encouraged their disciples to write to them about their difficulties and questions related to their practice of yoga. In these thousands of letters to Sri Aurobindo and various talks with and questions to the Mother, they dealt with every aspect of the Integral Yoga of perfection, offering various sadhaks some psycho-spiritual guidance for behaviour and some understanding of the psychological difficulties of their spiritual journey. For many sadhaks the statement of their difficulties was a means of release.

A few of these letters will be quoted here to get a better understanding of the difficulties most sadhaks are confronted with during their practice. "All who enter the spiritual path have to face the difficulties and ordeals on the path, those which rise from their nature and those which come in from outside. The difficulties in nature always rise again and again till you overcome them; they must be faced with both strength and patience. But the vital part is prone to depression when ordeals and difficulties rise. This is not peculiar to you but comes to all sadhaks. But you must train yourself to overcome this reaction of depression, calling in the Mother's Force to aid you...It may be said generally that to be over-anxious to pull people, especially very young people, into the sadhana is not wise. The sadhak who comes to this yoga must have a real call, and even with the real call, the way is often difficult enough. ... Or else the unfit adhar tends to suffer under the stress of a call for which it was not ready, or at least not yet ready."[2]

The reason why difficulties happen Sri Aurobindo explains as follows, "In every human being there are two parts, the psychic with so much of the thinking mind and the higher (emotional, larger dynamic) vital that is open to the psychic and cleaves to the soul's aims and admits to the higher experiences, and on the other hand the lower vital and the physical external being (external mind and vital included) which are attached to the ignorant personality and nature and do not want to change. It is the conflict between these two that makes the sadhana so difficult. It is only by curing the duality that one can overcome them. That happens when one is able to live within, aware of one's inner being."[3] Alternating moods are due to two different elements in the practitioner, "On one side, there is trying to develop in you your psychic being, which, when it awakes, gives you the sense of closeness or union with the Mother and the feeling of Ananda; on the other there is your old vital nature, restless and full of desires and, because of this restlessness and desire, unhappy. It is when the desire and restlessness of the vital are rejected that the psychic in you comes forward and then the vital itself changes and feels full of the joy and the nearness."[4]

In another letter, he explains, "You should realise that these periods of clouding are not due to any incapacity or perversity in you—even the best sadhaks have them. It is the difficulty of human nature in getting transformed. The difficulty sometimes takes the form of a bad will in the vital somewhere or a tendency in the physical to cling to old mistakes and old habits or to shrink from the trouble of transformation. What is there is the mechanical habit of the lower nature, not voluntary, to repeat the old movements to which it has been or was quite recently accustomed when any strong wave of them comes in from the surrounding universal Nature. This creates a kind of recurrence of relapse into the states which the spiritual progress is pushing out and it is not easy to get rid of this recurrence altogether."[5]

Obstacles are usually due to "the too great activity of the intellectual mind and it's attachments to its own pride of ideas, its prejudices, it's fixed notions and it's ignorant reason may shut the doors to the inner light and prevent the full tide of bhakti from flooding everything; it may also cling to a surface mental activity and refuse to go inside and allow the psychic vision and the feelings of the inner heart to become its guides. So too the passions and desires of the vital being and its ego."[6] The ego and desires of the vital, its disturbances and upheavals have to be dealt with and if not at once expelled, at least dominated and prepared for a gradual if not a rapid modification, change, illumination. "The vital ego itself must become conscious of its own defects and willing to get rid of them; it must decide to throw away its vanities, ambitions, lusts and longings, its rancour and revolts and all the rest of the impure stuff and unclean movements within it. This is the time of the greatest difficulties, revolts and dangers."[7]

One of the other main obstacles is related to the practitioner's resistance, described by Sri Aurobindo as" there may be a resistance in the mind and the common form of that is the denial and doubt-which may create mental and vital suffering. There may again be a resistance in the vital nature whose principal character is desire and the attachment to the objects of desire, and if in this field there is a conflict between the soul and the vital nature there may be much suffering of the mind and the vital parts. The physical consciousness also may offer a resistance which is usually that of fundamental inertia...There is, moreover, the resistance of the Universal Nature which does not want the being to escape from the Ignorance into the Light. This may take the form of a vehement insistence in the continuation of the old movements....There are two ways to meet all that, first that of the Self, calm, a mind, a vital, a physical consciousness that remain resolutely turned towards the Divine and unshaken by all suggestions of doubt, desire, attachments, depression, sorrow, pain, inertia. This is possible when the inner being awakens... There is also the way of the psychic,- when the psychic being comes out of its inherent power, its consecration, adoration, love of the Divine, self-giving, surrender and imposes these on the mind, the vital and physical consciousness and compels them to turn all their movements Godward."[8]

"I believe that alternations of bright and dark periods are almost a universal experience of yogis, and the exceptions are very rare... and the second cause is some resistance, something in the human nature that has not felt the former descent, is not ready, is perhaps unwilling to change,- often it is some strong habitual formation of the mind or the vital or some temporary inertia of the physical consciousness and not exactly a part of the nature,- and this, whether showing or concealing itself thrusts up the obstacle. If one can detect the course in oneself, acknowledge it, see its workings and call down the Power for its removal, then the periods of obscurity can be greatly shortened and their acuity becomes less. But in any case, the Divine Power is working always behind and one day, perhaps when one least expects it, the obstacle breaks, the clouds vanish and there is again the light and the sunshine."[9]

The path of yoga is not a shortcut to the Divine, and it is necessary from the beginning of the practice to understand and accept the arduous difficulties the seeker must face. Despite all kinds of difficulties, it is clear that all those who are sincere and faithful in heart and rely on the Divine Will arrive at the Kingdom. In one of his letters, he writes, "It is a mistake to dwell too much on the lower nature and its obstacles, which is the negative sadhana. They have to be seen and purified, but preoccupation with them as the one important thing is not helpful. The positive side of the experience of the descent is the more important thing. If one waits for the lower to be purified entirely and for all time before calling down the positive experience, one might have to wait forever. It is true that when the lower nature is purified, the easier is the descent of the higher Nature, but it is also and more true that the more the higher Nature descends, the more the lower is purified. Neither the complete purification nor the permanent and perfect manifestation can come all at once, it is a matter of time and patient progress."[10]

On the sunlit path, when the seeker encounters difficulties, there is no hard labour, strain or tension, but one remains quiet and opens oneself to a Power behind, a Force that is there all the time, above and around, doing its work in peace. For Sri Aurobindo, the sunlit path is the path of the psychic leading the seeker to God; if one wholly relies on the Divine and accepts that whatever comes to the seeker comes from the Divine, then the path becomes sunlit. The sunlit path, however, requires the sadhak's recognition of his weaknesses first to renounce them, and not to identify the difficulties as part of one's real nature but to look at them as things imposed on them. After rejection, the sadhak becomes conscious of a separate being within, which does not identify itself with the difficulties. It is this inner being which guides the sadhak in the process of purification. "When we are in close contact with the Divine, it does not throw aside all difficulties, sufferings or dangers, but it carries us through them and out of them—except where for a special purpose there is need for the opposite."[11] "The sunlit path can only be followed if the psychic is constantly or usually in front, or if one has a natural spirit of faith or surrender or a face turned habitually towards the sun or psychic predisposition (e.g. faith in one's spiritual destiny) or if one has acquired the psychic turn."[12] Our incapacity does not matter- there is no human being who is not in his parts of nature incapable-but the Divine Force also is there. If one puts one's trust in that, incapacity will be changed into capacity. Difficulty and struggle themselves then become a means towards achievement."[13] Sri Aurobindo maintains that "the sunlit path can be followed by those who are able to practice surrender, first a central surrender and afterwards a more complete self-giving in all the parts of the being. If they can achieve and preserve the attitude of the central surrender, if they can rely wholly on the Divine and accept cheerfully whatever comes to them from the Divine, then their path becomes sunlit and may even be straightforward and easy. They will not escape all difficulties, no seeker can, but they will be able to meet them without pain and despondency.... But not all have this nature; most are very far from it, and the complete or even the central surrender is not easy to get, and to keep it always is hard enough for our human nature. When these things are not there, the liberty of the soul is not attained and we have instead to undergo the law or fulfil a hard and difficult discipline."[14] If failure happens, it needs an invariable and unflagging aspiration or effort. "The effort demanded of the sadhak is that of aspiration, rejection and surrender. If these three are done, the rest is to come of itself by the Grace of the Mother and the working of her force in you. But of the three, the most important is surrender of which the first necessary form is trust and confidence and patience in difficulty."[15]

As long as their lower nature is not purified, personal effort remains necessary. This personal effort which requires a triple labour of aspiration, rejection and surrender, is described by Sri Aurobindo as "an aspiration vigilant, constant increasing mind's will, the heart's seeking, the assent of the vital being, the will to open and make plastic the physical consciousness and nature; rejection of the movements of the lower nature- rejection of the mind's ideas, opinions, preferences, habits, constructions- rejection of the vital nature's desires, demands, cravings, sensations, passions, selfishness, pride, arrogance, lust, greed, jealousy, envy, hostility, to Truth......rejection of the physical nature's stupidity, doubt, disbelief, obscurity, obstinacy, pettiness, laziness, unwillingness to change, tamas... surrender of oneself and all one is and has and every plane of the consciousness and every movement of the Divine and the Shakthi."[16]

As the surrender progresses and the sadhak becomes more aware that the Divine Shakti is doing the sadhana, the more the sadhak becomes aware of this process, the more his own effort is replaced by the Mother's Force. The aspiration to be in contact with Mother's Force as a psychic feeling is an indispensable condition, for it is through the psychic that this contact becomes easy. Once the basis is firmly established, then the safety of the right guidance will be ensured. The advantage of being in the psychic consciousness secures the sadhak's right awareness of being in harmony with Mother's will and calls in Mother's Force to make the necessary changes. According to Sri Aurobindo, "it is certain that one's own effort is necessary, though one cannot do the sadhana by one's own effort alone. The Mother's Force is needed, but the sadhak must open himself to it, reject what opposes the Force, and put his full sincerity, aspiration, and willpower into the sadhana. It is only when all is open and there is the full surrender that the Divine Power takes up the sadhana so entirely that personal effort is no longer necessary. But that cannot happen at an early stage, one must go on opening oneself, consecrating oneself, making the surrender till that later stage comes."[17] It must be clear that the action of the sadhana does not depend on the Mother alone; her Force can do the work only when there is a complete openness and surrender to the Mother.

In the initial stages of the practice, the sadhak has to work using the instruments of his lower nature, but in a later transitional stage, one's personal and necessary effort is replaced by the action of the higher Nature. In the final period, there is no effort at all, no set method, and no fixed sadhana. The self-surrender of the individual self to the Divine does not exclude a human will for the participation in the Divine consciousness and the satisfaction of the Divine fulfilment in the sadhak, but the will, the aspiration, is the sadhak's because it is his will. But Sri Aurobindo warns disciples of the obstacles in the process of surrender when he writes, "It often happens when the forces of the lower nature are stimulated and excited by the descent and want to mix with it and turn it to their profit. It often happens too that some Power or Powers undivine in their nature present themselves as a Supreme Lord or as a Divine Mother and claim the being's service and surrender. If these things are accepted, there will be an extremely disastrous consequence.... This assent and a rejection of all egoistic forces or forces that appeal to the ego are the safeguards throughout the sadhana. But the ways of Nature are full of snares, the disguises of the ego are innumerable; the illusions of the Powers of Darkness are extraordinary, skilful; the reason is an insufficient guide and often turns traitor; vital desire is always with us tempting to follow any alluring call. This is the reason why in this yoga we insist so much on what we call *Samarpana*, rather inadequately rendered by the English word Surrender. If the heart centre is fully opened and the psychic is always in control, then there is no question that all is safe. But the psychic can at any moment be veiled by a lower upsurge. It is only a few who are exempted from these dangers and it is precisely those to whom surrender is easily possible."[18] For this process of the descent from above, it is most important not to rely entirely on oneself but to rely on the guidance of the Guru, trusting in the inner guidance and perceiving it more and more or else in the outer guidance of the Guru.

## The Mother as a Guru

Guru, as a Sanskrit term in the Chandogya Upanishad, is used as a teacher, mentor or guide of specific knowledge or a field. Still, other terms were also employed at that time, such as one who imparted the sacred Vedas or socio-religious knowledge, or a prophet as a teacher. This did not mean that every wandering ascetic or holy man was a teacher. The Guru is a spiritual preceptor, and his knowledge and teachings are of a transcendent and powerful origin. The discipline of the Guru is supposed to be efficacious, because just as the teacher is liberated, so too could he guide others to enlightenment.

In Integral Yoga, the obstacles and difficulties on the path to progress demand either endless patience or an unquestioning reliance on the Guru, who is the pathfinder and leader, or a predestined commitment to follow the path of Integral Yoga and cleave to Sri Aurobindo and the Mother as their Guru, with no one else. The various questions related to the role of the Mother in the chaotic present situation of Auroville are not meant to challenge Mother's unconditional teachings in any way; they are asked for clarity and understanding.

Mother's help in difficulties is described by Sri Aurobindo as, "Not to be disturbed, to remain quiet and confident is the right attitude, but it is necessary also to receive the help of the Mother and not to shrink back for any reason from her solicitude. One ought not to indulge in ideas of incapacity, dwelling too much on defects and failures and allowing the mind to be in pain and shame on their account, for these ideas and feelings become weakening things in the end. If there are difficulties, stumbling, or failures, one has to look at them quietly and call in tranquilly and persistently the divine help for their removal, but not allow oneself to be upset, pained or discouraged. Yoga is not an easy path, and the total change of the nature cannot be done in one day."[19]

The Mother, as a Guru, had the same spiritual experiences and realisations as Sri Aurobindo; she helped him give a concrete form to his yoga. There is no difference between the Mother's and Sri Aurobindo's paths that led to divine realisation. All the disciples who come to practice Integral Yoga surrender themselves to the Mother, who helps them on their path, and Sri Aurobindo supports her from behind. This difficult yoga requires the guidance of a Guru to warn disciples against various dangers and to avoid specific areas, enabling them to pass through safely. This yoga cannot be done without them. Although Divine Grace is essential for success in the sadhana, it also requires the effort of aspiration, rejection, and surrender, along with the process of inward reflection and becoming aware of this psychic activity that prepares the descent of the Grace. In Mother's guidance, all she asks is to open and receive, to have faith and an entire sincerity to follow the spiritual path. There is no general path; the way for each Aurovilian is personal; each citizen carries his truth in himself, which has to be expressed in his life, i.e., for the Mother, each person is an exceptional case to be dealt with specially, and each must be treated according to one's nature. "The relation of Guru and disciple is only one of many relations which one can have with the Divine, and in this Yoga the Divine is regarded as the Source....This is a greater and more intimate relation than that of the human Guru and disciple, which is more of a limited ideal."[20] Nevertheless, "if the mind still needs the more familiar mental conception it can be kept so long as it is needed; only do not let the soul be bound by it and do not let it limit the inflow of other relations with the Divine and larger forms of experience."[21] In describing Mother's Consciousness-Power of the Divine, Sri Aurobindo mentions "three ways of being of the Mother of which you can become aware when you enter into touch of oneness with the Conscious—Force that upholds us and the universe. Transcendent, the original supreme Shakti, she stands above the worlds and links the creation to the ever-unmanifested mystery of the Supreme. Universal, the cosmic Mahashakti, she creates all these beings and contains and enters, supports and conducts all these million processes and forces. Individual, she embodies the power of these two vaster ways of her existence, makes them living and near to us and mediates between the human personality and the divine Nature."[22]

The Mother is assumed to be an incarnation of the transcendent, cosmic and individual Divine Mother in a human body, just as Sri Aurobindo was an incarnation of the transcendent, cosmic and individual Ishwara in a human body. In the spiritual progress of man, it is difficult for him to believe in something unseen within himself; it is easier to imagine something extraneous to himself, a kind of external support, an object of faith outside himself. This can be an external image of God, a Prophet or a Guru, the Divine representing himself through a less marvellous intermediary. However, the practitioner of Integral Yoga needs a living example, for only a few can make the past Teacher and his teaching a living force in their life. The Guru should represent the disciple with divine wisdom and convey to them something of the divine ideal. What the disciples saw of her with their physical eyes was only her outer shell, but the Mother in her body was also the Great Mother, the external Divine Mother in the higher Nature. Those who approach her as a human Mother instead of going inside often get into trouble by their conception, making all sorts of mistakes in their approach to her.

When Sri Aurobindo describes the relation between the Mother and her disciples, he writes, " it is true that the Mother is one in many forms, but the distinction between the outer and the inner Mother must not be made too trenchant; for she is not only one, but the physical Mother contains all the others in herself and in her is established the communication between the inner and the outer existence. However, to truly know the outer Mother, one must know what is within her and not look only at her outer appearance. That is only possible if one meets her with the inner being.... the only safe thing is to communicate on the inner union foremost and altogether and to leave aside all claims and demands for anything external."[23] Mother's psychic and spiritual motherhood is a far more significant relation than that of the physical mother to her child, as it is a more complete relation. It includes human motherhood, but it replaces it in both the inward and outward life. When the sadhak remains psychically open to the Mother, all that is necessary for the practice of sadhana will develop progressively.

It is a mistake to put the whole emphasis on the external vital or physical relation with the Mother, insisting on a critical interchange. The mind, vital and physical, can participate in the union, but they must be submitted to the psychic, which is itself psychicised. The purer soul has easier access to the Divine. "Yogis whose progress does not depend on the personal intervention of the Mother need to have no personal relation with her- only the spiritual contact in distance.... There is a universal Divine Love which is equal for all. There is also a psychic connection which is individual; it is the same essentially for all, but it admits of a special relation with each which is not the same for all but different in each case.... whether one feels the Mother's love or not depends on whether one is open to it or not, it does not depend on physical nearness. Openness means the removal of all that makes one unconscious of the inner relation...She has not come to establish a 'physical relation' with people. Some have come with her to share in the work, others she has called, and others have come seeking light. With each she has a personal relation, none can say that she must do equally the same thing which each person.... She acts in each case for different reasons suitable for that case."[24]

The Mother is also represented as the power of the Divine universal Shakti, a representative Force of the Divine, the master of Yoga, which accompanies the growth of a new consciousness. This Force is the Yoga Shakti, and to this Force, the sadhak has to open himself to the Power of the Mother. The Mother is the Divine in its Consciousness-Force, a higher Divine Force that descends from above to transform the lower nature and where it replaces the ego principle with the principle of the Divine, it establishes a connection between the sadhak's consciousness and the Mother's consciousness. This Mother's Force will answer the calls from her disciples, but not in a similar way to an ordinary human action, but rather an action on the occult plane, "an interchange of psychic communication is quite sufficient to set the Force at work. At the same time, it is not an impersonal Force... it is something personal to the Mother and if she had not this power she would not be able to do her work; but this is quite different from the outside practical working on the material plane, although the occult working and the material working can and do join and the occult power give to the material working its utmost efficiency."[25] When the sadhak becomes aware of the divine Shakti, it draws her to us and calls her in to fill the whole system, it will take up the charge of all our activities, and there is no more sense of a little personal self as the doer, instead the divine Shakti will take up all our outer life, our Yoga and transform all the lower energies into the energies of her Supramental nature.

In the words of Sri Aurobindo, "The power of the divine universal Shakti which is behind our aspiration is illimitable, and when it is rightly called upon it cannot fail to pour itself into us and to remove whatever incapacity and obstacle, now or later, for the times and durations of our struggle while they depend at first, instrumentally and in part, on the strength of our faith and to our endeavour, are yet eventually in the hands of the wisely determining secret Spirit, alone the Master of the Yoga, the Ishwara."[26] When the devotee becomes aware of the divine Shakti and calls her in and takes up charge of all our activities there, then there will be no separate personal will to conduct our actions and no sense of a little personal self as the doer. The divine Shakti will encompass all our inner activities, our outer life, and our yoga, transforming all the lower energies into energies of her supramental nature. This needs a real opening to the receptivity of Mother's forces, to be so turned to the Mother that her Force can work in the sadhak without obstructing her action. The opening will usually come in short flashes, glimpses at first of brief duration, but afterwards, it grows and sometimes may be ready for permanence.

Mother's invisible Force of the yogic consciousness is the whole meaning of producing tangible inward and outward results, but this is not a power that acts without conditions and limits like the Supramental Force. It is not only in its results but also in its movements, and the Force is tangible and concrete, where the sadhak is able to direct and manipulate its movements, which is possible through the development of yoga. The conditions and limits under which sadhana must be practised are not arbitrary; they arise from the nature of things. The sadhak needs his receptivity, self-opening and surrender to receive the Yoga Force; only the Supramental Power, when it receives a sanction from the Supreme, can override everything, get something done and radically alter everything. The Supramental Force, a Yoga Force in its original totality of the divine spiritual Force, works absolutely because it creates its own conditions. However, Mother's Force is a Force that does not work absolutely, but miraculously; it works through given means and under certain conditions of the evolutionary world. Sri Aurobindo describes the yogic Force as "The Divine does not work arbitrarily; He acts upon the world along the lines that have been fixed by the nature and purpose of the world we live in by an increasing action of the thing that has to manifest, not by a sudden change or disregard of all the conditions of the work to be done. If it were so, there would be no need of Yoga or a Master and disciples or a Descent or anything else."[27] So in case of man acting as an instrument of the Force he must be able to work out what the Force puts through him and if he has the capacity and responsiveness he can work out the Force perfectly, if not he has to perfect his instrument first, before all man's potentialities works itself out automatically and the results will come.

This is an important issue that may require further explanation. The Mother, as a living Guru in Integral Yoga, is a representative of the Divine, and the disciple must open himself and be receptive to her divinity within, from where she guides him to grow. What the Mother can do for the sadhak depends on the receptivity of the sadhak, not upon any method or rule of sadhana. Could it be that most of her disciples have more faith in the method rather than in the Divine, though one needs to follow certain conditions, such as humility and sincerity towards the Guru, devotion and trust in the Mother, a right attitude increases the receptivity of the Mother's Force. When the intimacy grows, the relation with her changes. Whereas the Mother is an aspect or representation of the Divine, there is also something which is still more profound and more intimate, where the Divine is regarded as the source, the living supramental light of knowledge and consciousness. This is a more significant, more intimate relation than that of a human Guru and disciple relation, which is more of a limited mental ideal, unlike the direct opening to the Infinite. In surrendering to the Mother it is to the Divine in her that one surrenders. In the words of Sri Aurobindo, "surrender to the divine and surrender to the guru are not the same thing. In surrendering to the Guru, it is to the divine within him that one surrenders; if it were only to a human entity, it would be ineffective. But it is the consciousness of the Divine Presence that makes the Guru a real Guru, so that even if the disciple surrenders to him thinking of the human being to whom he surrenders that presence will still make it effective."[28]

In her relationship with the disciples, "Each sadak has to be dealt with according to his nature, his capacities, his real needs (not his claims or desires) and according to what is best for his spiritual welfare. As to how it is to be done, we refuse to be dictated to by the ignorance of those sadhaks who consider that the Mother must act according to their standards or their ideas of equality or justice or the demands of their vital or the notions they have brought with them from the outside world"[29] In her power during the work through the disciple she deals with each person differently according to his true need and his progress in the sadhana and not what he fancies to be his need. She intervenes with her yogic Force, enabling the sadhak to withstand the rigours and demands of the path. She places herself at the disposal of every aspiring soul who looks for help without any fixed mental rules. However, the form her action takes must vary with the different nature and needs of each, the demands of the work, and the necessities of their sadhana. For the Mother, human nature cannot be dealt with by a set of mental rules applicable to everybody in the same way; if it were so, there would be no need for a Guru. Much misunderstanding originated when Mother's concern for a specific sadhak was applied without discrimination to another sadhak. Similarly, a general statement that is true in itself cannot be used to everyone alike or applied immediately without consideration of circumstance or person.

It is essential to recognise Mother's Force when it acts and distinguish it from ignorance and egoistic forces. As Mother's Force gets mixed with the action of the present mind, vital, and body, it inevitably has to work upon it, and only after the transformation can it be fully the Mother's Force with no mixture of the lower instrument. Unless this change occurs, it keeps the disciple in the lower action, and the experience of doing the action by her Will is untrue. The unexceptionable mistake of Mother's words for the ego is a critical issue to understand and might be one of the causes of the present crisis in Auroville. As Sri Aurobindo wrote, "Apart from incomplete sincerity, there is the difficulty that the brain is clouded by egoism and desire and imagines it is doing the very thing when it is doing something else. That is why I spoke of the danger of the theory of all from the Mother. Some people have taken it that all that comes from the ego or the vital comes from the Mother, is her inspiration or what she has given them. Others have taken it as an excuse to continue indefinitely in the old rut, saying that when the Mother wants, she will change things. There were even some who on this basis created a subjective Mother in themselves whose dictates, flattering to their ego and desire, they pitted against the contrary dictates of the Mother here and came to think that this external Mother was after all not so much the real thing as the inner one, or that she was putting them through an ordeal by contradicting the inner dictates and seeing what they would do!"[30]

This tendency to distract Mother's words is almost universal in human nature, and not from dishonesty, because when the disciples listen to her or read her words, their minds are not silent, and they mix what they have heard or read and give it another turn. Often, the vital is exaggerated or reshaped according to desire or convenience. Sri Aurobindo meaningfully describes this as; "be on your guard and do not try to understand and judge the Divine Mother by your little earthly mind that loves to subject even the things that are beyond it to its own norms and standards, its narrow reasonings and erring impressions its bottomless aggressive ignorance and its petty self-confident knowledge. The human mind shut in the prison of its half-lit obscurity cannot follow the many-sided freedom of the steps of the Divine Shakti."[31] There will always be doubts and confusion of the mind and the vital when the Mother is approached from the wrong standpoint if the disciple insists on judging her by her response to his demands and ideas of what she ought to give to the sadhak. . This wrong interpretation of her messages, beyond their true meaning and deduction from a logical conclusion, is quite contrary to Mother's knowledge and experience, and as a result, the disciples listen and read something in their minds, which they follow and announce as the Mother's.

It is of no use to claim and revolt, 'Why do I not get it?', but to surrender and to receive with joy whatever the Divine gives, and then what one receives will be the right thing for the sadhak. By making it possible to change their attitude and move from the lower vital and physical planes, a union with the Mother on the higher or inner plane becomes possible.

Again and again, Sri Aurobindo warns the disciples not to misuse Mother as a Guru when the sadhak has self-centered and egoistic motives, "The theory that once you remember the Mother always everything you do flows from the Divine and therefore it does not matter what you do is rather a dangerous one. It may end by giving sanction instead of rejection to many things that ought to go out of the nature."[32] In passive surrender without aspiration and rejection, it is easy to claim, 'I (your disciple) won't do anything, Mother does everything, let her do all that to me.'

It needs a progressive surrender to call in her Force to work in the sadhak in its own way, which is the way of the Divine Truth and not work the way the sadhak wants, allowing some egoistic element of mind and vital which wants the Force, but only to use it for one's own purpose and not for the Divine purpose, without giving himself to the Divine. It is not only a one-sided surrender to the impersonal, or not only to the Divine in oneself, but also to the Divine outside, a complete, genuine spiritual surrender to the total Divine. However, "if there is ambition or other motive of the kind mixed up in the spiritual seeking, it may lead to a fall in the Yoga and the growth of an exaggerated egoism and megalomania. One cannot or ought not to plunge into experiences of this sadhana without a fairly long period of preparation and purification (unless one already has great spiritual strength and elevation). Sri Aurobindo himself does not care to accept many into his path and rejects many more than he accepts." [33]

Man is not bound by his outward nature, and the Divine is able to change it under any circumstance or develop something new in it, something not yet manifested, offering human beings a chance to become like the Divine. However, though the Divine Consciousness is omnipotent, it has put forth the instrumental personality in Nature, under the conditions of Nature, and it uses it according to the rules of the game. When the Divine takes on fully the burden of terrestrial nature sincerely, it does so without any conjuring tricks or pretence. There is a divinity in every man, and it can break through its coatings. It can manifest in ignorant and uncultured men and women, which is, for the Mother, a proven fact; all kinds of men and women can follow its path. The Divine assumes an outward human nature to reveal itself to human beings, but does not cease to be Divine.

The Mother, as the Divine in its Consciousness-Force, offers in her embodied physical action the opportunity of a constant Grace, but she can manifest in many other ways besides her physical one and acts according to the nature of the instrument. In her many forms, it is quite possible to have an inner, close relationship with her, even if she is not physically present. To truly know the outer Mother, one must understand what is within her, not just look at her outer appearance. The Mother works on the consciousness of the sadhaks through a silent occult influence, on which they learn to open themselves, to develop the psychic condition of surrender with an unshaken faith and rejection of the restlessness in the mind and the vital. When there is a demand for the Divine in the form of a sincere call, it is bound to have its fulfilment one day, provided there is no strong insincerity, such as power or ambition, that counterbalances the inner call, and something within oneself has to be overcome.

## The Role of the Mother as a Guru

In Sanskrit, the role of the Guru is often applied to a teacher who claims special spiritual insight based on personal revelation and who offers their disciples new ways of life and self-development. These spiritual revelations of Truth are unshakable and cannot be criticised; they are only accepted. Faith in the Guru's spiritual vision, though unsupported by proven evidence, does not accept rational judgment or any form of questioning. As the Guru, Sri Aurobindo and the Mother are pathfinders who advise the devotee to "Follow my path, the way I have discovered for you through my own efforts and example. Transform your nature from the animal to the spiritual and grow into a higher divine consciousness. All this you can do by your own aspiration and by the force of the Divine Shakti... I have said, 'I have opened the Way,' now you, with the Divine help, can follow it. I have not said 'Find the way for yourself as I did."[34]

The Mother was born in Paris in 1878 to Turkish and Egyptian parents and came to Pondicherry for the first time in 1914, settling there in 1920. In 1926, when Sri Aurobindo retired into seclusion, she supervised the organisation of the Ashram and later established Auroville. It was her task to implement Sri Aurobindo's vision, and her only aim in life was to give form to Sri Aurobindo's spiritual experiments. The Mother experienced a very high incarnation of the Divine Mother (Avatar) and spent her life manifesting a new consciousness in the terrestrial atmosphere, and by relying on this higher Consciousness (Force), Aurovilians became her instruments and would function as her willing servitors. As a feminine aspect of the Divine, the Mother is entirely equal to Sri Aurobindo in consciousness; the two aspects are not gross manifestations of sexuality in the lower worlds, but a division-in-unity—a spiritual thing, not a physical or vital indulgence. Without Sri Aurobindo, she cannot exist; without the Mother, the Divine cannot be manifested.

The Mother chose Auroville as an experimental laboratory, bringing together people of all backgrounds, characters, temperaments, and nationalities to subject its citizens to the workings and realisation of the inner consciousness and to understand its action. The disciples had to envision how the Force acts. While still guiding the Aurovilians from the start, and a few years after the inauguration, before her passing, she nurtured the residents to uncover their souls and realise human unity and fraternity. As a fundamental spiritual premise, she offered the unfettered freedom of the individual to follow the path and truth of one's unique inmost being in contact with the divine Will. In any form of spiritual discipline, the Guru's inspiration, guidance, methods, and presence are indispensable for avoiding errors in the practice. As a master and representative of a higher consciousness, she not only guides the disciples on the path through her method of teaching or, even more, by her example, but also by a power to communicate her own experiences to others.

The practice of Integral Yoga aims to evolve from man's animal humanity into a diviner race by opening all the various parts of the being to the descent of the higher, still concealed supramental principle. As a first step towards this transformation, the devotee needs to become aware of his inner being within and to live from there outward. Within us, we have the potential of a practical principle of our inmost being, the psychic being, as a representative of the Divine. For the Mother, our mental instrumentation is insufficient for the realisation of the ideal utopia; it appears utopian only because of our limited mental capacities. This soul is not an outer mixture of the mental, vital and physical elements, but it is like a spark from the Divine. After the psychic being comes to the forefront, an upward opening and descent of a higher principle toward the Supramental Truth consciousness may follow. The Mother showed the devotees an integral path to reach the inner and higher consciousness, aiming at divine perfection in a divine body on earth. A sustained preparatory period of personal effort needs the invocation and surrender to the Divine Shakti to gradually take over the disciple's sadhana. The practical steps on the path concern the practice of all one's actions and surrender to the Divine. As an aid to progression on the path, the Mother did not demand ascetic practices or the development of miraculous powers. However, in her yogic techniques, she emphasised living a disciplined, righteous life of truth in a spirit of humility, mutual respect, and tolerance. On the journey, the Mother advised her disciples to focus more on the process rather than merely looking for results. In Karma yoga, all the results and fruits of one's everyday actions are offered to the Divine, i.e, focusing on the action itself rather than looking for the result as a goal. For the Mother, the way of yoga is a living thing, not a mental principle or a set method to be applied against all necessary variations. She was never a guide bound by absolute and rigid principles and rules; instead, she demonstrated her practical flexibility in response to the requirements of each individual and each situation. With her practical attitude, she made innumerable exceptions for all kinds of established rules while communicating with Ashramites and Aurovilians. She encouraged the various

Aurovilians to follow the path which was best aligned with their inner nature.

All kinds of difficulties and doubts are inherent in a future city that transcends ordinary human aspirations. These difficulties can take an infinite variety of forms, and how to utilise them for progress depends on the nature as well as the practitioner's state of consciousness. The difficulty does not necessarily need to be a challenge for more intense effort; it may be an opportunity to question, in quietude, the fundamental validity of the attempt and eventually revise our attitude. The real cause of the difficulty is not external but due to some defect within ourselves, such as disharmony, impurity, or weakness, and in conquering this defect lies the progress. Outside circumstances only create the occasion to manifest itself. Often, the nearer the sadhak arrives at his goal, the difficulties become more intense, and this is true not only of the individual's sadhana but also in the collective sadhana. It is not easy to change our lower nature, our old habits, and other vital, mental movements of the lower instrumentation.

Entering the spiritual path is, therefore, extremely difficult; the path is strewn with the opposition of various forces, such as the limitations and incapacities of human nature, insufficient faith, egoism, inertia, or even the resistance of universal nature; they all stand in the way of inner and higher consciousness. However, too much concentration on the lower nature discourages the sadhak and may obscure a less vigilant mind easily. It is better to establish a connection with the inner or higher consciousness before delving into the areas of imperfection in the lower consciousness. Even this can be rather risky, and the best and safest way for the sadhak is to aspire to Mother's divine grace.

Mother's vision to develop an ideal community practically depends on the attitudes and beliefs of her disciples concerning the future, and the practice of their faith in her hypothesis affects its realisation. Such a transition needs a starting point, and her disciples are only able to move the world when they first have some stable ground on which to stand. The Mother hoped to find a circle of some sadhaks who gathered around her and who opened themselves to their true inner consciousness. She would like her disciples to choose to remain in the old jumbo, in the hope of stumbling upon some discovery or seeking the light within and finding the Divine within and without. On the journey, her emphasis is on action, which is inspired by spiritual knowledge and experience. She does not want us to parrot her views as an intellectual exercise, but rather to put them into practice and experience an inner change, thereby living an authentic life.

## A Critical Estimate

There is a universal Divine Mother and the Mother as a living Force who is carrying on the sadhana, both are one in different poises. With her Grace, she leads the disciple's soul to its divine destination, like a seed out of which a beautiful tree would grow, if not this life, then next. When worshipped by her disciples as an Avatar, she is an embodiment of the Divine in a materialised living form, i.e., a direct incarnation of the Divine on earth. As a universal Force, she has brought the Divine Self as Love into this manifestation. The Mother never referred to herself as an Avatar, she regarded herself more as an evolutionary pathfinder in the descent of the supramental consciousness on earth, those who want to contact her as an Avatar need an advanced psychic development, beyond the senses and thoughts to perceive her as the Divine Shakti and all other aspects of the Divine.

Glorification of Mother's spiritual insights should not disregard various considerations about the practical difficulties and credibility of her vision. Her human unity as an ideal to be realised is not something to accept passively as a metaphysical principle of faith. The guarantee of the practical credibility and success of the transformation of her ideals needs human action and social organisation. The field of action often proves to be much more complex than that of thoughts and ideas; through action, ideas become more refined and get meaningfully articulated. For the Mother, utopia is not simply a new utopian place; it is more a utopian practice of developing ways to deal with obstacles during the process of building the city, under the guidance of gradually awakened psychic change that transcends these obstacles. Only this change of consciousness, along with the necessary human effort, creates the condition for the existence of utopia and is the very possibility that inspires other citizens to change their lives and continue their efforts.

In the process of sadhana, the practitioner aims to actualise the various aspects of Integral Yoga, and the Mother emphasised the practitioner's experiment through the integral method of spiritual practice. Without applying her spiritual practice, the sadhana becomes mechanical and may finally deteriorate her vision into a rigid vision of formulas. The Mother was aware that practitioners of Integral Yoga, when they got stuck somewhere on the path, might be inwardly advanced in yoga but outwardly still unconsciously behave under the influence of a magnified ego and often show confused and mean characteristics in their behaviour. A primordial condition of inner work requires a certain psychological balance to avoid distortions which may accompany the sadhak during the inner exploration. She cautioned against spiritual arrogance and warned that spiritual commitment is like fire when the instrument is not sufficiently purified. It is not only by becoming irrational that the sadhak can move beyond states of consciousness, but it must also pass through reason to the light of infinite reason.

In the multiple interpretations of her dream, the pace of present-day changed reality, with its unpredictable breakthroughs, creative thinking, and useful and constructive but also, at times, inconvenient discoveries, offering new possibilities and contemporary insights, cannot be held back and may uncover new meaning. In her forward-looking approach, does it require first the study of the accumulated wisdom and new knowledge in various fields before transcending the present limits? Every devotee needs a certain degree of blind fidelity to specific goals and pursue these goals and actions, but what to do with those devotees who refuse to discuss complicated dogmatic issues and who project their desires into Mother's charismatic personality, while in their blind adherence to Mother's spiritual vision they refuse to implement new knowledge and developments? The Mother did adjust and revise some of her ideas about Auroville throughout the latter part of her life, in response to changing circumstances and situations, but these revisions were always accompanied by her own new insights, rather than as a consequence of criticism from her disciples. The disciples always accepted her messages without criticism, because they needed her as a leader, and they did not expose 'her truth' to the dangers of critical evaluation. Could it be that the meaning of her words after more than half a century may require a re-examination in the context of the historical moment? Is there sufficient space in Mother's speculative vision for future incalculable and unpredictable stress of circumstances and other practical limitations that would make new needs desirable?

In pursuing this point, are disciples able to handle the increased complexity inherent in her model without deviating from the path? When circumstances are not favourable, we may need to follow a different course to derive something valuable from it. This requires contemplation on making the right choices at the right time, and the impact these choices have on those around us as we learn valuable things on the journey towards realising her dream. In that dream, did the Mother offer her future plan as a blueprint, or is there scope for the devotee's own free will to offer them choices related to the changed situation? The citizens have deep faith in Mother's vision, but each new generation must learn to relate to the historical event, incorporating new facts, making necessary adjustments, and integrating them with the existing knowledge. Her views are not immutable; they are the result of her spiritual experiment, which requires no dogmatic approach from her disciples. An ideological approach requires a more spiritual way of practice, which enriches one's way of life and possesses intrinsic values. Although the details may change, the essence of her vision remains the same. To explain Mother's vision as unassailable limits that vision to a faith where facts are subordinated to experience.

In her excessive specification while planning every detail of the city, did the Mother in her vision sufficiently implement the shifting contingency of all human endeavours and shifting ambiguities of life? Are some Aurovilians able to shift their anchor in response to changed actual events? Reading her concepts related to a spiritual utopia may also require the extrapolation of the function and use of her original terminology. Her great vision is itself always ready in the process of flux and, therefore, subject to continuous challenges and revision. Her dream of the last century may need to be reasserted by re-examining the past in the light of newfound evidence more grounded in present-day facts. The Mother, in her pursuit of her goal, never presumed easy solutions; it included conflicts, resistance and even rebellion.

What is the core of her message, and what is still relevant in a century that looks so different compared to the period in which she lived, or is her spiritual message eminently radical, especially in our time? It is not difficult to conform to the wrong misconceptions of certain members of the community, and their influence may easily be exploited by charismatic leaders who present themselves as saviours. The idealistic managers continuously share Mother's aim with the community, utilising new laws and regulations, along with an increase in supervision and control, to protect the unity of the system and prevent any risks. These interpreters often omit the context in which her vision was written. There are contexts where the disciples cannot simply wave their hands and make the discrepancy between expectations and reality disappear. A crucial distinction should be made between the Mother's spiritual vision of Auroville and the renewed condition experienced by those living within the city with an authoritarian leadership who leave issues of differences unaddressed and do not encourage the cultivation of a method for managing dialogical interaction; engaging in the process of sharing ideas without the fear of condemnation. This loss of human concern may lead citizens to perceive a diminished sense of shared citizenship. The Mother emphasised entering the dialogue with a moral dignity without prejudices against each other, the will to see each other as one's equal and to be initially aware of what makes the other culturally, socially and religiously different, but simultaneously be mindful of their shared humanity which connects them and make them mutually dependent of each other to transcend these differences ultimately.

She aimed for a non-violent approach to conflict resolution, utilising a non-hierarchical decision-making process based on spiritual insights, innovative technology, and economic self-sufficiency. Such an attitude can only be realised when the citizens endeavour to change their consciousness and ask themselves difficult questions. It is too easy to pay lip service to the greatness of Mother's complex spiritual vision and use this to whitewash one's less enlightened ideas and behaviour. That's why Mother's radical spiritual message may become a form of conformism where authorities in power dutifully honour the memory of Mother's message. At the same time, they maintain their own ideas, which are directly opposed to Mother's vision. Paying lip service to her radical vision and thereafter going one's own way, misusing her words to digest an entirely contrary message. When the Mother's spiritual vision of life criticises tradition, it may be confusing when her spiritual views are made absolutistic and exclusive by some of her disciples. It may become an institute with a hierarchy whereby such devotees, in their faith, are inclined to determine their thoughts and actions to outsiders rather than being critical of themselves and the struggle against their oppressive tendencies. Rather than getting lost in endless hair-splitting arguments, it may be helpful to explore the essence of Mother's messages and move beyond endlessly parroting her words, often out of context. Each individual is different, and each disciple must discover their own path to self-discovery. However, will the Mother, as a human Guru, relieve seekers from the burden of their personal responsibilities? The Mother, far from acting like a conventional Guru, would be delighted when some of her devotees make some original contributions, which may be necessary for the present situation in Auroville. The Mother never wanted to become an object of blind worship or a cult figure who transformed herself into the leader of a movement where she was accepted as a Guru. Rather than deifying her, should she not be more honoured for her principles and methods on the path of the journey?

Too much blind faith and relying excessively on her dream relinquishes the disciple's autonomy and discernment. To have faith in the Mother, one needs to be able to believe passionately and have the necessary faith in Mother's guidance, but should one also simultaneously laugh at the absurdity of one's own blind faith, thereby ignoring one's own rational direction?

Faith, as a fundamental principle and dynamic conviction in Integral Yoga, must be free from attachment to the forms of the disciple's endeavour and the successive stages of their realisation. In contrast to blind faith of inert passivity, dynamic faith needs the cultivation of personal effort in refusing doubt and scepticism. Doubt has its utility and necessity only in the lower knowledge to get out of an ignorant belief and to be able to escape from its errors. The Mother did not ask for indiscriminate faith; all she asked was a fundamental faith by quiet discrimination, a faith in the soul's witness to something not yet manifested, achieved or realised, but which the knower within us feels to be true. For the Mother, faith is indispensable to man; he needs it to proceed forward in his journey through the unknown. However, does this mean that the practice of Integral Yoga and full faith in her complete spiritual vision determine Auroville's success or failure? If the sadhak's faith is rooted in an emotional attachment rather than in the assessment of evidence, then a critical, rational, analytical mind of the uninitiated will not contribute much to a fruitful debate about the flaws and hypocrisies in their integral practice.

Too much faith can be rather dangerous and have disastrous consequences, as it may blur one's judgment and lead to fanaticism. The inadequacies of Auroville's professed faith in the perfectibility of human nature can be traced to the errors committed by those who misused their faith, which have led to many absurdities. Perhaps some of her statements were only intended as a catalyst for action and as gateways to be explored by citizens guided by their psychic intuition.

The Mother created Auroville as a spiritual experiment in human unity, founded on her vision for a future spiritual society through yogic practice. In this process, did the Mother overestimate the spiritual capacities of her disciples, even when, in the early 1970s, many disciples did not meet her expectations? As a faithful Guru, she repeatedly requested her disciples to find their Guru internally and receive guidance from within, where the psychic force itself becomes the infallible inner guru of the yoga rather than being worshipped as an external physical presence. Deifying and worshipping the Mother in her perfection, where she is far above us as an example of unchanging perfection, the disciple may hand over his responsibility of making progress himself, living off her energy without creating his own. Are some of her devotees in their devotional practice making an increasingly exaggerated image worship of her as their Guru? If Mother's Force is used as a guide, implementing her statements as a gateway in the exploration of the development of our psychic being, then we don't need to repeat her words. Could their practice of Integral Yoga turn her vision into a mere personality cult and a religion, and create a dogmatic attitude? In the words of the Mother; "It is their own mental and vital formation of me that they love, not myself. More and more I am confronted with this fact. Each one has made his own image of me for himself in conformity with his needs and desires, and it is with this image that he is in relation, through that he receives the little amount of universal forces and the still smaller amount of supramental forces that manage to filter through all these formations. Unfortunately, they cling to my physical presence, otherwise I could withdraw into my inner solitude and do my work quietly and freely from there; but this physical presence is a symbol for them and that is why they cling to it, for they have very little real contact with what my body truly is or with the tremendous accumulation of conscious energy that it represents."[35] For the real devotee, it appears catastrophic to humanise her personality and her activities, as any doubt or self-willed behaviour on the path is assumed by them to distort their spiritual development.

Unfortunately, the Mother did not choose a formal successor to guide the citizens in the multitudinous needs of her project after she passed away, and there was no leader anymore whom the collective community could lean on. She left it to be executed by the citizens themselves, who were now dependent on their own divine guidance. This raised numerous questions for the future when it became apparent that not all her helpers were competent and appeared unreliable, often fixated on their own creative faith in self-government and impractical ideals. The Mother showed her disciples a path of transformation based on her own experiences without creating exaggerated expectations. Unfortunately, multiple interpretations of her words regarding the development of the future city led to a wide divergence within the community. As a result, a laissez-faire attitude pervaded social life. In contrast, her messages were intended to guide citizens in their spiritual practices and be put into action while simultaneously building the city. The gulf between her spiritual ideals and the present reality of human affairs seems to grow wider only. Who can replace Mother's role as a qualified, authentic Guru in the present chaotic situation? Even with the Guru's company, there are no guarantees, as it requires the blessings of Divine Grace beyond comparison; it comes to those who are ready to prepare the ground for the psychic experiment. This requires a challenging process of engagement in the practice of Integral Yoga, transcending habitual patterns and mental obstructions and opening the inner subtle psychic energy currents.

The questions from the disciples to the Mother primarily dealt with matters related to clarifying every aspect of Integral Yoga, and they asked for her support in the unpredictable outcomes that arose during the inner exploration of the psychic experiment. For the Aurovilians, Mother's statements regarding their difficulties during the practice of their sadhana served as a means of releasing their lethargy as they transitioned from an area of darkness into some light. In offering her guidance, she did not merely find direct solutions to the sadhak's problems related to the practice, but also for the development of the sadhak's enhanced inner psychic consciousness. Sri Aurobindo is quite clear about this when he writes," As for the Mother, you will not find in her this blind adherence to an arrangement once made....These methods of interviews are not promises, contracts or engagements-they are arrangements only and can be altered... There is a plasticity needed in the movement of time and the Shakti of life cannot afford to be rigid in its movements, otherwise Life would either be turned into a mere mechanism or break to pieces." [36] What the Mother was daring to envisage in her vision, some of it is now realised and carried into effect; lofty speculations of a partial change do not need the estrangement of the purity of her original vision, even with all its failed noble persistent efforts of its citizens and their dissatisfaction.

The author's comments about Mother's spiritual vision are not always compatible with everything she wrote, as with such an attitude, her vision becomes a religion with all sorts of inevitable fixed doctrines. Mother's spiritual vision of Auroville's future was not fixed; she knew very well that there is no single transcendental point of view that can be defended in the face of all sorts of changing problems and claims to be superior to various facts.

## Mother's Utopia

As discussed already before, the Mother's and Sri Aurobindo's consciousness are the same Divine Consciousness in two; they are one in two bodies because it is necessary for the play. In the words of the Mother, "Sri Aurobindo and I are always one and the same consciousness and one the same person."[37] Their paths on their journey of the supramental change and divine realisations were the same; she had automatically converted his realisations into a material form for the earth, too. He put her in charge of the disciples of the Sri Aurobindo Ashram, where she was called the Mother. Sri Aurobindo, as the masculine, remained in the background and worked from there, whereas the Mother, as the feminine Shakti, converted Sri Aurobindo's spiritual acquisitions into practical facts of growth. Before elaborating more on Mother's utopia, it might be useful to explain Sri Aurobindo's future vision and his description of a Divine utopia beforehand.

For Sri Aurobindo, those individuals who contribute most to the future of humanity will be those who recognise spiritual evolution as the destiny and the great need of the human being; an evolution of the present type of humanity into a spiritualised humanity, which is surely the need of the race and the intention of Nature. Sri Aurobindo is certain that this change cannot be effected by machinery, social adjustments, or outward institutions; it must be lived out by each person inwardly, along with the external readjustment. The outward unity of the human race can only be secured if humanity spiritualises itself, and the spiritual religion of humanity becomes the general inner law of human life.

Sri Aurobindo questioned "whether past analogies are a safe guide in a problem so new and whether something else might not be evolved more intimately and independently arising from it and suitable to its complexities. But, even in dealing with its new problems, mankind works upon past experiences and, therefore, upon past motives and analogies. Even when it seizes on new ideas, it goes to the past for the form it gives to them...On the other hand, it is quite possible that human thought and action may take so new a turn as to bring in a number of unforeseen possibilities and lead to a quite different ending. And one might upon these lines set one's imagination to work and produce perhaps a utopia of a better kind. Such constructive efforts of the human imagination have their value and often a very great value; but any such speculations would evidently have been out of place in the study I have attempted."[38]

Only a spiritual religion of humanity holds out hope for the future, as the growing realisation that there is a divine reality in which the human race and the human being are the means by which it will progressively reveal itself here. This implies bringing about a kingdom of the divine Spirit upon earth. Such a realisation must proceed for the time being through mechanical solutions, with the hope that the growing number of men will realise the truth of the Spirit, which will lead humanity to the path of perfection. "The perfectly spiritualised society will be one in which, as is dreamed by the spiritual anarchists, all men will be deeply free, and it will be so because the preliminary condition will have been satisfied. In that state, each man will be not a law to himself but the law, the divine Law, because he will be a soul living in the Divine Reality and not an ego living mainly, if not entirely, for its own interest and purpose. His life will be led by the law of his own divine nature liberated from the ego. Nor will that mean a breaking up of all human society into the isolated action of individuals.... Therefore too is a growing inner unity with others a necessity of his being and perfect unity the sign and condition of the perfect life. Not only to see and find the Divine in oneself, but to see and find the Divine in all." [39] There is this dream of a fulfilment exceeding the individual transformation, a new earth, a city of God with a divine descent upon earth, a kingdom of God within and outside in a collective human life. This miraculous and occult picture of utopia is nothing extraordinary or irrational, and Sri Aurobindo described his spiritual society as, " there would be nothing supernatural or miraculous in such an evolution except, in so far as it would be a supernature or superior nature to ours just as human nature is a supernature or superior nature to that of animal or plant or material objects...yet it would seem impossible if we took our stand of the limited animal consciousness and its capacities; for there is nothing there to warrant so prodigious a progression."[40]

The critical issue confronting humanity is not related to the outer manifestation; these outer manifestations have physical, ecological, political, cultural, and social implications, but they all arise due to the constraints on our consciousness, which require a change. It will be difficult for a few individuals to live in a spiritually oriented society when still confined to the life of the lower nature. It is for this reason that Sri Aurobindo advices, " At a certain stage it might be necessary to follow the age-long long device of the separate community, but with a double purpose, first to provide a secure atmosphere, a place and life apart, in which the consciousness of the individual might concentrate on its evolution in surroundings where all was turned and centred towards the one endeavour and, next, when things were ready, to formulate and develop the new life in those surroundings and this prepared spiritual atmosphere. It might be that, in such a concentration of effort, all the difficulties of the change would present themselves with concentrated force; for each seeker, carrying in himself the possibilities but also the imperfections of a world that has to be transformed, would bring in not to only his capacities but his difficulties and the oppositions of the old nature and, mixed together in the restricted circle of a small and close common life, these much assume a considerably enhanced force of obstruction which would tend to counterbalance the enhanced power and concentration of the forces making for the evolution. This is a difficulty that has broken in the past all the efforts of mental man to evolve something better and more true and harmonious than the ordinary mental and vital life."[41] This advice is certainly applicable to Auroville's present dilemmas, and these difficulties would be overcome if the power of the Spirit descending from the higher planes is sufficiently strong.

The key to understanding Sri Aurobindo's concept of utopia lies in his concept of true spirituality, which involves subjectively exploring the individual's powers and potentialities within themselves after realising the inadequacy of the objective view of life. This form of true subjectivism is a confluence of transcendental self-affirmation and the identification of the self with the collective in the world. This vision of utopia will face the necessary scepticism of modern scientists because their views do not conform to the present-day scientific conception of nature and their preconceptions, which are based on limited experience. However, Sri Aurobindo counters such criticism by arguing that the kingdom of utopia, in the evolution of the utopian divine within us, does not depend on external methods. His spiritual humanism is the hope for the future, and the realisation of the highest human potential must be worked out from the inner truth to the outer forms. In the realisation of the ideal utopia, our mental capacities are not sufficient; they need the development of our inmost being.

Auroville's name refers to Sri Aurobindo and carries the meaning of "dawn," the French word for aurore. A utopia, as envisioned by the Mother, was meant to be a "universal city" where its citizens built a utopian community and where her utopian dream became a living reality under her spiritual guidance. As a complex experiment where its inhabitants create something new, it resists any definition and cannot be easily categorised neatly. The Mother proposed a utopian experiment in living beyond the normative structures of the 20th-century capitalist-liberal democracies. This self-proclaimed utopian experiment integrates a mixture of biological evolutionism, socialism, and spirituality in a common effort towards perfection. The Mother founded Auroville as a collective experiment for the progress of humanity, aiming to be free to explore new ways of being and living together without being led down the same paths as before and free from external interference. Auroville has no reason to exist for those who are satisfied with the world as it is; such people interfere in something they don't understand, they lack a sincere attempt at a new future life, and they are not willing servitors of the Divine. The Mother envisioned "the city the Earth needs" as "a centre of transformation, a small nucleus of men who are transforming themselves and setting an example for the world."[42] She envisioned a city, not a mere village or community, as the smallest collective unit that encompasses all the activities undertaken by the citizens without personal desires. In the city, "humanity should be variously represented. For the problem of transformation, one has to deal with all sorts of elements, favourable and unfavourable. The same man indeed carries in him a mixture of these two things. If only sattwic (virtuous) and cultured men come for yoga, men without very much of the vital difficulty in them, then, because the difficulty of the vital element in terrestrial nature has not been faced and overcome, it might well be that the endeavour would fail."[43] This letter was intended to describe the population of the ashram, but it may also be applicable to the citizens of Auroville. As an intentional community, the Mother adds an occult dimension to Auroville, where participants are taking part in this work, and though she may have wanted a city of 50,000 people, it seemed sheer numbers were finally not her priority; she was more concerned with the influence of the occult dimension of the project. In the Mother's utopian dream, she presented Auroville as an intentional community to realise a new society to be achieved in all its details and a place where she offered the citizens the possibility of a future change that makes life better and inspires others to bring about a better world. In this entirely new type of spiritual utopia she offered the disciples a method of practice and a plan for realising her vision, and she described in detail what life in the community would look like. She did not believe in external decisions; it is the Divine who makes decisions for each of us; otherwise, one is the slave of one's habits, desires, and all kinds of outer rules. To be a true Aurovilian, "one lives in Auroville to be free from moral and social conventions; but that freedom must not be a new slavery of the ego, its desires and ambitions." True freedom is obtained by union with the Divine when the ego is transcended. This means that a citizen's life should not be organised according to external and artificial rules, but rather according to one's inner consciousness.

In Mother's words, "At present, all human organisations are based on: the visible fact (which is a falsehood), public opinion (another falsehood), and moral sense, which is a third falsehood!... To be an organiser should be there; no more desires, no more preferences, no more attractions, no more repulsions- a perfect equality for all things. Sincerity, of course, but that goes without saying: wherever insincerity enters, poison enters at the same time."[44] For the Mother, the proliferation of written rules was anathema to progress; the rise of bureaucratic rule-making institutions only causes atrophy of the Divine inspiration.

All attempts at the great utopian dreams have, to some extent, failed to materialise. Outer social reform was intended to replace inner ethical reform, but this effort often failed and frequently ended in disaster. This inner change aims at the perfection of life on earth, a diverse out-flowering of life's capacities and the individual's potentialities. This perfection of the individual is inseparable from the perfection of the society at large. Mother's spiritual perfection is characterised by a process of purification of the lower instrument by the divine psychic consciousness. Mother's predominant preoccupation was, unlike the utopian socialists, the cultivation of community-wide development of a collective soul through collective solidarity, unity, and liberty with the help of divine Grace. When she established Auroville, she was aware that the world would not improve as long as human relations were founded upon old ideas; it required a spiritual transition into a new world and a new man. The terrestrial transformation is brought about by each citizen's individual transformation through their inner development toward union with the Divine, which requires support from external action, and thereafter, by the collective social transformation through the creation of an environment favourable to the growth of the individual. Both proceed simultaneously.

Its realisation calls for collective effort in terms of an integral perfection of man. Regarding the possible failure of the concrete materialisation of the spirit of Auroville, she wrote, "As the formation descends in order to manifest, all oppositions arise, contradictions arise, complications arise, and within you clearly see that they [the residents] don't understand. So I spend my time telling them, Don't try to organise, don't try, you are going to fossilise the whole thing before it's begun... Anyway, we'll muddle along as best we can. It's all an attempt, that's all."[45] Individuals who will most help the future of humanity in the new age are those who recognise spiritual evolution as a great need of the human being. However, the Mother advised the disciples that the special work to achieve a new realisation is for the earth and not for ourselves. "It is necessary to stand apart from the rest of the world so as to separate ourselves from the ordinary consciousness in order to bring down a new one. It is not that love for all is not part of the Sadhana, but it has not to translate itself at once into a mixing with all- it can only express itself in a general and when need be dynamic universal goodwill, but for the rest it must find vent in this labour of bringing down the higher consciousness with all its effect for the earth." [46]

However, even if there is much goodwill, the collective life also needs to be properly organised and coordinated. It does not seem that the Mother knew exactly how Auroville would develop in the future, and although she did offer a detailed plan, it seemed more that she decided to undertake it as a great adventure. Over the last nine years of her life, she traced the developments into the unknown step by step, exploring the evolutionary nature of the Auroville experience. From the beginning, she expressed her concerns about the quality of the people who wanted to join Auroville. In 1972, she did not want many men; she wanted some people, but true people, and she could give Auroville a hundred thousand people in a moment from South Africa. It seemed the Mother definitely revised her policy regarding the 50,000 future Aurovilians when she wrote in 1971, "Twelve good men would be better than hundreds of stupid persons. Auroville is not for comfort but for the servants of the Divine. People in Auroville should not shirk hard work. They should not think of escaping from the outer control until the Divine control is there."[47]

The Mother selected every future citizen who represented a possibility and a special difficulty that had to be resolved, but it was the maturity of their soul that made them into new citizens of Auroville, ready to participate in the great adventure. In order to fulfill the realisation of the divine purpose the Mother needed, at that time, a diverse mixture of people which, though necessary, may also be complicated, because it seems that the mixture of today's Aurovilians is not advanced enough in their practice, struggling with their own difficulties, or some or many are collectively not in Auroville to realise Mother's divine purpose but are here more for the gratification of their own selfish needs.

Mother knows "it's not easy, but we are not here to do easy things; the whole world is there for those who like an easy life. I would like people to feel that coming to Auroville does not mean coming to an easy life-it means coming to a gigantic effort for progress. And those who don't want to keep up with it should leave.... People should know that coming to Auroville means an almost superhuman effort for progress... We are here to prepare a superhumanity, not to fall back into desires and an easy life."[48] Those pragmatic Aurovilians who attempt to improve the community according to Mother's vision must remember that we live in a different era, where certain unanticipated historical circumstances inevitably limit their aspirations. None of the community members can definitely anticipate Mother's ideal plan, as much depends on the realities of the contemporary world. Mother's utopian speculation was less risky during the time when she described her vision of a barren landscape, comparing the attempts which are now made in the growing complexity of the changed large-scale present problems in the real world, i.e., the gap between the Mother who seriously wrote about her future vision of Auroville as a new society and those who attempt to build it, where human progress itself seems to be gradually equated with technological progress if the citizens are seeking only to alter the speed and ignoring the direction and the transformation of the spiritual utopia, through technological development. In their empirical pragmatism, as they strive to build the concrete city of 50,000 people as soon as possible, the builders need not lose sight of the possibilities of material progress; however, they should not overlook the spiritual virtues of Mother, which are integral to the process of 'how' building the city. The goal of her utopian future city is to create a new consciousness, a new person, and the city serves as a means for the development of this new consciousness. She offered the citizens a multiplex spiritual practice, not based on a strict, linear, systematic closure of a single alternative or her authoritarian guidance of a static blueprint, but rather as the emancipating possibility of her dream. She warned her disciples not to lapse into a rigid system.

Her concern is not only the fixed structure of the future city but also the fluid integral practice needed to develop a changing consciousness, being constantly open to new ways of experimentation while building the future city. To reach new ways of being through a willed human transformation, she emphasised active participation, initially through a collective and non-hierarchical effort, in the hope of finding some enlightened individuals later on.

The Mother, as a subject of devotion and dedication, is, for many devotees, the representation of the Divine energy or the incarnation of the Supramental Consciousness into the earth-consciousness. Her spiritual teachings based on her spiritual experiences are not religious, exclusive or partial; however, she warned her devotees not to formulate her system in a way to impose it and make it a religion; she rejected any form of religion as it is a hindrance to the evolution of the Spirit and Auroville should not be sectarian. The Mother did not impose her dogmatic beliefs on her disciples, and she did not expect blind faith. Her teachings originated from the Divine and were based on her direct spiritual experiences, rather than being inspired by religious authorities. Religious authorities lack the understanding of the higher truth of universalism and the material and spiritual evolution of the Divine.

Is there any flexibility within the community where Mother's dream of Auroville as a city of the future can be characterised as an ongoing process of the disciple's critical dialogue, in which her illuminative vision is continuously nuanced and adjusted to present-day circumstances? Do the inhabitants have to surrender to her vision down to the smallest details and cling to her original vision in terms of the detailed physical manifestation of Auroville? Could the Mother foresee the totality of Auroville's material unfolding, and are some of her ideas no longer relevant today? Could it be that the Mother was more interested in realising the key elements and fundamentals of her vision and left the details, without ignoring the essence, to the citizens?

Advances in knowledge, in any sphere of human endeavour, should it be allowed to criticise Mother's accepted authority? Could it be that some of her illuminations appear delusional in the context of modern knowledge and in total disregard of accepted scientific evidence, without detracting from the value of what she thought her disciples? Her emphasis on real change from within elevates her teachings far more than prescriptions for outward conformity. Her authority, as an important attribute of her charismatic leadership, may have occasionally elevated her status due to the self-absorption and high expectations of her disciples. For various disciples, a complete passive submission to her spiritual vision is attractive because, in obeying her divine Will, the devotee abrogates responsibility and doubt.

Mother's utopian vision may have been partly realised, but in an entirely different spirit from the one she had visualised in her dream. Her aim at transforming Aurovilians shows flaws which, for many of its citizens, are intolerable. As a work in progress it seems its citizens are unable to come to a consensus on important matters, and they are constantly divided on vital issues which do not contribute to the fulfillment of the citizen's hopes, on the contrary, it often appears more hope of a secularised and angelism than Mother's gradual development of a perfect society.

Are human geniuses who manifest new ideas, machines, and social institutions the new lever by which the Millennium of abundance will be built from Auroville's down-to-earth planners, engineers and technicians in a secular future utopia and not from a divine intervention from above? Is there still, deep inside Auroville, the original divine spark to protect its future existence? There have been attacks from outside, but nowadays, attacks also come from within. Aurovilians are aware that acting on the outer world without aiming to transform themselves inwardly will not lead to removing the real root causes of long-term suffering. However, such an approach seems to have a relatively low rate of success, because among the many who follow this path, none of the citizens has reached a specific destination that enables them to act and alleviate the present crisis within Auroville. While celebrating Auroville's successes in various fields, where new ambitions inspire the community, citizens should not overlook the foundational principles that remain the codes of survival and success. Challenges and non-adherence to the Charter's basic tenets have led to the intervention of governmental authoritarianism.

## Notes

1.) Sri Aurobindo; *The Hour of God*, p 154

2.) Sri Aurobindo; *Letters on Yoga*, p 1615

3.) Ibid., p 1647

4.) Ibid., p 1649

5.) Ibid., p 1674

6.) Ibid., p 1623

7.) Ibid., p 1626

8.) Ibid., p 1616-161

9.) Ibid., p 1666

10.) Ibid., p 906

11.) Ibid., p1628

12.) Ibid., p 1610

13.) Ibid., p 1676

14.) Ibid., p 621

15.) Ibid., p 1643

16.) Sri Aurobindo; *The Mother*, p 6

17.) Ibid., p 220

18.) Sri Aurobindo; *Letters on Yoga*, p 1169

19.) Sri Aurobindo; *The Mother*, p 294

20.) Sri Aurobindo*; Letters on Himself and the Ash*ram, p 395

21.) Ibid., p 396

22.) Sri Aurobindo*; The Mother*, p 20

23.) Ibid., p 483

24.) Ibid., p 505-509

25.) Ibid., p 314

26.) Sri Aurobindo*; The Synthesis of Yoga*, p 752

27.) Sri Aurobindo; *Letters on Himself and the Ashram*, p 484

28.) Sri Aurobindo; *Letters on Yoga*, p 615

29.) Sri Aurobindo; *The Mother*, p 116

30.) Ibid., p 330

31.) Ibid., p 25

32.) Ibid., p 138

33.) Sri Aurobindo; *Letters on Himself and the Ashram*, p 398

34.) Ibid., p 42

35.) The Mother, *Collected Works of the Mother*, Vol 13, June 11

36.) Sri Aurobindo; *The Mother*, p 360

37.) The Mother; *Mother's Agenda*, p 121

38.) Sri Aurobindo; *The Ideal of Human Unity*, p 575

39.) Sri Aurobindo; *The Human Cycle* p 259

40.) Sri Aurobindo; *The Life Divine*, p 1042

41.) Ibid., p 1026

42.) The Mother; *The Collected Works of the Mother*, Vol 13, p 225

43.) Sri Aurobindo; *Letters on Yoga*, p 335

44.) The Mother; *Mother's Agenda*, 25-3-1970

45.) Ibid., October 1967

46.) The Mother; *Collective Works of the Mother*, Vol 15, p 114

47.) Ibid., Vol 13 p 240

48.) The Mother, *Mother's Agenda*, April,1972

*CHAPTER SIX*

# WHY AUROVILLE

The desire for a paradise on earth is as old as humanity. Auroville's name is derived from Auro, in Sanskrit, 'dawn', the city of dawn, inaugurated by the Mother on the 28th of February 1968. The Auroville concept was created as a city originating from the ideals of the spiritual philosophy of Sri Aurobindo, i.e., for the creation of a new world expressing the Divine perfection. Auroville is the place where Sri Aurobindo's ideals are to be realised in the form of a collective identity, and where its citizens aim to demonstrate that Sri Aurobindo's spiritual philosophy is viable. In a vision, the Mother visualised that there should be a place where people from all over the world could live together in peace, and together with the support of the Indian government and UNESCO, she planned to realise her dream, which had to be expressed in a material form. In Mother's words, "Auroville, as an experimental field, can be seen as a step towards establishing a spiritualised society, where the future Aurovilians belong to the enlightened portion of humanity."[1] The city of dawn, as the new utopia, did not come out all of a sudden; the vision of a new future city appeared several times in Mother's life. In August 1954, she published' A Dream'. She did not want to remove the established order but to transform it, and in the aim of the city, she emphasised the realisation of human unity based on the spiritual insights of Sri Aurobindo. As the collective ideal for creating a new world, a new society, and a new humanity on earth, it calls for a collective effort in which citizens can set aside their egos and relinquish all personal desires. Each citizen has a role to play in the collective transformation of humanity through the mastery of their ego and a progressive manifestation of their psychic being. The Mother envisioned Auroville as a city the earth needs, with a small nucleus of citizens who are transforming themselves and setting an example for the world. All activities undertaken in the city are to be carried out in the spirit of Integral Yoga.

Integral Yoga, as a form of sadhana, forms the psycho-spiritual practice underlying the aim of Auroville. As "all life is yoga," the practice emphasises engagement with the material world, infusing everyday existence with spirituality and pushing evolution beyond the limits of the present terrestrial creation towards the creation of a more advanced, higher, and truer supramental world. According to the Mother, "Humanity is not the last rung of the terrestrial creation. Evolution continues and man will be surpassed. It is for each individual to know whether he wants to participate in the advent of this new species.... For those who are satisfied with the world as it is, Auroville obviously has no reason to exist." [2] Though the Mother did not enforce the practice of Integral Yoga as an absolute necessity for Aurovilians, life in Auroville was meant to develop the inner quest of the members, which would have a determining effect on their outer lives. Auroville is intended to be the meeting point between the inner and outer worlds; the two are one, and Auroville aims to be a living example of this truth, providing concrete proof that Spirit and Matter are one. To realise the nature of this ideal, Aurovilians need to be determined to subordinate their personal convictions to the common goal of Auroville, a collective life that strives to grow and perfect itself, yet each individual does so in their own way, with goodwill for all.

Auroville was inaugurated in a makeshift amphitheatre on an empty plateau, where people from 124 countries and 23 Indian States met, each carrying samples of soil from their country, placed in a sculpted urn as a symbolic act of human unity. As a center of accelerated evolution, man must change his world utilising the power of the Spirit within and work individually at one's self-perfection, and as a consequence, collective perfection follows thereafter spontaneously. The citizens are ready to collaborate with the latest and most advanced contemporary discoveries in technical, psychological, economic, social, cultural, and spiritual sciences, mostly utilising human resources rather than relying only on mechanical labour. However, Auroville is not only a project to build a new city, but it is also essentially an experiment in a new consciousness where the community functions through the action of the Divine Consciousness-force in each individual, which is the means to accomplish their inspiration. A fundamental change in consciousness manifests itself in changes to various aspects of human life.

From 1968 to 1973, the Mother guided the Aurovilians as an authority; they followed her advice regarding the practice of Integral Yoga and other specific aspects of life. Many of her children (disciples) still believe that her spirit is still alive, and 'beyond' she is still running the daily affairs of the city where the citizens function as instruments to fulfill a divine plan she still supervises. However, there are also those Aurovilians who believe that Auroville is an open secret, and none of them know whether this experiment will ultimately become a utopian city of the future or gradually fall apart. Without her Force, most likely, Auroville will suffer the same fate as all other utopias, so the Aurovilians need to draw ceaselessly on the source of this Consciousness-Force. It is this inner psychic consciousness that holds the community together, and as long as the citizens don't connect with each other on this level, Auroville may fall apart.

For the Mother, it is not the citizens who build Auroville; rather, they are the instruments under the divine guidance of a divine process that is unfolding itself in and through the citizens. Sparks of the soul, as a play of forces, are the first stones of the city, and many developed psychic beings are able to carry within themselves a collective soul, where the city, as a collective body with a soul, mirrors the future destiny of man and his union with the Divine. This is how the construction of Auroville is built, on a totally new basis guided by the values of the soul rather than the old basis of the comfortable world. On the journey to discover their true center they make themselves the vessels of the divine consciousness. The city with a soul becomes an experiment in human living, and with its applied spirituality, it aspires to be a new creation, expressing the dawn of a new consciousness through its own new innovative methods. It is not an institution, but a vastly complex, collective experimental process aimed at some kind of transformation. It is not easy to describe this process; glimpses of its effects and movements can be offered, but there are no grand panoramas.

The experiment must be lived through as an ongoing process, beginning with the inward level, which forms the basis from which outer activities and development can be known and realised. The process of moving inward and acting from there is often accompanied by the exploration of one's capacities and incapacities, the latter of which, as destructive potentialities, need to be faced, understood, and transformed into creative, purposive potentialities. This whole process requires a stable and reasonably developed ego as the starting point of sadhana, where the sadhak is capable of exploring inner realms and being confronted with conscious and unconscious traumatic contents of the psyche. As long as the sadhak is not in contact with the action of the Force from a deeper will within, the mental will is essential for cultivating control and detachment. This attitude of the mind should not be prematurely abandoned. In their shared vision and collective purpose, the collective growth that emerges from within can be relatively unstructured, with little outward instructions in the nature of the vision. As a laboratory of experimentation, there often exists, initially, a considerable amount of chaos before ultimately reaching a genuine unity. In this human unity, disunity cannot be ignored, and difficulties must first be experienced not by adding more disharmony but by gradually moving inwards to the psychic being in order to overcome them.

On the journey into the unknown, while experimenting with different models related to the reinvention of a new society, Auroville's most utopian aspects navigate between the search for perfection rooted in idealism and the inescapable limitations and constraints of imperfect human nature, grounded in realism and pragmatism. During this journey towards a new reality that transcends old oppositions, the release of old ideas and the emergence of a new, evolving reality mustn't remain opposed to each other; instead, the old ideas are transformed and integrated into a broader context. The Mother expected all those citizens who participated in the development of the new city to strive for this common goal, and in their diversity, they offered their energy and commitment to this experiment. In the process of building the city, Aurovilians are provided an opportunity to participate in the project according to one's means and capacity, and one's activity for the welfare of the community must not be something mechanical but in the truer and deeper spirit of the community. As a complex process, community development initially relies on the participation of its citizens, which may require the creation of new forms of leadership and the need to transcend existing potentialities that differ from the current state. It is not a blueprint for a new society; the details of the utopian experiment, as envisaged by the Mother, will have to be worked out by the community.

To gain a better understanding of Auroville's current development, it is helpful to provide a more detailed account of the city's history. Due to the failure of the mid-20th-century system, the valuable ideas about manipulating nature and the numerous problems and obstacles that humanity in the West encountered could not be resolved by its existing potentialities. The market economy could not deliver social justice and was not something to be justified by some consensus or transcendental principles. The explosion of technological inventions, globalisation, and organisational abundance would generate a new imagined place in features of modern life, where a perfect solution in human affairs could be possible, even though it seems that men at present may be ill-suited for such a utopia. In the 1960s and 1970s, out of acute dissatisfaction with social ills, some groups rejected the prevailing values as morally unacceptable and initiated the reconstruction of their own lives by inventing small, new utopian worlds founded on experimentation and the belief in the capacity for human transformation and infinite potential for human perfection. They demonstrated how a comprehensive utopian vision can move the separate ambitions of other diverse groups into a shared collective vision. As a result, a wave of utopias emerged during the economic boom that followed World War II.

In the 1960s, a few busloads from France arrived in Auroville with people who stood for antibureaucratic individualism, accompanied by a spontaneous expression of their high-spirited way of living, which contrasted with any form of social control. Bureaucrats tend to operate under the fiction that rules apply equally to everyone, although they are often deployed as a means to exert their own arbitrary personal power. These first citizens, with their ideology of reforming various aspects of social problems in a complex society, attempted to implement their mature ideals in a new social and cultural environment. Breaking ground in the wilderness and building a new society under Mother's guidance, they began from scratch, dedicating their tireless efforts to the city. As long as the early Aurovilians believed that Mother's dream might be realised one day, they laboured with heroic energy, gladly bearing immense hardship.

Many of these earlier settlers in Auroville came to escape their affluent, consumerist suburban lifestyle and joined Auroville as an intentional community to undertake developmental work for a self-organising spiritual society envisioned by the Mother. Initially, many of them were young, middle-class Western individuals, and their withdrawal from their society was not an escape into fantasy; instead, it was used as a means of adopting a new way of living within an international spiritual community. Their attempt at socio-cultural reformulation and building a new society required a balance and maintenance of the unifying vision that the Mother initially provided. Auroville, as a spiritual intentional project, offered them a form of spiritualism for a broken industrialisation and economic materialism. The first Aurovilians, in their utopian experimentation, had to learn survival methods while preparing the ground for Mother's new ideology. They questioned traditional authority and shared their disillusionment with the older society; they not only came to Auroville to learn more about sophisticated forms of life adjustment but also for the inner exploration of higher forms of consciousness. In its initial stages, Auroville grew into existence with its three Charters, "Mother's Dream", "the Charter" and "To Be A True Aurovilian" together with a City Plan. With this founding vision, the Mother set about establishing Auroville as a guiding force for a new and sustainable way of life where the universal city would not be just an ordinary developmental project but an evolutionary experiment. Mother's city plan, the Galaxy plan, looked quite different compared to most modern cities and had other priorities beyond all existing social, political, and religious convictions.

In its first decades of existence, the focus had to be on fundamentals, including housing, land cultivation, education, agriculture, and industry. The first priority focused on regenerating the severely eroded land, followed by environmental and sustainability issues. In its early existence after the Mother left her body, a vacuum of authority caused an extreme situation within the community, and the Aurovilians encountered some clashes with the Sri Aurobindo Society, a group of Ashramites previously established by the Mother, who controlled Auroville's administration. In their struggle for independence, a legal entity was established to continue the Auroville project. In 1979, the Indian government initiated a process to protect and preserve the development of the international Township. This ultimately led to the establishment of the Auroville Foundation Act, and its assets were initially transferred to the Indian government. Under this Act, an autonomous institution, the Auroville

Foundation Act, has been established with a Governing Board, an International Advisory Council and the Residents Assembly. All the activities of Auroville are vested under the Foundation to make long-term arrangements for better management and future development. The Act envisaged that these three authorities would work together in harmony and coordination.

## Back to the Present

At present, Auroville barely qualifies as a Township. Despite its impressive achievements and the lush surroundings, Auroville still appears fragmented, and the city of 50,000 people is still approximately 47,000 people short of its target. After more than 55 years since its inauguration, the world and humanity have witnessed various developments in new information technology, A.I, digitalisation, climate change, globalisation, capitalism, consumerism and environmental issues that are reshaping the world at an unprecedented pace, and it is not always clear how the citizens of Auroville respond to these changes. How do they bridge the gap between their ideal vision and this factual reality? By continuously experimenting with different collective structures by its participating citizens and engaging in their journey towards a psychic consciousness which shapes the outer manifestation, the Aurovilians are attempting to bridge the gap between their spiritual practice and the present-day factual reality. By the reward of their strenuous aspiration and partial realisations, a temporary approximation to their goal is possible.

Unlike other intentional utopias, which are based on economic, environmental, social, or religious ideologies and have their own constitutions, rules, and regulations governing the lives of their members, Auroville insists on an understanding of and faith in the Divine within the ideals of Auroville. In Auroville, the largest intentional community in the world, its citizens follow the teachings of the Mother and strive to lead a way of life in accordance with the Mother's vision for Auroville's future. The Mother's predominant preoccupation was not, unlike the utopian socialists, on ordinary social reform but more on the cultivation of an outward expression of the individual's potentialities and community-wide development of a collective soul within through solidarity, unity and liberty. Envisioned as a laboratory and a field of experimentation, it is a place where the first results of the laboratory for a new humanity are being challenged in the outer reality of the world.

As a multidimensional and living experiment, the project serves as an intentional community that challenges the inner awakening of a new society and a new consciousness. Each of its citizens represents a particular set of problems which need to be transformed in Auroville's evolutionary experiment. As a spiritual anarchy, the development of Auroville is a never-ending process and not a ready-made product, it includes instability, the freedom of expression of severe differences of opinions, and it needs an open society with sufficient space for the development of new ideas, i.e, Auroville's necessary renewal should not be contrary to the latest accepted universal world views.

Nevertheless, in due time, conflicts arose due to issues related to citizens' ideological differences with the original ideals, organisational and financial matters, individualism, impatience, competition, and various other problems that occur in society outside Auroville. Often, these conflicts intensify when working towards an abstract notion of the common good, which gradually dissipates and demands a return to Mother's more spiritual principles. Auroville became ideologically divided into one part of 'the moderates' who wanted the activities of the city more based on profit and self-maintenance who, losing touch with much of Mother's dream, are commercialising her dream more with the gratification of their basic human needs, authority, rules and power, and on the other part 'the purists' who prioritised more the city's non-material ideals and agreed spiritual principles, devotees with a belief in Truth and faith in Mother's guidance, dedicating to perform their work and duties for Auroville's spiritual survival.

During this time of polarisation, the critical question remains more pressing than ever: is Mother's spiritual vision immune to the present-day challenges regarding the continuous clashes of citizens' differing opinions? Group formation has its advantages as long as the group remains alert to the inclination towards the glorification of their arguments without being open to criticism. When groups are formed that are not reasonably transparent, and members of the various groups approach each other in an atmosphere of criticism, factionalism becomes one of the most important causes of rupture. There can be no answer to the growing group polarisation within the community, where truth seems to become privatised and where fact and fiction are mixed.

How to equalise the confrontation between the different groups that polarises such great forces of conflict; the collapse of the ancient regime and its old establishment, which is still concerned with the excitement of the evolution of the new man, and the new establishment who resolve, often by order, in a drastic fashion and proud self-confidence the utopian dream according to their innovations under the pretext of Mother's vision? It appears that the earlier spiritual ideology in Auroville has gradually waned and is being gradually replaced by those with a more secular approach, who, in their quest for a new world, are less doctrinaire and less rigid in their ideology. These difficulties can be encountered in the accustomed way, but perhaps citizens will be able to try something different from how it has been done in the past. Should Aurovilians go round and round in fixed circles on the way to the centre, or move to the centre directly with an enhanced inner consciousness and then look at the roads outward? When these conflicts of an abstract notion of the common good gradually evaporate, they may demand a purifying return to Mother's more spiritual principles. Though faith in these principles certainly has its nobility and its positive effects, when the citizens go too far in their faith, they might become an obstacle for the secularists who don't have such spiritual ambition.

Building the planned city rapidly, prioritising collectively with external support, or building the city where individuals with Mother's guidance will do what has to be done? What needs priority when building the city? Should the city be finished at any cost and at any speed, and then the Mother will do what she intends to do, or should the city be developed by cultivating the collective inner consciousness of the citizens while the city is being built? The Master Plan is an ideal goal, but is the work not as much related to 'how' to plan,' how' to achieve it, as well as ''how' to get there? One of Auroville's aims is practical human unity, which is only possible through the development of one's inner being, one's identity with the Divine within, and becoming a willing servitor of the Divine consciousness. As a collective yoga of transformation, the development of a more ideal society and a more perfect town becomes one of the means to achieve Auroville's aim. In this context, it is not merely about building a new city but about building a new city with a new consciousness in a new person, and the city will evolve in tandem with the evolution of its citizens' consciousness. Only by the perfection of the inmost psychic being the outer environment can be perfected, and to improve the quality of Auroville's environment, it needs progress in some individuals' consciousness first, whereafter the collective consciousness follows, and not the other way around by developing a more perfect city first and creating a more perfect soceity afterwards.

In Mother's vision, the universal ideal of humanity through societal reform must begin with the development of the individual's psychic, where the spark of the Divine inspires citizens to strive for higher spiritual values and modes of behaviour. Based on a series of precepts given by the Mother, each citizen is invited to participate in Auroville's development and shape a new society, both physically, psychologically, and spiritually. Could it be that instead of building an ordinary, cement-filled city rapidly, it may be more important to create a spiritual society first? That is, how is Auroville, as an ideal society, going to be built as an expression of spiritual consciousness? In the final days of her life, she expressed her concern about the arrival of all sorts of people who wanted to join Auroville. She changed her mind about 50,000 people within two decades, and in a reversal of her policy, she wrote, "12 good men would be better than hundreds of stupid persons. Auroville is not for comfort but for the servants of the Divine. People in Auroville should not shirk hard work. They should not think of escaping from the outer control until the divine control is there."[3] To solve this oppositional difficulty, Mother's force will not be able to prevent this conflict between those who aim at building the city first and those who emphasise the cultivation of an inner process first. To avoid the source of a tragic wrong turning the warring groups should not be left to an inevitable fate; they need the strength to transcend the path of those who decide to wait confidently for the unexpected and those who actively want to finish building the city at the earliest. The city needs to be built, but nothing will ever change its confusion and feelings of impotence unless a change of consciousness precedes it, making it possible to think and act differently.

To better understand these issues, it may be helpful to pose a few questions that urgently require dialogue among the argumentative groups. There is not a single intentional community that has survived for more than fifty years. Although any utopian ambition need not always end in inevitable failure, it certainly requires care to avoid the side effects of a failed perfect world, such as forms of collective cruelty, indoctrination, dogmatism, and fanaticism. Human progress toward a spiritual society will initially occur in the 'here and now,' and it will be a gradual change toward a new man in a transformed society. However, could it also ultimately involve a divine experiment with emotional absolutism, leading to the possibility of its own decay?

What could have possibly gone wrong? Where is the source of error? Who will manage to collect the faith for a noble struggle in Auroville's far-fetched spiritual anarchy under the shadow of its failures? How to judge Auroville's success or failure? Does this depend on the extent to which the community meets the needs of its citizens and how it improves, or does it require the inner development of their everyday lives, taking into consideration that their needs also change, as well as the changes in the internal organisation of the community? Is Mother's spiritual vision infallible, and are some Aurovilians able to overcome various inconsistencies? What happens when her visionary dream is confronted with the gulf between contemporary discoveries, new knowledge and the reality of present-day human affairs, which are in contrast with Mother's planning of her future utopian city? To survive, the community may have to significantly weaken its approach or even abandon some fundamental elements of Mother's original ideology about Auroville's future development. The citizens find themselves confronted with divisive issues, including their adherence to the purity of Mother's vision versus syncretism, or a focus on inward concerns versus social outreach. These issues might determine a permanently changed basic structure of the community. This may require a gentler process of inward arrangements, initially with the highest perfection of their moral ideals, and no longer be associated with the governmental institutionalisation in its long-awaited spiritual society.

To create a new life on earth, distress often becomes an unwitting part of the journey; as long as there is hardship, it attracts the strong Aurovilians in their quest. However, they may finally become a victim of their own success when their succeeding generation of Aurovilians use the results of prosperity and comfort of their predecessors, which gradually intrude on the present life in Auroville, causing a deviation of their initial quest for perfection, i.e., the cultivation of an inward and outward life that is consistent with their spiritual development. On the one hand, the optimism and creativity of the utopian predecessors can be rather infectious for newcomers when everything within the familiar social institutions is rejected, but on the other, Auroville's new generation and newcomers increasingly ignore the values of the original members and become more secular-minded transforming the utopian experiment into a commercial enterprise. Are some of the earlier utopians stumbling over their rigid vision of the perfect society, or are they lost in an extreme absolutist vision of the future? Is the new generation able to avoid the pitfalls of their forebears, or is Mother's grand utopia of the past replaced by those utopians who are pressing their secular ideals, commercial self-interest, and modest values upon like-minded seekers? The foundation of Auroville as a utopia rests mainly on the participation of a spiritual society, and in Mother's dream, she envisioned a community of 50,000 people where each individual would fulfil their defined role alongside all their fellow citizens. Her vision had nothing to do with today's utopian Hindutva movement, which would like to re-establish India as a purely Hindu nation.

The various activities in which citizens are engaged need to be viewed as a means to develop a new consciousness, rather than as ends in themselves. Auroville is not a mere city for the future as a city, it is as much its direction, and for the Mother, it is somewhat naive to think that an individual and collective transformation and the next stage in human evolution could be accomplished only with technology, such transformation needs as much the intervention and descent of the divine Grace. Unfortunately, as previously mentioned, Mother did not choose a charismatic successor in the organisational structure as the authoritative leader of the city with whom the devotees could communicate. As a disciple of the Mother, her authority is now vested in the inner Spirit that resides within each individual. According to R. Minor, "following the Mother, what if their individual perceptions of the direction of that inner Spirit apparently disagree?"[4] What happens with those who claim to be in touch with their psychic being and disagree among themselves in which direction Auroville should move? Who is the authoritative interpreter? Auroville's present difficulties, do they indicate its limited spiritual capacities to overcome its problems, and is its utopian experiment still stimulating and relevant in today's hype of the ambiguous modern technological society? Other spiritual communities of the past created favourable conditions for their members to discover their lives, but Auroville was established on a different principle; here, the citizens have to embrace the world in order to experiment with the opposition between spirituality and material life, to discover previously unimagined possibilities. Auroville cannot be built solely by human efforts; its creation requires the citizens' response to the play of soul-force, which moves them, and where new forms for the new consciousness will emerge.

Though Auroville's future may be heading in a different direction due to closed-door policies, nevertheless, many of its hard-working idealists, who have been present from the beginning, still influence and overwhelm the city with their highest idealism and are trying not to succumb to external pressure. All citizens are aware that they must reflect on the changing circumstances and maturing perspectives, but the radical restructuring should not result in a comfortable ongoing existence that loses the essence of what Mother's vision is all about. The materialisation of the city depends on the consciousness of the Aurovilians, who bring the collective psychic being to the forefront. This emphasis is on the individual's inner development rather than merely manifesting outer reality. This may need some necessary collective introspection on the journey, where all kinds of failures and inconsistencies are as crucial as its achievements. Only the future will show if Auroville is able to live up to its ideals or will become a usual creation where Aurovilians romanticise the past and become another spiritual exotic tourist destination and attract those people who come to fulfill their basic needs without dynamically engaging in the herculean task of building a spiritual utopian society. To conclude in Mother's words, who believed in the open-endedness of Auroville when she said," Even if you don't believe in it, even if all circumstances appear to be quite unfavourable, I KNOW THAT AUROVILLE WILL BE. It may be 100 years, it may be 1000 years, I don't know, but Auroville will be, because it has been decreed."[5]

## Planning

Intentional communities are characterised by conscious planning, which makes an uncertain future more specific. The planning is related to a purpose and meaning in terms of values and beliefs of the group, though this is not the same when used as blueprints for action in realisable social projects. In a decision-making body, the good of the community transcends personal selfishness, as the individual's fulfillment can only be achieved when the community functions harmoniously. The work involved in planning is a communal enterprise, rather than being the domain of specialists; it requires joint endeavours and opportunities for the participation of the whole community to work together in a spirit of experimentation. It is a means of exploring new ways of social experimentation and new approaches to doing things in a manner different from the conditions of the prevailing outside world. This requires a high level of intentional quality within the community, where citizens' own internal affairs and expression of their ideals are often more valuable to the community than demands from outside society. The planning of the practical utopia must be possible and not violate nature. The degree of possibility varies and may not always be immediately achievable; however, this does not mean it is intrinsically impossible.

Most utopians reject the concept of blueprints as detailed recommendations related to every aspect of life. Describing utopia as blueprints often leads to totalitarian planning, which overlooks constructive social theorists and ignores the complexity and diversity of utopia.

Mother's utopia is based on a spiritual ideology, but was her detailed utopia rather vague and specific only in certain parts, and were problems gradually created when her disciples seized power to fill in their own details and bring the community into line with their ideals? The town development plan as a kind of a blueprint provided by the Mother as a perfectly planned city is the means for realising the ideal city. She was reluctant to offer Aurovilians a strict blueprint. In the development of Auroville, she refused a single plan, and the community life also revolved around the development of the psychic being and the ignition of the psychic being in others while building the city. Auroville, as a spiritual utopia, is not Mother's authoritarian guidance of a static blueprint or a rigid system. Still, she offers the possibility of realising her dream, a dream that challenges present insufficiencies. The utopia Mother has created is not a blueprint to be imposed by her; on the contrary, it embodies a vision in which she anticipates a new concept of humanity in a new society through psycho-social and spiritual change. She emphasised a strategy of non-hierarchical and collective effort, all working together in all their diversity and disagreements, breaking down old values and views and developing a new way of life with new attitudes. All she wanted was "a hierarchical organisation grouped around the most enlightened center and obeying a collective discipline." In the words of the Mother," Auroville functions as a spiritual experiment in conscious evolution, any form of the future organisation will emerge out of this process. The outcome of such a process, a heightened level of Auroville's collective consciousness, cannot be anticipated or described. The citizens strive towards a new paradigm of society and unlike limiting themselves to some specific aims such as social, environmental, artistic, educational or research."[6] Its development must be progressive, flexible, experimental, and responsive to evolution, and it must evolve according to the new consciousness of each individual to create a collective change. It appears that her vision for building this city was not based on a fixed and predetermined plan, but rather on inherent connections with the existing tendencies of reality at that time.

Her statements on Auroville are disputed, and the citizens are rather divided in the controversial issue of whether Mother's vision for Auroville laid down in the Master Plan was 'approved' by her or had the Mother only 'blessed' the Galaxy model of the Auroville Township. The master plan itself is only a first framework and needs to be followed by a detailed development plan. The detailed planning is an ongoing process, and the latest Master Plan specified that it should be revised every five years. It may be questioned whether the Mother was more concerned with the challenges Aurovilians faced on the way to attempting individual and collective transformation simultaneously, or if she was more concerned with building a concrete city of 50,000 people within two decades. Both were necessary, but she certainly would not have agreed with any form of a preconceived mental plan. In the words of the Mother, "Men always make plans and mental constructions and attempt to create on that basis, but not one human creation is a total realisation of their mental construction. They always add something, or else it is always altered by a force they do not understand; they think it is chance, fortune, circumstances, all sorts of things, but it is in fact the Truth-force which is trying to manifest on earth and which is exerting a pressure and of course this changes the mental and vital creations which are only superficial ones."[7] She insisted on replacing the mental government of intelligence by the government of a spiritualised consciousness. This power of the spiritual consciousness "is capable of ordering material things in a MUCH TRUER, happier and better way for everyone than any material power, all those participating in the experience would have to be absolutely convinced that the highest consciousness is the best judge of the MOST MATERIAL THINGS... The highest consciousness, when it is put in contact with Matter spontaneously has... a power of conviction greater than that of all intermediary regions. Through simple contact, its power of transformation is greater than that of all the intermediary regions."[8] The construction work of building a city with 50,000 citizens serves as an opportunity for inner growth, and in the process of building the city, all aspects of human nature must be developed and perfected.

In the development of the Master Plan two sides are opposing each other, even though they need each other, as both sides have to deal with the practicalities of planning and ground realities and come back to the original aim of building Auroville as a city to realise human unity and not only to live in Auroville as a spiritual community. Planning in Auroville is the manifestation of an experiment in its totality and is not limited to building infrastructures alone. The two sides, the ones who rigidly adhere to Mother's plan, which is unmodifiable without the flexibility for new ideas versus those with a lasses-fair attitude; the eco-supporters and their environmental sustainability together with those who want to build the infrastructure at the earliest, need a tendency to go 'beyond 'for and against' attitude and co-exist together. A top-down mental planning process without proper engagement of the entire community lacks equal participation and involvement from Auroville's professional planners in the planning process. This approach is questioned and opposed by many Aurovilians who support Mother's spiritual planning, which relates to social, psychological, cultural, economic, and spiritual aspects. Aurovilians acting as her instruments "are only puppets in the hands of large Forces. Nothing depends on human beings- neither the planning nor the execution." [9] In Auroville, as a laboratory of evolution for a new form of organisation, the building of an inner character of its citizens is as important as building the city. The creation of a future city links consciousness with matter and integrates the knowledge of both inner and outer experiences, past and future. There is no opposition between material life and spirituality, and it is through physical work that the spirit must be manifested.

Seriously working with matter as a form of Karma Yoga is necessary for the practical and pragmatic survival of the city, but this requires simultaneously the divinisation of the inner being before there can be divinity in outer existence. In Auroville, the Mother was primarily concerned with the practice of Karma Yoga and how Aurovilians should integrate their spirituality into their lives and work. In her last message to Auroville, she wrote in March 1973, "Auroville is created to realise the ideal of Sri Aurobindo who taught us the Karma Yoga. Auroville is for those who want to do the Yoga of work. To live in Auroville means to do the Yoga of work. So, all Aurovilians must take up a work and do it as Yoga."[10] When the Mother refers to Karma Yoga she does not mean work being done ordinarily with the ordinary consciousness, but the spirit in which the work is done, i.e., as a sacrifice to the Divine without egoism or desire, not for the sake of any personal gain but for the sake of the Divine. All the different types of activities undertaken by the sadhaks are a part of their yogic endeavour. Each activity must be pursued in the true spirit and with the right attitude, i.e., the activities are pursued with a spirit of sincere dedication and with a sole motive of making them fit means of manifesting the Divine Truth in life. This process needs to be developed gradually, and it takes time to grow from the lower forces and open oneself to the higher divine Force.

The work done in Auroville is not intended to showcase one's capacities, but rather as an opportunity for Karma Yoga. It is a process of learning to work in the true Yogic way through practical selflessness, discipline, order, patience, and becoming an instrument of the Divine. It is not work as something done for its own sake, but one's way of doing it, in the spirit of dedicating it to the divine; as such it does not matter what work it is. Only as the disciple's inward connection with the Divine grows, when the self-offering becomes more complete, the sadhak develops the feeling that he is guided by the Divine who is carrying out the work or action and the individual functions merely as an instrument i.e., when work becomes an integral part of Yoga done as a service to the Divine, then the human instrument becomes a better instrument, where the sadhak, under the guidance of the Divine presence around him, is able to overcome obstacles and limitations of the outside world. Desire and ambition can be significant sources of obstacles and problems in the workplace. Work done for the Divine without attachment brings freedom. The sadhak works according to his essential nature and law of being in tune with the Divine Will, and gradually he becomes aware of the Divine Force supporting him in his work with the right energy and correct intuition. When the truth perception grows due to the influence of the psychic, the sadhak gets tuned to the Divine Force, and he gradually realises that the Divine initiates all works and that he is only an instrument in the hands of the Divine.

Mindlessly sticking to past tradition and static repetition, regardless of changed circumstances and new requirements, does this attitude oppose a reinterpretation of Mother's creative spiritual vision about Auroville's future development, and does communication through Mother's direct one-liners offer solutions for the present-day social dormant discomfort of the citizens? For the Mother, action is more important than the loftiest adoration of her metaphysical insight, and the first step following the Divine life is Karma Yoga. The building of the town through the current Master Plan, with its emphasis on circular roads and large stretches of concrete buildings outlining the shape of the Galaxy model, is not merely a mechanical placing of bricks upon bricks. Still, if it is a form of Karma Yoga, then it becomes a means to develop another higher consciousness. The act itself is not the truth, it is only a consequence, but it is the intention behind the act. Mere credulity and faith in her vision is not a reason to escape the necessary practical aspects of her vision.

Could it be that one of the difficulties in Auroville is related to those sadhaks who want to work according to their own personal ideas and plans and expect that these are to be sanctioned? According to the Mother, "If those who are in power are puffed up with their own importance, they disturb the true working. Whatever their abilities, their achievements are not genuine. But it is not that they are always lacking in good-will. They have fake ideas of what is proper. If they become more conscious of the divine aim, they can surely succeed and carry it out."[11] When there are difficulties in work, they are often related to something wrong in the sadhak's inner attitude, like egoism, ambition or vanity. To correct this disharmony, the Mother advised her disciples to look for the cause of the difficulties within themselves rather than in others or due to the circumstances of the situation. The external situation could be an extension of one's inner consciousness expressed in the outer world.

The Galaxy, as the city's material physical map, needed a specific type of people who wanted to participate in an adventure to build the city for the future with their goodwill. Goodwill, as an innocent concept of altruism, has many traces of egoism; however, the Mother initially used it as a starting point for an individual's and collective's higher and more authentic life. In the words of the Mother, "All those who wish to live and work at Auroville must have an integral goodwill; a constant aspiration to know the Truth and to submit to it; enough plasticity to confront the exigencies of work and an endless will to progress to move forward towards the ultimate Truth."[12] However, those with goodwill may develop their own preconceived ideas or methods, but without a spiritual connection, the citizens may limit themselves to the worldly domain and the fulfillment of their own basic needs. In a similar way, when Karma Yoga is not practised with a spiritual connection, where the fruits of one's efforts are not dedicated to the Divine. In Mother's earlier messages, she indicated that having goodwill was a sufficient quality to become an Aurovilian, but later, she expected Aurovilians to be open to the practice of the Divine consciousness that is seeking to manifest itself, i.e., 'to live in Auroville one must be a willing servitor of the Divine consciousness.'

In previous blueprint conceptions of utopia, the ongoing transformative aspects were often overlooked. It was assumed that if people were just organised differently, then an ideal society would be achieved. In Mother's spiritual vision of the future city, she links her dreams with reality and imagines a better life for all humanity through volitional human transformation. In a simplistic reading of Mother's planning for the future utopian city, the present planners in charge should not overlook the fact that Mother was not a futuristic technocrat envisioning some technological transformation, creating an exotic, unreachable, and otherworldly imagined place. Her other place is a realistic and complex alternative rather than an unreachable heaven. In her transformative vision, she envisioned a new society in the future that would lead its citizens, through collective spiritual prefigurative practice, to fundamental and social-spiritual change. Urban renewal through city planning and architecture can help reinforce particular social relations, but community development is not directly related to the city's structural design problems. A holistic process of community design requires the integration of all facets of a community's life, including social, cultural, economic, technical, artistic, and spiritual dimensions, which are all part of a whole and reinforce one another.

Auroville is not a place for escapism; it does not offer opportunities for daydreaming. On the contrary, in building the new city, it provides many challenges for progress by supplying an alternative spiritual way of life through the gradual, practical realisation of the Mother's ideal vision. Are the disciples aware of the open-endedness and limits of Mother's portrayal of her ideal society where the results are not pre-ordained? She certainly championed the citizens' choice of new innovations in the face of various unpredictable challenges. Certain developments are subject to fixed causal laws, and with mere references and paying lip service to Mother's divine

Providence, are disciples ignoring connecting events with their immediate causes? In planning the future city according to Mother's portrayal of an ideal spiritual future society, is there sufficient space for various impracticable determinants, for limits imposed by the complexity of incalculable natural situations, entirely new changed circumstances, unanticipated historical forces, interactions between innumerable variables and processes of coincidences, and major catastrophic effects of environmental, climatic and ecological changes, or discovered counter facts in the dynamic pattern of evolutionary progress? What about the unpredictable characteristics of human nature, their non-conformity, and their individual goals for the overall good of the community?

When Guiles Guigan, who managed the Auroville Archives and conducted an extensive study of documents related to Auroville's history, was asked if the Galaxy still mattered, he said, "I believe not." Our community and its planners need to acknowledge the present reality and adapt their plans according to the existing situation. They shouldn't plan more than 20 years ahead (all over the world planners never plan more than 20 to 25 years in advance, simply because' life' tends to modify even the very best plans) and speak no more of 50,000 inhabitants (although we should do our best to increase our population quickly and harmoniously). I am well aware that some of us need a plan/ framework as, without it, they feel lost. So, they won't let go of the Galaxy until some other plan, even more visually appealing than the Galaxy, is presented to them. Yet, on the 10th of July 1957, Mother invited us to join a Great Adventure but warned us that a road would need to be created step by step in the unexplored. Mother repeatedly told Udar, "Don't Plan". But we don't need any 'preconceived mental plan' (neither a 50-year-old one nor a brand new one) because too many questions about Auroville's future are left unanswered. Life has shown that answers come only when the questions are really there-and not when we speculate about them well in advance"[13] He proposes Auroville needs "a third way" between full organic development and some detailed master plan (new or old ), though for Gilles it is not guaranteed that Rogers Galaxy plan signed by the Mother is sure to manifest.

## The Mother on planning

The Mother often emphasised the evolutionary nature of the Auroville experiment, and any changing local or global realities would have modified some of her earlier insights. She could not foresee everything in the future, and she was not always clear about what she expected to happen in terms of the detailed material development of Auroville. The Mother never knew exactly how Auroville would develop; it was part of a gradual adventure where the road was unknown and had to be outlined step by step in the unexplored. While modifying or updating details of Mother's future vision of Auroville, nobody should overlook the essence of her proposals. It is one way to cling to Mother's original words based on her Truth and materialise what she said about the detailed material manifestation, which has to be worked out by her disciples in a spirit of collaboration, or the other way, change or modify some of her indications due to the process of evolutionary nature of Auroville's experience and changing global realities though the Charter is unlikely to change. During the last nine years of her life, she sometimes retracted her future plans for Auroville in response to the various developments of that time. It seems Mother's earlier messages dealt more with plans for specific projects, whereas in her last years, she communicated more about her concerns about Aurovilians' incorrect and bad behaviour. All such adverse conditions may weaken the dynamics of building the city.

In the struggle for a new society, she remained open to the continuous changes in the world of daily practice and social and historical change. The Mother was always very flexible and adapted her plans according to newly perceived needs, possibilities and changed situations. She left the developments of the details of her plan to the citizens. The Mother would have certainly championed the citizens' choice of innovations when faced with various unpredictable challenges, and in the open-endedness of a plan, she never generated a claim for absolute truth or being infallible. Life has uncertainties that can overwhelm even the greatest prudence and spiritual foresight.

Did the Mother anticipate unintended consequences in her ideal planning because she lacked the foresight to evaluate all the results of her vision? While building the city as much as possible according to Mother's plan, the builders should not neglect the gap between the present practical effects and what works or has organisational and social value in the context of Mother's ideal vision. Some of Mother's ideals may nowadays be pragmatically impossible due to changed circumstances. Science may not be able to reveal an underlying plan or purpose built into the universe and the belief in a divine purpose, and man's role in fulfilling a divine plan of spiritual progress need not be abandoned, but the insight of modern sciences, as a system of generating hypotheses and testing them against facts leaves room for the emergence of a more realistic view of our present position in the world. Some parts of her vision may need new planning, which can be tested against an ever-expanding realm of evidence.

According to Krishan Kumar, changes in planning utopia "has temporal and spatial as well as conceptual boundaries... the concept is defined by its appearance at a certain point in history, within a certain point in history, within a certain intellectual and cultural tradition. Unlike the case with the natural sciences, concepts in the human sciences have no timeless essence. They are the products of particular histories and particular interpretations of those histories. Their meaning can change with time and with the diversity of uses to which they may be put. This does not mean that usage can or should be arbitrary... But it does mean that we should neither expect nor seek some universal or essentialist definition valid for all times and places. In the case of utopia, in particular, we need to acknowledge the importance of distinctions of time and place in establishing its character"[14] Though in Kumar's utopic interpretation he is more concerned with his faith in the future city of human beings and not the future city of the Divine humanity, are some of his boundaries applicable in the limitations of Auroville's future perspective?

Implementing a detailed development plan requires the accountability and meaningful participation of all its citizens, as it is the collective consciousness within the community that will indicate its direction. Mother's conception of Auroville as an ideal place of freedom to experiment is a laboratory and adventure, and not a usual, well-organised, planned project. If Auroville is to change, the change cannot be imposed by outside interference; the real change must come from within. Any change brought about by external pressure is unlikely to be an enduring one. Perhaps the most essential point of change lies not in the direct and final realisation of Auroville as a product of a blueprint but in the process of building it. No doubt, this city has to be built, but maybe it is not so much where the Aurovilians stand at present, but in which direction they are moving. When the Aurovilians turn their views too much to the past, their mimesis patterned on the old days, the inhabitants become conformists, not examining and investigating new means for reaching their divine utopia. Is Auroville, as a spiritual utopia, a relatively timeless and unchanging entity of human social-spiritual imagination and an ideal society that imposes certain unavoidable constraints on its members or is the utopian good life affected by the contemporary reality in which it appears?

The present tense polarisation offers Aurovilians an opportunity for self-reflection and the possibility of questioning themselves about the root causes and their own involvement in the inadequate organisational processes. As it is today, are Aurovilians more concerned with their daily consumption and profit-making production, a kind of spiritual entertainment project which offers its citizens and tourists opportunities for the gratification of their basic needs and other exotic experiences or has its utopian idealism still its own distinct features different from other utopias that aim at the possibility of human betterment? When speaking about the gratification of needs, the Mother writes, "One who is all the way up necessarily has the least amount of needs; his material needs decrease as his capacity for material vision increases. And it's perfectly true. It's automatic and spontaneous. It is not the result of an effort: the vaster the consciousness and the more things and realities it embraces, the smaller the material needs become- automatically so- because they lose all their importance and value. It's reduced to a minimum need of material necessities."[15]

Auroville should not be judged by an appeal to contemporary life for its validity; however, it cannot ignore the root cause of the threat to the very existence of Auroville as a spiritual utopia. To agree on an acceptable plan, Mother advised her disciples to re-establish unity on a higher level where each Aurovilian has his own place within a harmonious unity. What we see now is a situation where various members pull in different directions, representing their own interests without any cohesion. This lack of unity is one of the main causes of the multiple difficulties, and there is an urgent need for the Aurovilians to become united again, rather than preaching about unity while constantly opposing each other and quarrelling among themselves without a common discipline of action.

In one of her messages regarding this lack of unity, Mother writes, "Instead of a combination where each one has his place within a harmonious unity, instead of that, everyone pulls in his own direction. The real progress to be made is a moral one.... lack of unity is the cause of all the difficulties.... From the beginning, there has been this lack of unity, and also because of the action I no longer perform. No matter how much I tell them, You are not here to represent your own interests. You are all one and the same"—they just don't understand!"[16] While building the city the process is as important as the result, and in its physical development, the city ought to be an expression of a spiritual consciousness following the evolution of the resident's consciousness so that new human beings will grow. In her vision of Auroville's future Master Plan, are her planned details shared as set patterns without considering the creation of new forms as the force evolves, and is the Master Plan able to adapt to ground realities?

The Mother said many things about Auroville on various occasions and often in different contexts. She left various utopian details of a new city and a new society for the future generation in which she was guided and inspired by the Divine Force, but she never attempted to force a rigidly defined set of spiritual ideals to be used as a strict dogma for the future citizens in their process towards the transformation of a perfect society. There are those Aurovilians who may tend to become encrusted by a dogmatic attitude, lacking openness in their experimentation with her vision, including the secular, rational mode of inquiry in planning the future city.

Should her vision be supplemented, at present, by more rigorous arguments about the challenges posed by experimental results of natural, human and technological sciences, having learned from them what is possible on the way of human development, implementing their ingenious creative inventions in new possible future forms of social life without wild speculations? We now live in a quite different world in which humankind functions; how well are the realistic possibilities of the fulfilment of Auroville's future able to confront the realities of the contemporary world? The Mother did not envision her vision as an exact intellectual blueprint for a new society, but she sketched a utopian vision for a society that would ultimately emerge through action. As mentioned before, the Mother did not stress the need for a preconceived mental plan; she remained very flexible and adapted her approach to achieve her aim according to newly perceived needs, possibilities, and constraints. Similarly, the Master Plan may need to be adapted to the present reality, respecting what Auroville has already accomplished while adventuring on the unknown roads of her ideal town.

## Organisation and its Leaders

Auroville belongs to nobody in particular, it belongs to humanity as a whole, and it seems that in today's reality,

Aurovilians have not reached the spiritual authority needed for the organisation of Auroville as envisioned by the Mother. Many of Auroville's problems are related to its ambivalence, distrust, and opposition to authority, as well as the community's resistance to rules and regulations imposed by outside entities. The Mother warned against any interference from outside in the whole developmental affair of Auroville, as this would reverse a divine creation into a human realisation. However, as explained before, due to serious clashes between officials of the Sri Aurobindo Society of the Ashram and the Auroville citizens, governmental interference within the organisational structure of Auroville became necessary to protect Auroville from its decline. Various working groups have been instituted to administer the town on a day-to-day basis. These groups are primarily peer-based in their organisational structure and participatory in their processes. In the absence of structured laws, governance is based on sets of guidelines that depend on the goodwill and cooperation of the citizens, adopted by the community. As there are practically no collective structures to enforce decisions, one can imagine that decision-making procedures are extremely slow due to a lengthy process, as different viewpoints are taken into consideration before a consensus is reached.

The present-day reality of Auroville bears little resemblance to the vision envisioned by the Mother. She visualised the replacement of the mental government of intelligence by the government of a spiritualised consciousness. According to the Mother, "Men always make plans, mental constructions and attempt to create on that basis, but not one human creation is a total realisation of their mental construction."[17] Somewhere else she says, "Usually men establish mental rules according to their conceptions and their ideal, then they apply them. And that is absolutely false, arbitrary, unreal, so the result is that things revolt, or else waste away and disappear. It is the experience of LIFE ITSELF that must slowly work out rules AS SUPPLE AND FAST as possible, in order that they ever remain progressive. Nothing must be fixed...When the body is subjected to rules, it is a slave to those rules and its possibilities are limited by them. But when it is governed by the Spirit and the Consciousness, that gives it incomparable possibility and flexibility."[18] She was aware that such an aim is not easy, and that's why she proposed that a small number of people with intuitive intelligence govern Auroville as representatives of spiritual consciousness. Nothing should be fixed, and discipline should not be used to organise one's life according to external and artificial rules, but as the process of arriving at the discovery of an organised, more accurate inner consciousness. For the Mother, the proliferation of written rules was anathema to progress, and the rise of a bureaucratic rule-making institution only caused an atrophy of the living divine aspiration. The quality of human perfection requires no prescriptive discipline to grasp divinity in a spiritual experience; however, every utopian community maintains some form of discipline. Communities that manage to invent specific rules that enhance the initiative of their members are considered successful.

There is a controversy surrounding freedom, which is linked to surrender to the Divine and the rules of the formal collective discipline within the organisational structure. To be free from all moral and social conventions does not mean a free license and blind satisfaction of one's desires (vital freedom) but the replacement of moral rules by the obedience of the inner Divine, where they organise themselves spontaneously without fixed external regulations and laws. To live freely as citizens in Auroville, Mother expects her disciples to obey the Supreme Truth, and our freedom is directly linked to our surrender to the Divine. In the new humanity, as an intermediate link between the present mental humanity and future supramental humanity, enforcement of authority has no place at all, the leaders, as voluntary agents and instruments for executing the divine Will, do not impose anything on others, they are like elder brothers and sisters to less evolved ones and help other Aurovilians to develop. "The ones who are in charge should regard the others as one's associates and helpers in the work; he should not try to dominate or impose on them his own ideas and personal fancies, but only see the execution of the will of the Mother."[19]

When authority remains within a limited area, it is beneficial, but once that power is situated outside the area of authority, it may easily be misused. There is nothing inherently wrong with authority, but when authority becomes a form of paternal power, then everything gets out of control.

The Mother hardly framed any rules or laws; rules should arise according to the requirements. One is free only when somebody is no longer a slave of one's ego, desires, ambitions, old habits and mental laws and rules, and where one is united with the divine Will, which makes decisions in each of us. Individual and collective discipline, willingly accepted, is indispensable and starts with mastering one's lower nature and its desires. This requires personal effort, sincere commitment, and a willingness to progress in the essential unity of humanity and goodwill towards all. In the right organisation, there is an antagonistic tendency between freedom and moral laws and regulations related to order, but such conflict does not manifest itself in the psychic consciousness. True freedom is obtained only by union with the inner divine, which needs mastery over one's ego. For the Mother, there is no contradiction between the ideal and the real, and it is the ideal that allows Aurovilians to put them on the path of their new, actual course of life. For the Mother, mental idealism is ineffective; it has to be converted into a spiritual realism, in which the higher reality of the Spirit takes up the lower reality of one's physical, vital and mental nature and its activities.

However, in the activities since the early days of Auroville, there has been a lack of a proper, internal and efficient organisation, and up till now, it seems Auroville has not succeeded in discovering a new form of organisation in the light of Mother's vision where the individual freedom and authority are reconciled. Many attempts have been made in the past to create a new model of organisation for Auroville, but none have gained approval from the community up to now. In its pursuit of self-governance, Aurovilians often become entangled in endless discussions about contrary ideas and arguments, rather than concentrating on governance guided by the divine Will, where decisions evolve gradually with the guidance of the divine. The Mother was aware of such difficulties when she wrote "If there is no representative of the supreme Consciousness (which can happen of course) if there isn't any, we could perhaps (this would be worth trying) replace him with the government by a smaller number- we would have to choose between five and eight, something like that: four, seven or eight-a small number having an INTUITIVE intelligence. Intuitive is more important than 'intelligence': they should have an intuition that manifests intellectually."[20] Those who have reached this higher intuitive consciousness have the right to govern and should be given responsibility. Why did it not happen to move beyond the artificial organisation? Did the Mother not want an organisation that is the expression of a higher consciousness working that manifests the truth of the future? The Mother refers to the self-organisation of Auroville's governing structure in terms of the individual's inner Divine consciousness, and some Aurovilians have faith in the real invisible authority in the form of her Grace that rules over its organisational groups through all its difficulties and guiding the Aurovilians to the real freedom of the psychic consciousness. It is the spontaneous working of the Force of the inner consciousness and the control of this Force that causes the inner change beyond artificial organisations. For the Mother, "Organisation is a discipline of action, but for Auroville, we aspire to go beyond arbitrary and artificial organisations. We want an organisation which is the expression of a higher consciousness working to manifest the truth of the future...A hierarchical organisation grouped around the most enlightened centre and obeying a collective discipline.... In order to be workable, this requires all workers of Auroville to be yogis conscious of the divine Truth."[21]

However, Mother agrees that organisational methods that have proven effective, based on human logic and the use of machines, should be flexible, progressive, and tolerated, but only for a very temporary period. Could it be that a disordered ambiguity in the organisational system causes, again and again, the diffuse dispersion of responsibilities, where nobody takes the final responsibility, and nobody makes anyone responsible? In this way, the involved prefer to perpetuate rather than denounce the system. In improving a better, more suitable organisational structure, specific rules and protocols are essential to reach a compromise and align citizens with a better agreement on the solution to the problem. However, a negative spiral of excessive rule proliferation with overly detailed clauses limits diversity, even with the participation and involvement of its citizens. It may lead to a replacement of the inner, psycho-spiritual discipline with the outer, imposed areas of bureaucratic rules, where Aurovilians may easily lose interest and trust in their sometimes power-driven leader

The reality of Auroville as an intentional spiritual community with all its accomplishments, its conflicts and struggles is a fascinating chronicle of its achievements and failures. It has undertaken numerous innovative projects and creative activities, but behind the scenes, not all is well, and often, the citizens are at odds with one another. In 2007, Michael Murphy, on a visit to Auroville, put it rather aptly, "The organisational structure within the Auroville community needs something like a Center for Organisational Yoga where you can draw upon what has been learned elsewhere. He advises the citizens to set up some kind of a center of advanced transformative work for those who want to ramp up their practice."[22]

Does the present-day bureaucratic organisation of the Aurovilians organise themselves too much on the need for proper authoritarian governance to put some order in the decent functioning of the community, rather than the need for an efficient collective organisation where "it is the experience of life itself that should slowly work out rules"? For the Mother, organisation is discipline in action; discipline is indispensable, but it is a discipline of transformation where one aspires for a true life, responsive to the influence of the inner consciousness. Any action centred around this psychic centre will change disorder into order. This inner foundation of psychic development is not a self-contained process; rather, it should express itself in outer activity and become a driving force for the betterment of one's actions and reactions. The actions of the leader are for the sake of the Divine and have to be seen as acts of sacrifice undertaken without the indulgence of one's own will, which the leader may seek to impose on the other members of the group. Mother's leadership does not focus on managing external change; she emphasises inner change as the foundation of effective leadership. She maintained that external circumstances are the objective projection of what is inside oneself. When the leader changes himself, the circumstances will also change.

The charismatic Aurovilian leader, though his inner power may be under pressure, should not surrender to his own complacency and merely be concerned with quick results of his own policy and prudence, on the contrary, it needs the leader's crucial coherent strategy to work with a cohesive vision and penetrate the deeper root causes of the problems rather than the success of the leader's short-term policy. Even though there are hardly any leaders with psychic consciousness, the leader needs to be at least a charismatic guide, heroic, fearless, and stable, even if their hope goes up in smoke. Otherwise, they will not reach what is still reachable. The leader's difficulty is not always related to making plans or organising, but the leader's test often lies more in holding opposite groups together. When the transforming phenomenon in Auroville causes a crisis and develops polarisation, it may lead to the degeneration of the authority of its leaders. Healthy criticism may gradually pass from exaggeration into deception and lies. The symptom of polarisation is the ability to proliferate through the accommodating and indulgent attitude of present leaders who are unable to capitulate to these polarising powers. When polarisation becomes prominent and confronts the spiritual aim, then the moderation needed for grounding the plural human society disappears. A debate about this issue may be a stimulus for change; it thrives on abrasion and disagreement, but this need not be problematic because, in times of polarisation, citizens explore issues more dynamically and deeply rather than passively suggesting a neutral middle ground. Just before the Mother left her body, she wrote a message for future leaders, "As long as I was physically present among you all, my presence was helping you to achieve this mastery over the ego, and so it was not necessary for me to speak to you individually. But now this effort [her guidance to the sadhaks in overcoming their ego] must become the basis of each individual's existence, and they are supposed to free themselves from their old ego, more especially for those of you who have a responsible position and have to take care of others. Leaders must always set the example; they must practice the virtues they demand from those in their care. They must be understanding, patient, enduring, full of sympathy, warm and friendly, and goodwill, not out of egoism in order to win friends for themselves, but out of generosity so that they may understand and help others...To forget oneself, one's own thinking and preferences is indispensable in order to be a true leader." [23]

In times of extreme polarisation and lack of unity it may be questioned if Mother's Force is still effective, and in a reply to Shyam Sundar who complained about the lack of unity and infighting amongst the early settlers, she writes, "there is not only a harmony, there is no unity, no sincerity, no consecration to the Divine, no faith, no confidence in the Divine." Her protection, after a fire accident, was not effective because the atmosphere there was very bad. There was no harmony, no sincerity, no faith, and no confidence in the Divine. Each one worked for his own power satisfaction and not with an aspiration to the Divine. We should start again with the right attitude of working for transformation." [24] Manifesting a spiritual organisation in Auroville is not an easy task when people are not organised by their psychic consciousness. Mother, time and again, envisaged her vision related to Auroville's organisation as "a small group with intuitive intelligence governing Auroville who are representatives of the spiritual consciousness, wherein the general organisation intellectual, moral and spiritual superiority will find expression in the enhancement of the pleasures and the powers of life, but in the increase of duties and responsibilities. "[25]

It appears that there are currently no charismatic leaders who are in touch with their psychic consciousness and are recognised, appreciated, and viewed as trustworthy by the entire community, capable of transforming the present crisis while navigating Auroville through its development, achievements, failures, and difficulties. Are some present-day Aurovilians able to identify chronic developmental blockages in the community and envision a new direction towards Auroville's fundamental spiritual ideals and values? There is a sense of urgency to agree, but how can this be achieved? Do we need other kinds of leaders, as Mother predicted, or the pressure of court cases? Does this have a significant impact on today's problems? Nobody wants the relationship between the inhabitants of Auroville's project and the government to collapse into future chaos. Both groups need leaders who support Mother's ideals, not their own well-intended vision. To solve this problem, there needs to be more space for a sense of urgency to agree and more space for negotiation, which does not currently seem very promising. It is certainly possible, but it is unlikely to happen at this time. Now that the city is gradually growing and problems have become more complex, perhaps Aurovilians should learn from the experiences of others elsewhere in the world.

## The Government's Interference

In Mother's vision of Auroville, she does not aim at mere human harmony in a general sense; her goal is more related to a change of the individual's and collective consciousness in a new society, which corresponds to the insights of Integral Yoga and the collective practice in Auroville's community. There are two psychological convictions necessary to become an Aurovilian. "1) To be convinced of the essential unity of mankind and to have the will to collaborate for the material realisation of the unity; 2) To have the will to collaborate in all that furthers future realisations. The material conditions will be worked out as the realisation proceeds."[26] The final Charter has to be envisioned in the context of Mother's creation of a new world with a new consciousness.

The Mother did not want an outside government to take the direction of the Auroville affair, as it would be more a human realisation rather than the realisation of a Divine creation. The Mother did not want an artificial organisation for Auroville; she wanted an organisation that is the expression of a higher consciousness, "a hierarchic organisation grouped around the most enlightened centre and submitting to a collective discipline." She was deeply concerned that the absence of laws had become an excuse for some to fulfill their egoistic desires. Even before the Mother left her body, she complained frequently about the undisciplined and misbehaving behaviour of some of the early Aurovilian settlers. In January 1970, as written in Mother's Agenda, "it must be said that almost all the first newcomers, with a few remarkable exceptions, made up a rather heterogeneous group seeking holidays of sorts on an exotic Riviera and dragging behind themselves a number of unsatisfactory habits. That is what Auroville's enemies later based themselves on to spread all kinds of mischief. It took a few years for the situation to settle and change completely, and for most of the undesirable elements to go away on their own, while fresh newcomers brought a truer aspiration."[27] Again on the 30th of March during the final years of her life she wrote, "they turn freedom into license, they use it to satisfy their desires. And all the things that we have truly worked all our lives to master, they indulge in a dissipation. I am absolutely disgusted."[28]

After the Mother left her body in 1973, a committee of trustees took over the management of the Sri Aurobindo Ashram. However, there was no official, institutional or organisational structure in place where Aurovilians could accept any authority as the leader of the community. As a result, a confrontation arose between Aurovilians and representatives of the Sri Aurobindo Ashram, which was responsible for the administrative affairs of Auroville. This contributed to several court cases, ultimately culminating in the Auroville (Emergency Provisions) Act, where the government assumed management of Auroville for a limited period. It became effective in 1980, and Auroville was officially placed under government control. After the force of the Act continued through "Amendment Acts", a final resolution was reached. It came into full force in 1988 when the central government became the owner of all property and assets. The government appointed a Governing Board as the main authority within the foundation. The Foundation Act comprises three bodies that ensure the government's final and permanent authority. The central government even reserved the right to make additional rules for implementing the provisions of the Act and to provide the infrastructure for realising Mother's dream. The Governing Board has nine members, two of whom are representatives of the central government, and seven of whom render service to Auroville. This Board is the ultimate authority within the Foundation and is responsible for the general direction, supervision, and management of the Foundation's affairs, including developing future plans, promoting Auroville's ideals, and approving decisions of the Residents Assembly. In the second body, all the registered residents of Auroville, the Residents Assembly, will advise the Governing Board on all activities related to the residents, to develop a Master Plan (the Galaxy Plan) for the Board's approval, admit new residents, and take care of fundraising. The third body consists of the Auroville International Advisory Council, where five members, also appointed by the central government, are devoted to the ideals of human unity, peace, and progress. It is an advisory body to the Government Board. They are supposed to ensure that the ideals of Auroville are encouraged and that Aurovilians are allowed to grow in freedom and fulfil their aspirations envisaged in the Charter of Auroville.

From the moment the changes took place in the organisational matters of Auroville up to today, Aurovilians have not been able to create the spiritual authority needed for its organisation as envisioned by the Mother. It appears that there are no charismatic leaders capable of bridging the gap between the various groups within the community and the governmental authorities at present. Part of Auroville's governance problems is related to its ambivalence, distrust of and opposition to authority, and citizens' resistance to rules and regulations. The Aurovilians live in Auroville to practice Integral Yoga in freedom, but if the government as a controlling authority limits this freedom where the officials do not give the citizens their own way of expressing themselves and do not appreciate plurality and disagreement, Auroville as an experimental laboratory for the practice of the Integral Yoga becomes more a relic of Mother's dream. The Mother emphasised that Aurovilians are free agents, not to be micromanaged by bureaucrats or regulated by outside governments. The latter should not only protect the Aurovilians but also respect and leave them as much as possible to make their own collective choices. Perfection cannot be achieved merely by outward rule-keeping; it needs the psychic consciousness to annihilate the selfishness in the heart and the mind of the devotees. The ideal of human unity is not an autocratic superstructure of a rigid organisation where prosperity and safety are secured by emphasising the uniformity of its citizens at the cost of their freedom and the variety of their lives.

For the Mother, unity is not the same as uniformity or mechanical association for unity, where the Aurovilians subjugate themselves for the sake of the collective. Mother's unity supports an infinite diversity, which is as necessary as unity for our true completeness. Mother's divine anarchy is "the anarchic state of self-government of each individual, and it will be the perfect government only when each one becomes conscious of the inner Divine and will obey only him and him alone." [29] The Mother refers to the inner Divine, the psychic being, where the citizens organise themselves spontaneously without fixed rules and laws. This results in an integral unity where the individual and society experience a mutually beneficial relationship. She believed that man's realisation of his deeper unity of existence among themselves can provide independence from external authority; however, the individual may need the authority merely for a practical purpose, which otherwise may remain unrealised. While building the city Auroville, as a separate community, needs to provide a secure atmosphere in which the individual's consciousness will be able to concentrate on his development in a surrounding where all is centred towards that goal, and thereafter to develop the new life in the prepared spiritual atmosphere. The practice of Integral Yoga can accomplish the preliminary step necessary for societal change through changes in the collective psychic being

As general external laws were absent, the community adopted a set of guidelines in which governance was dependent on the goodwill of its citizens, though this often resulted in a slow and lengthy decision-making process within the experimental manifestation of the different forms of organisation. Instead of struggling with each other about the correct way to live, everybody has a certain right and freedom to find their own individual fulfillment. However, with an emphasis on personal freedom, one may easily lose sight of the collective responsibility we share with one another. It is not a freedom to do what you like without the involvement of others, including the government.

Aurovilians strive for the freedom of collective self-rule, driven by growing awareness of mutual responsibility and the right of citizens to determine their own rules in accordance with Mother's guidelines, rather than being subject to government regulations. But how does such a liveable and justifiable society look like, where Aurovilians are mere consumers running after the private fulfilment of their basic needs, and where the government becomes our customer service, while at the same time, the officials are not allowed full play to perform their duties? As mentioned before, various Secretaries of the Governing Board have warned the Aurovilians about the consequences of their ambivalence towards rules and regulations, despite their attempts to guide and protect them from the disorganised structure. They also complained about the lack of cooperation between the various working groups and the Secretary. Nevertheless, does the government's intervention need to restrain itself a bit more from rushing precipitously into Mother's new paradise?

To address Auroville's serious problems effectively, it is first necessary to understand them. In its forward-looking approaches, does it need to first study the accumulated wisdom of the past and incorporate new knowledge from various fields before transcending the present's limits? Mother's utopian dialogue needs to be an ongoing participatory process, not giving way to the dictates of outside technocratic experts or governmental leaders. The members of the Governing Board may reframe major policy issues affecting the majority of citizens, but what happens to the community when various changes are primarily based on specific, limited empirical information, whereas all other information in a new paradigm of society appears to be mere speculation, possibly tainted with wishful thinking? Although collective action in the service of unproven theories can bring large, diverse groups of people together in a harmonious society, it also involves various risks. In Utopia, it is the size that makes all the difference, and the present stage of Auroville's small-scale and grand ambitions may offer a clear insight into the practical cultivation of their psycho-social and spiritual experimentations. This experimental vision cannot be implemented in a short time, as if human nature can be transformed overnight; it is a well-known fact that within utopian communities, declaring victory prematurely is a common occurrence.

There are no signs of the completion of Auroville's experiment, but it seems there are tendencies towards restructuring Auroville, where the emphasis shifts gradually from a spiritual, mystical principle towards a more social, secular utopian society in the spirit of devotion to the common good. Challenges to the ideals and founding principles of the Charter may arise in the form of governmental authoritarianism, necessitating a dialogue about adherence to the Charter's fundamental principles. The Governing Board may finally guide, regulate, and approve, but it may not determine Auroville's direction true to the Charter.

Though the State strives for the individual's achievements and individual freedom, its ultimate aim is more interested in the collective achievements of the nation and national unity. The secular government is not concerned with traditional spiritual issues, such as Karma Yoga or the evolutionary becoming of the Supermind. It promotes spirituality only in the context of its own concerns and interests. In this context, how will the government use or even misuse the Charter in terms of its own limited approach to Reality and its own ultimate human concern, unable to integrate Mother's spiritual ideals and her promotion of spiritual perfection, i.e., Mother's emphasis on the experiential and practical aspect of Integral Yoga, and Auroville as a living laboratory, where sadhana becomes a means for this perfection. No doubt, during the eighties, it was the government's intervention that saved Auroville's survival when internal struggles between Aurovilians and representatives of the Sri Aurobindo Society escalated out of control, and the Foundational Act was established. But what are the various interests of the secular and spiritual parties involved in the present disputes about promoting their perceived interests in Auroville? What is the secular government's interest in a spiritual project like Auroville, which does not deal with spiritual issues? According to R. Minor in the discussion of the secular and the religious; "Founded by the inspiration of two gurus and culture heroes [Sri Aurobindo and The Mother] the government of India is now committed to promote (could we say propagate?) the goals for which it was founded in some form, and the Parliament, the courts and even an international organisation, the UNESCO, were involved what appears to be government interest in promoting the teachings of an Indian guru and his followers."[30] He continues about the nature of the government's interest in the success of Auroville, "The Government and members of Parliament came to have their own stake in Auroville's success, an interest based upon Indian pride and prestige in the international arena...Auroville's success came to represent India's success at such a commitment, the promotion of human unity and international cooperation. Auroville's failure would reflect badly on India's image. In the midst of the debates over Auroville, it was clear that the government's interest was different from that of the Mother or the Aurovilians....Auroville's success then was a matter of national pride."[31] The project was not only of interest for the government because its national and international prestige was at stake, but also due to the funds of the central and state governments that had invested in. One of the supporters of the Sri Aurobindo Society pondered during one of the debates, "how the government takeover of Auroville could possibly promote 'through a bureaucratic machinery' the Mother's three ideals of individual perfection, social transformation, or human unity in rich diversity through service to the Divine."[32] He concludes; "With the state in control and with these as the dominant state interests in their minds, whether they accept or merely tolerate the system of thought and practice taught by Aurobindo and the Mother, these interests that are now in place through legislation and judicial approval will have the power to decide the activities and status of the city of Dawn."[33]

Do all kinds of disciplinary measures really result in steps towards dialogue to combat polarisation, or do they render only treatment of symptoms? It may take a thousand years, and could it be that governmental authorities profit more when they slow down their efforts to build the city instantly? What they lose in time, they gain in experience, making someone pause for a dialogue and sharing questions, which enriches and offers a progressive insight into the complexity of the present crisis. Could it be that in building a new spiritual model city of the future, according to a developmental plan which envisions a high-density and self-sustained city, need not be only a matter of setting a time limit, 'how fast' we urbanise, but maybe also as much 'how' we urbanise, i.e., building the city as an experiment, a means related to build a new man through a change of consciousness which would gradually ripple out to the outside world?

Auroville's development cannot be simplified; the present-day reality is more complex than some Aurovilians would like to assert, and its enemy cannot be attributed only to an outside intruder. There are some Aurovilians, nobody knows how many, who are fascinated by the government's future plans, who offer them all kinds of promises to build a city of 50.000 people within a certain time frame and who take the law into their own hands under the umbrella of the Governing Board, with the possibility to throw out their opponents, or subjugating their old soul-mates to their grills. However, it is a misconception to believe that Auroville's desirable future city can be established only by the power and efficiency of the government, and though it can be certainly very effective in its actions to avoid all kinds of failures of the past on so many fronts, but when the Governing Board tries to improve too many things in a short time it expands its own instrument at the disadvantage of the interests of many citizens. To transform the basic structure of Auroville's community through direct intervention in its processes, it needs to incorporate not only a technical analysis of the present state of affairs but also its historical context and its philosophy for social and spiritual change. It requires a new consciousness that enables a massive current of change to dismantle and sweep away everything built up from the past, thereby alienating itself from the sentiments and needs of ordinary citizens. When dealing with today's external circumstances of Auroville's current reality, it is therefore necessary for the Aurovilians to move inward and witness the psychic change and establish harmony within and without. That is easier said than done, given the present outer circumstances; can Aurovilians really expect the psychic to act visibly in a world surrounded by all kinds of oppressive forces? Even when some Aurovilians claim to be in contact with their psychic being, how are they able to deal with the notion of indomitable enthusiast human spirits who, without divine intervention, penetrate the community?

The idea that the citizens are able to live in a small community with no fixed rules is possible only when it is based on an accepted authority, but experience shows that an egalitarian group within the shortest time establishes a hierarchy in which those with the most authoritative attitude grant themselves various privileges, i.e., exchange their authority for power. In their current movements of reform, the Board members, while being concerned with the welfare and reform of Auroville's future, could it be that they neglect the full problem in all its implications, to the total situation in which they crudely simplify the difficulties? In their haste to arrive at solutions and remedies, are they too ready to neglect a complete tally of the facts, the full problem in all its implications, or are they crudely simplifying the difficulties, ignoring the spiritual values of many Aurovilians and their environment? It appears the Board members are more involved in a model city for the future, which will attract thousands of daily visitors and tourists.

Auroville's citizens are not used to being directed by leaders who cause restrictions in their freedom to do whatever they want. The government's overwhelming interference due to its dissatisfaction with the results of Auroville's achievements may be a shock for the attempted self-government of dedicated citizens and awake some of them of their complacency, unbalanced behaviour and lack of self-control, however, at the same time, this interference has led to the gradual breakdown of the unity of its citizens. As competent managers, they may claim to represent Mother's vision, functioning as promoters of entrepreneurship and technology to complete their project at the earliest. They focus on crafting successful stories by evoking respect and awe with the help of some of their supporting citizens. Assigning all kinds of subtasks to external consultants makes them dependent on too many parties, and if other citizens object to their vision, they create more rules and laws. It requires not only professional expertise but also experiential proficiency to gather knowledge from all Aurovilians, initiate small steps towards a long-term goal, and formulate collective tasks rather than pitting different groups against each other. Perhaps these Aurovilians, who in their preoccupation with themselves, must not only strive for ideal material progress but also look inward with the same motivating power as the collective utopian ideal of progress envisioned by Mother, aiming for a better man and a better world. It may require a whole new generation to recover Mother's dream with a transition to a new, progressive order of affairs, and perhaps these new utopians have their eyes and sweet hopes for the future fixed on a renewed, glorious vision of human perfectibility.

Currently, the expression of emotional and rational argumentative involvement takes precedence over gaining contemplative insight, as the distinction between fact and fiction is often abolished. Instead of a free exchange of ideas, insights, and arguments, group polarisation exists. When the concept of truth turns out to be merely a matter of perspective, then anyone can create their own truth. The fact that people believe what they want to believe and the fact that we often misinterpret things is not so much due to the way we think as to what others make us believe. In addition to one's own critical mind, one needs an unsparing eye for those who abuse our fragile relationship with facts and the idea of truth for their own ideological agenda. Either the residents resign themselves to a future where building the city as a concrete object as soon as possible will mould their fate, or they cultivate a collective aspiration under the sun's grace to release what remains involved in their inner and outer consciousness. It is easier, when confronted with problems while building the city, to arrive at a fixed material idea rather than approach the whole project of building the city as a learning process of Karma Yoga and a means to develop a psychic consciousness. One of the results of Auroville's deep crisis may be a combination of intellectual pessimism, practical and useful to avoid sleepwalking towards Auroville's own demise, and optimistic hope of Auroville's strong will-power, creativity and divine Grace

Coercive measures to align the Aurovilians with the government's vision might cause much resistance from many citizens. In its aim to improve building the city, it needs to recognise the limits of what is possible, and perhaps more importantly, officials should be vigilant about how their idealism can turn into authoritarianism and exclusion when they seek to forcibly reshape Auroville. It requires a critical awareness of its own idealism in promoting the city's development, and to remain grounded and open to the complexities of citizens' lives and their human limitations during the journey of their individual and collective social transformation. The Mother would like the Aurovilians to find solutions independently, without a rigid structure that might hinder their freedom to experiment. If Auroville wants to change, then the change must come from within the Auroville community; it can hardly be imposed from outside. They need the freedom to conduct their activities in conformity with the Auroville Charter, i.e., the need for Aurovilians to develop along the lines envisioned by the Mother, where they are free from external interference.

At present, it appears that government officials, along with some of their supporting Aurovilians, are attempting to direct Auroville along familiar lines. In this way, they gradually attempt to control Auroville's future destiny. However, *in their claim, government officials have made it clear to all citizens that they are in Auroville because the Aurovilians are unable to govern themselves, lacking the necessary organisational structure and needing to become more practical and logical in their organisation.* Although the officials may lack genuine spiritual objectives and may not be familiar with human unity in diversity, this is because they are not practitioners of Integra Yoga. The citizens are supposed to be the practitioners, and the results of their practice cannot be applied to the officials; these officials have different jobs to do while building the city. While building the city as a spiritual experiment under the present control of governmental officials, when the polarisation between the citizens and the officials is subdued and manageable for all parties involved, then the project may, hopefully in the future, be gradually turned over to a more appropriate body that could better implement various aspects of Mother's teachings related not only in building a new city but also how to build this new city.

## Notes

1.) The Mother; Collected Works of the Mother, Vol 13, p 211

2.) Ibid., Vol 13 p 197

3.) Shyam Sundar Jhunjhunwala; Down Memory Lane on 9-6-1971

4.) R. Minor; The Religious, the Spiritual and the Secular p 126

5.) The Mother; Mother's Agenda, 21-9-1966

6.) The Mother; Collective Works of the Mother, Vol 13

7.) The Mother; the Agenda, 1966 p 4

8.) Ibid., Vol IX 10-4-1968

9.) The Mother; the Collective Works of the Mother, September 1969

10.) Ibid., Vol 13 p 227

11.) Ibid., Vol 14 p 273

12.) The Mother; Mother's Agenda, 6-2-1969

13.) Auroville Today; January 2018

14.) Krishan Kumar; Utopianism, p 33

15.) The Mother; Mother's Agenda, 10-4-1968

16.) The Mother; Collective Works of the Mother Vol 13 March 10

17.) The Mother; The Mother on Auroville, 26-8-1966

18.) The Mother; The Mother's Agenda, 30-11-1967

19.) Sri Aurobindo; The Mother, p 238

20.) The Mother; Mother's Agenda, 10-4-1968

21.) Ibid., 25-3-1970

22.) Auroville Today April 2007

23.) The Mother; Collective Works of the Mother, pVol 13 p 169-170

24.) Shyam Sundar Jhunjhunwala; Down Memory Lane, p 135

25.) The Mother; Collective Works of the Mother, Vol 12 p 94

26.) Ibid., p 43-44

27.) The Mother; Mother's Agenda, 17-1-1970

28.) The Mother; Collective Works of the Mother, Vol 13 March 30

29.) The Mother; Mother's Agenda, Vol 11 p 76

30.) R Minor; The Religious, the Spiritual and the Secular, p 17

31.) Ibid., p 78

32.) Ibid., p 85

33.) Ibid., p 149

*CHAPTER SEVEN*

# THE PSYCHIC BEING AND ITS OBSTACLES

When coming to Auroville, the discovery of and unification with the psychic being was not made a condition to live in Auroville, but the Mother often referred to its necessity when she was in touch with Aurovilians who were encountering difficulties on the practical journey towards psycho-spiritual transformation. The paths on the journey to the psychic being are vulnerable to contradictory views and opinions due to the disciple's mental limitations and dogmatic attitudes. In the Mother's talks, messages, classes, and personal Agenda, she described to the disciples, among other things, her experiences of the psychic being in detail and depth. Attempts to explain the psychic experience are illusory expressions, as they demonstrate some effects of the experience that others understand according to their preconceptions, but they do not explain the experience itself. The psychic being, as the inner guide of Integral Yoga, is that part of the human being that possesses transformative powers, illuminating and purifying the dark areas of our ignorant personality. When not ready and without guidance, a condition may result in serious psycho-spiritual difficulties. Without the required purification of the lower instrument, entertaining powers beyond one's comprehension can be rather dangerously delusional. On the spiritual journey inwards, it is not easy to delve within to discover one's psychic being. The seeker often needs to overcome various psychological obstacles on the path before entering into these inner realms of being. By removing the psychic experience from the psycho-spiritual context and by simplification of complex concepts without the deep metaphysical framework found in Mother's and Sri Aurobindo's works, could it be that this experience loses much of its meaning? Have Mother's disciples ever critically analysed the basic assumptions of their yogic psychic experiment, and what are the reliable effects as a means for secular social improvement? Aurovilians often lack the willingness to invite sympathetic observers who are familiar with the subject and who investigate critically the obvious discrepancies between the psychic reports from various practitioners. Most observers politely refrain from studying the psycho-spiritual condition of these practitioners.

The author aims to elaborate on various possible misunderstandings regarding the psychic experiment, and he humbly aspires to explore this issue in depth to benefit communal challenges and dialogue. He does not deny or affirm the truth of Mother's spiritual insights related to the experience of the psychic being, in his detached approach, he prefers to leave this issue to the Aurovilians themselves. In his analysis, he does not want to omit or downplay the often-neglected negative side effects of the psychic experiment, as warned against again and again by Sri Aurobindo and the Mother. While attempting to describe Mother's and Sri Aurobindo's exposition of the nature of psychic experience and its numerous valuable applications in daily life, he also explores essential issues related to various misunderstandings and misapplications of this concept. While navigating through the complex inner landscape, abuse of developmental problems should not be ignored or justified by anyone who claims to be in contact with the psychic being. The psychic being, as a direct, intrinsic, occult, and intangible experience of a transcendent reality, not cut off into fragmentary pieces of experience and unmediated by individual, social, and cultural structures, can be grasped by intuition but can hardly be interpreted and verified by the rational mind. The experience can be described differently in different people, but does this mean that these disciples can claim the absolute validity of their private experienced truth claims? They may often be more accepted as a matter of faith. According to Sri Aurobindo, "we must not apply to the soul a logic which is based on the peculiarities of matter.... the soul is not divided from God by these barriers of material dimension. What is true of matter is not true of Spirit, nor do the standards of form become facts applied to the formless. For matter is conscious being confined in form, the Spirit is conscious being using form but unconfined in it."[1]

The Mother developed occult powers in her early years when she joined an occult group in Paris with Max Theon, an adept occultist who could command material forces. Here, she learnt how to unite her experience with her psychic being, a term used by Theon to describe the personal, evolving soul — the soul that incarnates through various experiences. As a spark of the Divine within each human being, the soul personality is based on this Divine spark, though it is different from the eternal soul. It is the Mother who provided Sri Aurobindo with the concept of the psychic being as the evolutionary soul, an evolving being at birth and leaving the body at death. According to Peter Heehs, a disciple from the Sri Aurobindo Archives, "The 'psychic being' was a new element in Sri Aurobindo's yoga...He (Sri Aurobindo) used the word 'soul' for the divine element in each person.... Up to 1926, Sri Aurobindo had no name for this evolutionary soul. The Mother provided him with one. Theon had distinguished the *center divine or divine center* from the *etre psychique* or psychic being. When she mentioned the latter term to Sri Aurobindo, he took it up and adapted it to his needs...Eventually, he realised that the transformation he envisioned would be difficult, if not impossible, for others without a preliminary awakening of the psychic being, a development of such qualities as sincerity, devotion and inner discrimination. To bring about this awakening was the primary aim of the sadhana under Mother's guidance."[2] In his later life, Sri Aurobindo started to change the forms of his sadhana, as he realised the difficulties his sadhaks encountered during their practice. He placed less emphasis on the role of the mind in sadhana but advised the sadhaks to follow the emergence of their psychic being. During his sadhana, Sri Aurobindo experienced the extension of a conscious divine Force, and he looked at the Mother as representing this Force element, and that's why she could best guide the sadhaks in their sadhana during their day-to-day practical difficulties.

Goodwill to make a collective experiment for the progress of humanity is sufficient to gain admittance to Auroville, but Mother also said, "They may not practice themselves, but if they do not know about Yoga, how do they understand the purpose of Auroville?[3] "It is not for the comfort and satisfaction of desires that one comes to Auroville; it is for the growth of consciousness and concentration of the Truth that has to be realised. Unselfishness is the first need to participate in the creation of Auroville" [4] In a preparatory process the Mother gave the Aurovilians some advice and disciplinary steps on the path towards the psychic discovery; it needs untiring persistence of effort, the sadhak should never forget the purpose and goal of life and he should abstain from all mental opinions, personal comfort and while building the city do the work as an offering to the Divine so that the consciousness develops best and our bodies become physical vehicles connecting our inmost psychic being with the world of material objects and events. Ultimately, it is the contact of that inmost Consciousness-Force, which is the main reason, the ultimate sustaining principle of Auroville.

To gain a better understanding of the concept of the psychic being, it may be helpful to elaborate in detail on its meaning, function, nature, and development, as well as the difficulties encountered along the way, before analysing the various pitfalls on the journey towards psychic realisation and its role in the process of psychic transformation.

In the initial stages of sadhana, the sadhak needs first to concentrate and become conscious of all the disparate parts and chaotic instincts of his surface being and then, by a progressive purification, achieve some order and unity, which will facilitate the purifying influence of the psychic being. This requires total sincerity and self-surrender, as the ego's self-deception may attribute the results of the Divine power to itself. According to Sri Aurobindo, "Men do not know themselves and have not learned to distinguish the different parts of their being; for these are usually limped together by them as mind, because it is through a mentalised perception and understanding that they know or feel them; therefore they do not understand their own states and actions, or, if at all, then only on the surface. It is part of the foundation of yoga to become conscious of the great complexity of our nature, see the different forces that move it and gain control of directing knowledge. We are composed of many parts, each of which contributes something to the total movement of our consciousness, our thought, will, suggestions, feelings, actions, but we do not see the origination or the course or their impulsions; we are aware only of their confused and pell-mell results on the surface upon which we can at best impose nothing better than a precarious shifting order."[5] The first step is to learn to distinguish the multifaceted parts of our being for the sake of clarity and to avoid pitfalls such as mistaking the psychic being for the mental or vital parts that are only influenced by it or carried away by one's ego.

In Mother's spiritual experiment, she classified three realms that form together the three dimensions of inner consciousness, i.e., the inner, the true, and the central (inmost) being. The inner being (the subliminal) opens to the subtle plane, the true being, the actual physical, emotional and mental being (the Purusha), where the Atman is represented on all these levels. The central being, the Jivatman, is, in its essence, that portion of the Divine that supports all the rest of the manifestation and survives through death and birth. "This central being has two forms- above, it is Jivatman, our true being, of which we become aware when the higher self-knowledge comes,—below it is the psychic being which stands behind the mind, body and life. The Jivatman is above the manifestation in life and presides over it; the psychic being stands behind the manifestation in life and supports it."[6] The soul, as a representative of the central being, is a spark of the Divine supporting all individual existence in Nature and the psychic being is a conscious form of that soul growing in the evolution. "The soul or psyche is immutable only in the sense that it contains all the possibilities of the Divine within it, but it has also to evolve them, and in its evolution it assumes the form of a developing individual evolving in the manifestation, the individual Prakrti (nature) and taking part in the evolution."[7] This psychic principle, variously referred to as '**psychic entity**', 'psychic essence', or 'soul-element' is fundamentally always the same and functions as a non-individualised portion of the Divine consciousness that descents into the evolution to support to individual's evolution out of darkness into light. In its origin, the psychic being is a spark of the Divine consciousness, and through successive lives, it develops a conscious individuality. This evolving psychic being temporalises and individualises what is eternal in potentiality. In the course of evolution, the psychic essence, entity, or spark-soul develops in the human being a psychic personality, which is called the psychic being.

According to Sri Aurobindo, "there is indeed a soul-personality, representative of this entity already, built up within us, which puts forward a fine psychic element in our natural being: but this finer factor in our normal make-up is not yet dominant and has only a limited action. Our soul is not yet the overt guide and master of our thoughts and acts; it has to rely on the mental, vital, and physical instruments for self-expression, and our mind and life force constantly overpower it."[8] To express it differently, the psychic entity, a flame born out of the indestructible spark of the Divine, grows as the hidden Guide or inner voice of the mystic. It is that which endures and is imperishable in us from birth to birth. As a deputy of the unborn Atman this inmost entity takes form in each of us personally, which changes, grows and develops from life to life. In its development, it is influenced and mixed with the errors of the lower instrument, but the psychic entity itself remains free from this mixture. The mixture of the emotive heart and sensational vital creates in man a false 'soul of desire', and this crude element, which is distrusted by reason, needs to be controlled, even though the actual control remains always uncertain and deceptive. In the words of Sri Aurobindo, "It is the psychic personality in us that flowers as the saint, the sage, the seer.... where the psychic personality is weak, crude or ill-developed, the finer parts and movements in us are lacking or poor in character and power, even though the mind may be forceful and brilliant, the heart of vital emotions hard and strong and masterful, the life-force dominant and successful the bodily existence rich and fortunate and an apparent lord and victor. It is then the outer desire-soul, the pseudo-psychic entity, that reigns and we mistake its misinterpretations of psychic suggestion and aspiration, its ideas and ideals, its desires and yearnings for true soul-stuff and wealth of spiritual experience." [9]

## Psychic influence

Before continuing with the psychic experiment, it is important to distinguish between the various experiences of the psychic consciousness. After the initial 'influence' of the psychic, there is the process of coming into 'contact' with the psychic being, when one feels oneself like an instrument and is aware of the psychic consciousness using it, and thereafter, the 'awakening' of the psychic being, when the psychic comes forward and where where the experience becomes more stable and frequent during the process of psychic transformation.

The seat of the psychic is behind the emotional heart and deeper within the inner heart centre. Its power is experienced as a spiritual feeling, a soul feeling that supports all the parts of the surface being, though it is also much veiled by them. It has to act upon them as an influence rather than by its rights of direct action. The psychic, when it influences the outer life, brings light, order, quietude, and the joy of the Divine contact. In the words of Sri Aurobindo, "A certain sensitive feeling for all that is true and good and beautiful, fine and pure and noble, a response to it, a demand for it, a pressure on the mind and life to accept and formulate it in our thought, feelings, conduct, character is the most usually recognised, the most general and characteristic, though not the sole sign of this influence of the psyche. Of the man who does not have this element in him or does not respond at all to this urge, we say that he has no soul. "[10] The Mother described the psychic influence as "There are parts of the being under its influence and manifesting something of it. So, very often, people enter into contact with these parts, and this gives them illumination, great joy, and revelations, and they feel that they have found their soul, but it is only the part of the being under its influence ... One has not touched one's soul. One had touched those parts of the being which are under the influence of the soul and manifest something of it but are not it.... And these things are very beautiful and give you very impressive experiences, but this is not the contact with the psychic being itself."[11] However, the psychic influence is often not very pure but mixed with the activities of the subtle body, mind and vital and as such are not received in their purest form. As this psychic influence or action does not emerge quite pure, after it reaches the surface, it clings to the outer nature in an impure formation, with the possibility of further deviation and mixture of its original, pure form. A detailed explanation of this confusion will be provided later in this chapter.

## Contact with the Psychic

The outer consciousness is not in contact with the inner psychic, and it lives in all kinds of external movements instead of looking within into the depths of the inner being and its inner inspirations. Contact with the psychic, like the influence of the psychic, is initially unconscious, and conscious contact with the psychic typically develops only through sadhana. With the growth of consciousness, contact with the psychic becomes more frequent and lasts longer. According to the Mother, "it is not easy to come into contact with the psychic being, because the contact is not spontaneous, it is voluntary. The psychic being always has an influence on the thoughts and actions, but one is rarely conscious of it. To become conscious of the psychic being, one must want to do so, make one's mind as silent as possible and enter deep into the heart of one's being, beyond sensations and thoughts. One must form the habit of silent concentration and descent into the depths of one's being."[12] As soon as one concentrates and aspires, one may get the contact, and though one may not have the power to keep it all the time, yet he can get it at will. As the psychic being grows and its actions become stronger, it helps the sadhak to advance on the path.

The Mother describes the psychic contact as "If impelled by the psychic being, when the psychic being is in front and ruling the consciousness, there is a psychic contact with people, everything seems beautiful and good to them, their health improves, their consciousness grows more luminous; they feel happy, peaceful and safe; they think they have reached their utmost possibility of consciousness. It fosters an openness towards the true consciousness that pervades here and works out everything. So long as the openness is there, the peace, the fullness and the joy remain with their immediate results of progress.... But it is difficult for a human being to keep up constant contact with this psychic. As soon as he settles down and the freshness of the new experience fades away, the old person comes back to the surface with all its habits, preferences, small manias, shortcomings and misunderstandings."[13] Somewhere else she said, "I knew people who have no knowledge, so to say, of anything, who were hardly educated, whose minds were altogether of the ordinary kind, and who had in them this capacity of gratitude, of warmth, which gives itself, understands and is thankful. Well, for them, the contact with the psychic was very frequent, almost constant and, to the extent they were capable of it, conscious-not very conscious but a little-in the sense that they felt that they were carried, helped, uplifted above themselves. These two things prepare people the most. They are born with one or the other, and if they take the trouble, it develops gradually and increases. We say: the capacity for enthusiasm, something which throws you out of your miserable and mean little ego; and the generous gratitude, the generosity of the gratitude which also flings itself in thanksgiving out of the little ego. These are the two most powerful levers to enter into contact with the Divine in one's psychic being. This serves as a link with the psychic being-the surest link."[14]

The psychic influence of and contact with the psychic being are two different things. In the former, the sadhak has not touched one's soul; he has only touched those parts of the being that are under the influence of the soul. When the sadhak enters consciously into contact with his soul and the union is established, this experience changes the very structure of his inner consciousness and leaves a touch upon the outer parts of the being. Even when the psychic being "is obliged often under the pressure of its instruments to submit to mistakes of action.... yet is there a divination within it, which makes it a surer guide than reason or than even the highest desire, and though apparent errors and stumblings, its voice can still lead better than the precise intellect and the considering mental judgement."[15] In the words of the Mother, "This voice (of the ordinary conscience as an ethical voice) is very useful in ordinary life until one is able to become conscious of one's psychic being and allow oneself to be entirely guided by it- in other words, to rise above ordinary humanity, free oneself from all egoism and become a conscious instrument of the Divine Will. The soul itself is above all moral and ethical notions."[16] All those who have had such an experience of contact should be aware that the experience is genuine and not a mental experience, a contact with the idea they have constructed of it, but a truly concrete contact.

## Awakening or Opening When the Psychic Being Comes Forward

Contact with the psychic is not enough to make it the leader of the being; the beginning of the psychic contact prepares the awakening of the psychic being, which is bound to take a very long time to come. The path to the psychic realisation is long and complex, strewn with problems to be solved, which demand an unfailing determination. Usually, the first contact with the psychic being is only partial; only part of the consciousness or the activity of any part of the being is united with the experience, and at the moment of that experience, the position of that part of the consciousness is completely reversed. However, the Mother warned against all kinds of causes that may be obstacles to the awakening of the psychic being. "You may be moved, pushed into action and used *as unconscious* instruments by the divine Force if you have a minimum of goodwill and sincerity. But to become a conscious instrument capable of identification and conscious, willed movements, you must have this inner organisation; otherwise you will always be running into chaos somewhere, confusion somewhere or an obscurity, an unconsciousness somewhere. And naturally your action, even though guided exclusively by the Divine, will not have the perfection of expression it has when one has acquired a conscious organisation around this divine Centre. It is an assiduous task, which may be done at any time and under any circumstances, for you carry within yourself all the elements of the problem. You don't need anything from outside, no outer aid to do this work. But it requires great perseverance, for every often it happens that there are bad "creases" in the being, habits- which come from all sorts of causes.... from education or from the environment you have lived in or from many other causes. And these bad creases you try to smooth out, but they wrinkle up again. And then you must begin to work over again, often, many, many, many a time, without getting discouraged, before the final result is obtained."[17]

When the sadhak is sufficiently advanced, the opening needs the receptivity of Mother's forces through aspiration, quietude and rejection of all that is obstructing the Divine forces. One needs to be vigilant and open to the Mother's forces without the movements of the ego, vital desires, or one's own mental ideas. In this new birth, when her force becomes more predominantly active, the chance of mental constructions and vital formations mixing with the true experience will diminish. By the opening of the psychic being, it comes forward and governs the mind, life and body, turning all to the Divine where they become instruments of the inmost within us, but only "when the sadhak has got rid of the mixture of vital motives with his sadhana and is capable of a simple and sincere self-offering to the Mother. If there is any kind of egoistic turn or insincerity of motive, if the yoga is done under a pressure of vital demands, or partly or wholly to satisfy some spiritual or other ambition, pride, vanity, or seeking after power, position or influence over others or with any push towards satisfying any vital desire with the help of the yogic force, then the psychic cannot open or opens only partially or only at times and shuts again because it is veiled by the vital activities; Also, if the mind takes the leading part in the yoga and puts the inner soul into the background or if the bhakti or other movements of the sadhana take more of a vital than of a psychic form, there is the same inability. Purity, simple sincerity and the capacity of an unegoistic, unmixed self-offering without pretension or demand are the conditions of an entire opening of the psychic being."[18] If the psychic is awake and in front, it becomes easy to remain conscious of the things that have to be changed in the wrong movements of the surface parts of the being, there is an automatic perception of the divine and the undivine and gradually the vital and physical as well as the mind get full of the psychic light and truth bringing in a true force.

When the psychic is in front and governs all the parts of the being, the sadhana becomes natural and easy, and with this true psychic opening, it is possible to call through it a strength from above. According to Sri Aurobindo, "In using the expression 'opening of the psychic' I was thinking not of an ordinary psychic opening producing some amount of psychic (as opposed to vital) love and bhakti, but of what is called the coming in front of the psychic. When that happens, one is aware of the psychic being with its simple, spontaneous self-giving and feels its increasing direct control over the mind, vital and physical. Especially there is the psychic discernment, which at once lights up the thoughts, emotional movements, vital pushes, and physical habits and leaves nothing there obscure, substituting the right movements for the wrong ones. It is this that is difficult and rare; more often, the discernment is mental, and it is the mind that tries to put all in order."[19] The psychic is awakened when the sadhak becomes conscious of his soul instead of identifying himself with the mind, vital, and body. As the psychic emerges more and more, the inner light becomes more apparent, and when the deeper psychic experiences become possible, then the psychic personality reaches its full potential. The psychic entity then manifests itself as the central being that upholds the mind, life, and body.

## Psychic Transformation

The process of discovering the psychic being and allowing it to integrate and govern the different planes of one's being is termed by Sri Aurobindo as psychic transformation. Sri Aurobindo speaks of three transformations: psychic, spiritual, and supramental transformation, and the psychic transformation is the first necessity because it facilitates the transformation of the ordinary human into the higher spiritual consciousness, and it makes the descent of this higher consciousness safe. The psychic transformation consists of "bringing vision into the mind, right impulse and feeling into the vital, right movement and habit into the physical-all turned towards the Divine... finally, the vision and sense of the Mother everywhere in all as well as in the heart, her Force working in the being, faith, consecration, surrender."[20] It means a prolonged modification of the substance of the consciousness till it becomes permanent, and these modifications make transformation possible. When the psychic individual becomes dominant over the nature and when mind, life and body take their true place as its instruments, the sadhak becomes aware of the guide within that knows the truth and the true delight of existence and leads his life and being towards spiritual completeness away from the vital passions and it's dark self-seeking. As the leader of the sadhana, when the psychic opening and the connection with the psychic being is made, the psychic transformation becomes possible and facilitates the spiritual transformation. The psychic, with its increasing direct control over the lower instrumentation, is in direct touch with the Divine truth, but if the true soul-power behind it does not come to the front, nothing genuine will be done. The inner guide of the divine spark within each of us allows it to influence our lives and actions. It involves a process of purification, where lower impulses are replaced by their higher values within the psychic being.

The presence of the released psychic being supplies a progressive guidance for the inner and outer life and action, its light illuminates the other parts of the nature; it gives to mind the intrinsic feeling of the thoughts and perceptions, to life the infallible sense of the movements that are misleading and gives a just direction for our acts. Above all, the psychic being imposes on life the law of sacrifice of all its work as an offering to the Divine. Sri Aurobindo describes the effects of the psychic transformation as "it takes up its greater function as the guide and ruler of nature. A guidance, a governance begins from within which exposes every movement to the light of Truth, repels what is false, obscure, opposed to the divine realisation: every region of the being, every nook and corner of it, every movement, formation, direction, inclination of thought, will, emotion, sensation, action, reaction, motive, disposition, propensity desire, habit of the conscious or subconscious physical, even the most concealed, camouflaged, mute, recondite is lighted up with the unerring psychic light, their confusions dissipated, their tangles disentangled, their obscurities, deceptions, self-deceptions precisely indicated and removed; all is purified, set right, the whole nature harmonised in the psychic key, put in spiritual order..... As a final result the whole conscious being is made perfectly apt for spiritual experience of every kind.... this is the first result but the second is a free inflow of all kinds of spiritual experience, experience of the Self, experience of the Ishwara and the Divine Shakti...a direct touch with cosmic forces and with the occult movements of universal Nature, a psychic sympathy and unity and interchanges of all kinds with other beings and with Nature."[21]

Though the psychic experience in the Divine Person may reveal itself in a long and large comprehensive work, sometimes luminous and sometimes obscure, it is not a smooth process. In the words of Sri Aurobindo, "A little of the Divine Person may reveal itself or some Light, Power, Bliss, Love out of the Infinite. .... A Divine power comes in front at times and leads and compels or instructs and enlightens; at others, it withdraws into the background and seems to leave the being to its own resources. All that is ignorant, obscure, perverted or simply imperfect and inferior in the being is raised up, perhaps brought to its acme, dealt with, corrected, exhausted, shown its own disastrous results, compelled to call for its own cessation or transformation or expelled as worthless or incorrigible from the nature. This cannot be a smooth or even process; alternations there are of day and night, illumination and darkness, calm and construction or battle and upheaval, the heights of hope and despair, the overwhelming invasion, the compelling deceit, the fierce opposition, the disabling mockery of hostile Powers or the help and comfort and communion of the gods and the Divine Messengers.... But if the equality and the psychic light and will are also there, then this process, though it cannot be dispensed with, can still be lightened and facilitated; it will be rid of its worst dangers; an inner calm, happiness, confidence will support the steps through all the difficulties and trials of the transformation and the growing Force profiting by the full assent of the nature will rapidly diminish and eliminate the power of the opposing forces. A sure guidance and protection will be present throughout, sometimes standing in front, sometimes working behind the veil, and the power of the end will be already there in the beginning and in the long middle stage of the endeavour. For at all times the seeker will be aware of the Divine Guide and Protector of the working of the supreme Mother-Force; he will Know that all is done for the best, the progress assured, the victory inevitable."[22]

Why is the psychic experiment not a smooth process? What are the fierce oppositions, what are the obstacles, and its pitfalls? As discussed before, the different parts of the surface being have each a separate function and are distinct from one another, yet all of these external aspects interact with each other. It is through the practice of yoga that the seeker discovers the extraordinary complexity of one's being and finds "that every part of us-intellect, will, sense- mind, nervous or desire self, the heart, the body- has each, as it were, its own complex individuality and material formation independent of the rest; it neither agrees with itself nor with the others nor which the representative ego which is the shadow cast by some central and centralising self on our superficial ignorance. We find that we are composed not of one but many personalities and each has its own demands and differing nature. Our being is roughly constituted chaos into which we have to introduce the principle of divine order."[23] In outer surface nature, all parts are present together, and a strong power of introspection, self-analysis, and close observation is needed to find out the composition of our nature and the relation and interaction of these parts with each other.

During the practice of sadhana, the sadhak discovers that the various parts of the being are all mixed up, and these forces of the lower mental, vital and physical nature can do what they like by stimulating experiences and building up unreal formulations. But when the seeker gets beyond this ordinary surface consciousness, he discovers their distinctiveness and their separate forces. According to Sri Aurobindo, "The outer instruments of human nature have no force to carry the seeker through the severe ardour of the spiritual journey, for the lower parts of the being have their own rights and, if they are to be truly transformed, they must be made to consent to their own transformation. This is difficult to bring about because the natural propensity of each part of us is to prefer its own self-law, its dharma, however inferior, to a superior law of dharma which it feels to be not it's own; it clings to its own consciousness or unconsciousness, its own impulsions and reactions, its own dynamisation of being, its own way of delight of existence...A complete and radical change can only be brought about by bringing in persistently the spiritual light and intimate experience of the spiritual truth, power, bliss into the recalcitrant elements until they too recognise that their own way of fulfillment lies there, that they are themselves a diminished power of the spirit and can recover by this new way of being their own truth and integral nature. This illumination is constantly opposed by the Forces of the lower nature and still more by the adverse Forces that live and reign by the world's imperfections."[24]

The outer being is by no means complete in itself. When the individual moves beyond the external being, with its confused mixture of mind formations, life movements, and physical functions, and enters the hidden planes of one's being, he discovers a vast inner or subliminal existence. But there is often a struggle between the inner and outer parts, the latter remaining attached to the things of ordinary life while the former wants the Divine. The inner being, unlike the outer being, receives and responds to the physical and universal world directly, through the subtle sense of its more subtle inner bodies. It has the power to enter into direct contact with other consciousnesses or objects and is able to achieve immediate knowledge of the occult. Sri Aurobindo distinguishes the levels of the inner being (the inner subtle subliminal physical, the inner vital and the inner mental) from the inmost psychic being. By entering into the subliminal or identifying oneself with it, the seeker can observe the springs of one's thoughts and feelings, as well as the sources and motives of one's actions. The psychic inmost being replaces the surface desire-soul (ego) with its vital cravings, desires, and happiness into soul images of what is true, right, and beautiful, which can be turned towards the real aim of life, the ascent into the spiritual existence. In the words of Sri Aurobindo, "A time must come for every seeker of complete self-knowledge when he is thus aware of living in two worlds, two consciousnesses at the same time, two parts of the same existence. At present he lives in the outer self, but he will get more and more involved till the position is reversed and he lives within this new consciousness, inner self, and feels the outer as something on the surface formed as an instrumental personality for the inner's self-expression in the material world. Then from within a Power works on the outer to make it a conscious plastic instrument so that finally the inner and the outer become fused into one."[25]

It is known that the movements of the lower human and the inner and higher spiritual nature pull in different ways and that the lower is at first much stronger, but sadhana does not leave the one for the other, nor can the sadhak live a double life. That's why the lower realm needs to be gradually remoulded in the light and joy of the inner and higher nature. For a psychic transformation, the lower nature must experience a change through the process of purification and quietening. It is difficult to change and purify the outer nature as it opposes the psychic movement and clings to its old, accustomed habits. Sri Aurobindo explains the sadhak that, "This long and difficult process needs the total surrender of the self and of all the parts of our nature to the Divine, which may be supplemented by the method of detachment from all mental, vital and physical claims and impulsions, austerity and the rejection of false needs and false habits."[26]

The experience of the soul's complete emergence requires *direct* contact between the surface being and spiritual Reality. To achieve this contact, the soul may use the thinking mind as an instrument and put a psychic impression on the intellect and intuitive intelligence. However, this direct contact of the soul with spiritual reality can also be achieved through the consecration of the heart when the approach is made through the spiritual Reality of love. The nascent spiritual person appears in their emotional nature first as a devotee and may later develop into a saint. A more significant change, however, needs a consecration of the pragmatic will, and its motive power of desire, which is possible by a gradual elimination of the ego-will and its motive power of desire. But even a combination of these three approaches, the mind, the will and the heart, needs a change to arrive at its widest totality and profound completeness, and the consciousness has to shift its centre from the surface to the inner being because the outer nature has to undergo a purification of its substance and energy first by which the obstacles in it are reduced or disappear before it becomes possible to enter, and to pass through to the inner consciousness.

Sri Aurobindo describes some of the obstacles on the journey within as, "even before the tranquilising purification of the outer nature has been effected or before it is sufficient, one can still breakdown the wall screening our inner being from outer awareness by a strong force of call and aspiration, a vehement will or violent effort or an effective discipline or process; but this may be a premature movement and it is not without its serious dangerous. In entering within one may find oneself amidst a chaos of unfamiliar and supernormal experiences to which one has not the key or a press of subliminal or cosmic forces, subconscient, mental, vital, subtle-physical, which may unduly sway or chaotically drive the being, encircle it in a cave of darkness, or keep it wandering in a wilderness of glamour, allurement, deception, or push it into an obscure battlefield full of secret and treacherous and misleading or open and violent oppositions..... If there is too much egoism in the nature of the seeker or strong passion or an excessive ambition, vanity or other dominating weakness, or an obscurity of the mind or a vacillating will or weakness of the life force or an unsteadiness in it or want of balance, he is likely to be seized on through these deficiencies and to be frustrated or to deviate, misled from the true way of the inner life and seeking into false paths.... These perils were well-known to a past spiritual experience and have been met by imposing the necessity of initiation, of discipline, of methods of purification and testing by ordeal, of an entire submission to the directions of the path-finder or path-leader, a guide who is strong to take by the hand and carry over difficult passages as well as to instruct and point out the way. But even so the dangers will be there and can only be surmounted if there is or there grows up a complete sincerity, a will for purity, a readiness for obedience to the Truth, for surrender to the Highest, a readiness to lose or to subject to a divine yoke and the limiting and self-affirming ego.

These things are the sign that the true will for realisation, for conversion of the consciousness, for transformation is there.... the process may never be entirely easy, but the way will have been made open and practicable."[27]

To conclude this rather complicated issue, it may be helpful to explain one of the psychic's limitations related to the action of the psychic being when it comes to the surface. In its action, the psychic being gets mixed up with the surface disabilities that it has to use to express itself, and for this reason, it cannot remain distinct in its purity. The psychic intimation gets jumbled with mental ideas, vital desires, and habitual physical tendencies. Under these conditions, the true psychic light gets diminished in the mind into a mere idea, the psychic feeling in the heart into a mere sentiment and the psychic will to action into a blind vital enthusiasm. It must be clear that it is the *action* of the psychic being, not the psychic being itself, that gets mixed with the mental, vital and physical disabilities because it has to use them to express what little of the true psychic feeling gets through the veil. It is by the heart's aspiration to the Divine that the psychic being gets free from these disabilities. When mixed and misused by the lower parts of the being, which try to turn it to their own use, what will happen when the psychic center is not sufficiently developed, and the sadhak mixes genuine inner love, peace and joy, with outer appearances of these experiences such as blind passion, restless energy or happiness based on desire?

In the words of Sri Aurobindo, "This psychic action does not come up to the surface quite pure and does not remain distinct in its purity;...An occult mental and vital and physical action intervenes, mixes with it, tries to use it and turn it to its own profit, dwarfs its divinity, distorts or diminishes its self-expression, even causes it to deviate and stumble or stains it with the impurity, smallness and error of mind and life and body. After it reaches the surface, thus alloyed and diminished, it is taken hold of by the surface nature in an obscure reception and ignorant formation, and there is or can be by this cause a still further deviation and mixture. A twist is given, a wrong direction is imparted, a wrong application, a wrong formation, an erroneous result of what is in itself pure stuff and action of our spiritual being; a formation of consciousness is accordingly made which is a mixture of the psychic influence and its intimations jumbled with mental ideas and opinions, vital desires and urges, habitual physical tendencies. There coalesce too with the obscured soul-influence the ignorant though the well-intended efforts of these external parts towards a higher direction; a mental ideation of a very mixed character, often obscure even in its idealism, sometimes even disastrously mistaken, fervour and passion of the emotional being throwing up its spray and foam of feelings, sentiments, sentimentalism, a dynamic enthusiasm of the life-parts, eager responses of the physical, the thrills and excitements of nerve and body,-all these influences coalesce in a composite formation which is frequently taken as the soul and its mixed and confused action for the soul-stir, for a psychic development and action or a realised inner influence."[28] Sri Aurobindo continues, "Moreover the psychic being, the soul personality in us does not emerge full-grown and luminous; it evolves, passes through a slow development and formation; its figure of being may be at first indistinct and may afterwards remain for a long time weak and undeveloped, not impure but imperfect, for it rests its formation, its dynamic self-building on the power of soul that has been actually and more or less successfully, against the resistance of the Ignorance and Inconscience, put forth in the evolution upon the surface. Its appearance is the sign of a soul-emergence in Nature, and if that emergence is as yet small and defective, the psychic personality also will be stunted and feeble. It is too, by the obscurity of our consciousness, separated from its inner reality, in imperfect communication with its own source in the depths of the being.... its power to impress what it receives upon the outer instruments is also imperfect; in its penury it has for most things to rely on these instruments and it forms its push to expression and action on their data not solely on the unerring perceptions of the psychic entity. In these conditions it cannot prevent the true psychic light from being diminished or distorted in the mind into a mere idea or opinion, the psychic feeling in the heart into fallible emotion or mere sentiment, the psychic will to action in the life-parts into a blind vital enthusiasm or a fervid excitement:....As the psychic personality grows stronger, it begins to increase its communion with the psychic entity behind it and improve its communication with the surface: .....this evolution would be slow and long if left solely to the difficult automatic action of the evolutionary Energy; it is only when man awakes to the knowledge of the soul and feels a need to bring it to the front and make it the master of his life and action that a quicker conscious method of evolution intervenes and a psychic transformation becomes possible."[29]

By now, the causes of the opposition are clarified, and how negative traits counter the successful sadhana of psychic awakening. Insisting on these negative traits of character needs to be balanced by positive factors which are conducive to the psychic emergence, such as "Purity, simple sincerity and the capacity of an unegoistic, unmixed self-offering without pretension or demand are the condition of an entire opening of the psychic being."[30] The seeker, after the psychic opening, needs to be patient, keep up his aspiration, maintain his faith in the action of Mother's Grace, and go inwards and learn to concentrate on the heart centre rather than relying too much on the efficacy of the sadhak's own personal effort.

## Difficulties in the Process of the Psychic Experiment

In almost all sadhaks, the psychic being is not at all active; in most cases, it is asleep, and only with sadhana and a very persistent effort does one succeed in having conscious contact with one's psychic being. It is only after a long and intense sadhana that the sadhak obtains a total identification with the psychic, i.e., it takes a very long time to attain a complete union with the psychic where the psychic is an entirely formed, liberated being, master of itself, though it is possible that sometimes the psychic being is partially contacted in the sense that the sadhak felt that he was carried or helped or uplifted above himself. The occult psychic experience is not dependent on outer conditions or circumstances, it is not an expression of the vital reaction, and it is free from psychological and egocentric disturbances. During the experience, the unconditioned beingness is detached from the sadhak's dependence on conditioned things. The experience of the psychic being is purely spiritual; there is no sensation of its presence, and when the disciple has to express the inexpressible spiritual contact, then he can only find his symbols in the sensual analogies of everyday life.

## The Pseudo-psychic Experience (the Ego)

Even though the mind may be brilliant, the heart of vital emotions strong, the life force dominant and the bodily existence fortunate, it is then the pseudo-psychic entity (the ego) that reigns, and we mistake its misinterpretation of psychic aspiration, its ideals, its desires for the true soul-stuff of spiritual experience. Who is able to distinguish the direct psychic experience, which is intrinsic to the true being, from the pseudo-psychic experience, which is related to outward influences and circumstances? Could it be that the sadhak confuses or misinterprets suggestions of the surface desire-soul (the ego) for the true psychic being, or confuses the pure psychic influence with his immature mental ideas, vital desires and habitual physical tendencies? Could it end up with an erroneous result of what is in itself a pure action? The perfect love can only be experienced in a heart that is completely free of desires and attachment. The sadhak must purify the vital nature itself and disentangle one's consciousness completely from the ego. If the psychic urge is not entirely pure but accompanied by a vital impure flame, then the vital nature may refuse to support the psychic call.

It needs sufficient knowledge and experience to distinguish the true psychic and the psychic opening to mental, vital, and other worlds, which contain not only true but also false and half-true things, as well as all kinds of thought suggestions, good, bad, and indifferent. Like Sri Aurobindo, the Mother warns that if the movement from the psychic depths of the being "comes to the surface it gets mixed with all sorts of things which have nothing to do with it, but which want to make use of it. As, for instance, *all the desires and passions of the vital, which as soon as a force from the depth rises to the surface, catch hold of it for their own satisfaction. Or else people who live in the mind and want to understand and evaluate their experience, to judge it: then it is the mind that sizes upon this inspiration or this force which rises to the surface, for its own benefit or its own satisfaction-and it becomes mixed, and that spoils everything.* (Italics the author's). And this happens constantly; constantly surface movements creep into the inspiration from the depth and deform it, deforming it to such an extent that it is no longer recognisable."[31] As this happens constantly, the ego is not transcended but strengthened, improved and enlarged. After a first psychic experience, it often happens that all that is egoistic in the vital being soon rises in revolt, creating confused desires, demands, and claims that contradict the psychic attitude. If the Divine is hindered by the ego's claim, it brings about wrong movements, which is a significant obstacle to spiritual change. When the constant demand of the vital is taken for psychic aspiration, then the cry of the vital ends finally in 'satisfy my desires only then I will seek and accept Thee'. In other words, the psychic influence gets mixed up with all sorts of things that have nothing to do with it but want to exploit it. The proportion varies and depends according to the individual, but what happens when the surface movements deform this constantly, i.e., when the sadhak takes egoistic advantage of these psychic influences and tries to capture the psychic power for one's own interest and degrade it into an aggrandised lower instrumentation for desire and ego? What happens to those sadhaks who have no pure heart, who lose their purity again and again and use the psychic experience for selfish motives which confirm their egoism? In the spiritual process, the qualitative ritual becomes a quantified rational practice.

In an interview with "Auroville Today," Doctor Alok Pandey, the psychiatrist from the Sri Aurobindo Ashram, was asked if the possibility of the ego-sense rupturing is larger in places such as Auroville and the Ashram; he said," These places attract all kinds of people. Some come for the higher Truth, but there are a good number who are drawn to Yoga for Power, and that is dangerous... even well-intended people can break down due to the pressure of transformation generated in the process of this Yoga. For the Force at work in this yoga- especially in these places- is of a thorough-going character and uncovers hidden resistances, so that they can be neutralised through offering them to the Divine. But if the Sadhak is not careful or if there is some fundamental defect in nature, such as strong ambition (spiritual) or excess of vanity and lack of humility or an access and perverse force of sexuality, then it may be challenging to keep the balance when these hidden resistances come into the open."[32] But those who have centered their whole being around the conscious control of the psychic, away from the impulses of the lower nature, are able to cure themselves from all kinds of obstacles during the journey. When they become conscious of their psychic being and organise themselves spontaneously, there is no need for fixed rules and laws.

## Aspects which may Function as Disturbing Factors During the Psychic Experiment

### The Subliminal

Besides the obstacles mentioned above, when entering within, before getting in touch with the psychic consciousness, the sadhak finds separate sources of his mental, his vital and his physical subliminal energies, where he can see the pure operations and the composing elements of each, and their interplay in a clear light of self-vision, and where there are no contrary discordant tendencies of mental, vital and physical parts opposing with each other. According to Sri Aurobindo, "we find in this inner or subliminal being the means of directly distinguishing between what rises from within and what comes to us from outside, from others or from universal Nature, and it becomes possible to exercise a control, a choice, a power of willed reception, rejection and selection, a clear power of self-building and harmonisation which we do not possess or can operate very imperfectly in our composed surface personality but which is the prerogative of our inner Person. For by this entry into the depths the inner being, no longer quite veiled, no longer obliged to exercise a fragmentary influence on its outer instrumental consciousness, is able to formulate itself more luminously in our life in the physical universe." But when these inner subliminal experiences come without the emergence of the psychic entity, without the right psychic will then " ....if it is with the vital-ego motive that we make the entry into the subliminal being, it may result in serious dangers and disaster or at the least an exaggeration of ego, self-affirmation and desire, an enlarged and more powerful ignorance instead of an enlarged and more powerful knowledge."[33]

Without the full emergence of the psychic entity, these inner subliminal experiences by a power of direct contact of consciousness might be of a mixed character," for there could be an emergence not only of the subliminal knowledge but of the subliminal ignorance. An insufficient expansion of the being, a limitation by a mental idea, by narrow and selective emotion or by the form of the temperament so that there would be only an imperfect self-creation and action and not the free soul emergence, could easily occur. In the absence of any complete psychic emergence, experiences of certain kinds, experiences of greater knowledge and force, a surpassing of ordinary limits, might lead to a magnified ego and even bring about instead of an out-flowering of what is divine or spiritual an uprush of the titanic or demonic, or might call in agencies and powers which, though not of this disastrous type are of a powerful but inferior cosmic character."[34] It requires the inner power of intuition to judge and interpret rightly the experience between the nature of greater Knowledge and self-affirming ignorance; otherwise, the subliminal becomes subject to the grosser desires of the mind and vital being, despite its wider range of power and capacities. In the words of Sri Aurobindo, " It should be noted however, that owing to this complexity the action of the subliminal sense can be confusing or misleading, especially when it is interpreted by the outer mind to which the secret of its operations is unknown; a greater inner power of intuition, tact, discrimination is needed to judge and interpret rightly its images and experiences."[35]

## Imagination

Is the psychic experience the result of being influenced by imaginary or special speculative aspects, and do they play an important role in the psychic experience? Are the sadhaks' convictions creations of their imaginations rather than an opening to the psychic experience itself? No doubt, imagination is a power of formation. It is a very powerful means of action and opens for the sadhak the path of realisation. However, imagination is somewhat complex and manifold; the Mother distinguishes two kinds of imagination, which she calls the 'mental' and 'higher' imagination. According to the Mother, "There are artistic, literary, poetic domains, domains of action, scientific domains, all belonging to the mind- not a very high and abstract mind, a mind above the physical mind which, without our knowing it, pours out constantly through the individual and collective mind to manifest in action. ...This power of expression is different in different people, but those who can open themselves to these domains....... are, according to the degree of their power of expression either very highly talented beings or else geniuses. There are higher geniuses still. Some people can open to a higher region, a higher force which, passing through the mental layers, comes and takes a form in a human mind and reveals itself in the world as new truths, new philosophical systems, new spiritual teachings, which are the works and at the same time the actions of the great beings who come to take birth on earth. That is an imagination which can be called 'Truth-imagination.' "[36]

However, mental imagination is an instrument of ignorance; it erects possibilities which it hopes or wishes it could actualise, though more optimistically, it may enhance the chance of realising one's own aim. When used at the service of the Divine, it can be formative and creative, but indulgence in mental imagination often undermines one's own future. For Sri Aurobindo, "imagination is the refuge of a limited capacity of knowledge, and it erects possibilities which it hopes and wishes it could actualise. Wandering imaginations in the mind, as a force of propulsion may be responsible for action, but this has absolutely nothing to do with the true consciousness of the psychic being."[37] When the disciple is unable to distinguish between what is true and what comes to him from the vital in his desire for spiritual progress, he may start imagining things. When the experience comes in a flash and then withdraws, the memory remains, and one is bound to imitate that experience. Are the practitioners' convictions creations of their imagination rather than an opening to psychic experience itself? Believes, caused by habits, the weight of authority or imitation, such subjective constructs, when used as spiritual fictions or free creations, are not data of observed reality but may be used as a play of unrestricted imagination for the sake of subjective convenience. When imagination is used at the service of the Divine, it can be formative and creative, but with indulgence in anticipating expectations, sadhaks may deceive themselves. Are the described effects of the psychic experience more related to the faith in the experience and not in the experience itself?

## Expectation

What is the role of expectations? The contribution of the psychic being's experience to sadhana is related to unconditional spiritual love, the purification of the surface consciousness, and unerring guidance from within. It opens and purifies the whole lower nature, encouraging not only the liberation of the surface consciousness but also the beginning of the complete transformation, which becomes possible. This needs perseverance, sincerity, and, above all, the guidance of Her Grace. Could it be that the expected effects are not genuine due to the faith the sadhak has regarding the expectation and not due to the experience itself? Noble ideals should be grounded in the present reality, where a gap exists between the near-perfect psychic experience and the imperfection of man's own world. This gap could create specific expectations of what the true spiritual life should or should not look like. A mental investigation may create rigidity, and in its attempt to control, the ego may create more separation.

## Autosuggestion

Those practitioners of Integral Yoga who believe they have attained a stage of contact with the psychic being or who are under its influence, is it possible that they are not infrequently experiencing the effects of autosuggestion or the repetition of the Mother's verbal messages which have been moved to the subconscious? Autosuggestion is a cognitive process that is believed to enable control over one's own cognitive and physiological states. It is a form of self-induced suggestion in which the individual guides his own thoughts, feelings or behaviour. As a self-development method, it can be used to cultivate new, positive beliefs about oneself, as well as an effective approach to breaking bad habits. Autosuggestion works by placing one's ideas into the subconscious and making them believe they are true. This is achieved by repeating Mother's words with feelings, again and again, to change the sadhak's perception on a subconscious level. The autosuggestion should be in line with one's goal, and the sadhak should convince himself that Mother's chosen words are believable to him. The more meaningful the autosuggestion is to the sadhak, accompanied by positive thinking, the more effective it is. One's own created autosuggestion needs practice and patience, whereas the sadhak suggests a positive statement as if wanting to convince himself of it. When unconscious narcissistic needs capture the psychic experience, the guidance may be used as a cover-up for the opening of unconscious needs. Misinterpreting the psychic centre's guidance may limit the ability to discern psychic discrimination from the vital desires dictated by one's outer nature.

## Placebo Effect

Autosuggestion as a psychological technique is related to the placebo effect. Could there be a placebo effect in the psychic experiment? Could similar effective positive results of the inner illumination also be attained when the sadhak is carried away in his self-deception and his desire for this experience, with an attitude," if he believes it works, then it works." Whatever the sadhak imagines, believing his ideas may be a result of his incorrect self-knowledge. He may have had a psychic experience in a flash, and then it withdrew, but the memory remains, and later, he imitates that experience.

## Spiritual Bypassing

Setting out on a spiritual path does not clear up all psychological problems; the sadhak may misuse the spiritual impulse in order to avoid dealing with hidden unconscious defensive patterns or other psychological problems. The sadhak may commit himself to a dogmatic clinging to a spiritual path for defensive purposes to evade sincere, specific inner exploration. They use their stage of inner/inmost being as an excuse to dismiss their valid emotional and rational challenges in themselves and others, or the defence by which the ego protects itself from forbidden impulses, thoughts or feelings, which may hinder authentic personal growth. When entering denial, they refuse to acknowledge everything they see in their nature and avoid confronting the real problem, instead offering a spiritual explanation for what is happening, which obscures the issue. When people unquestioningly trust the words of the Mother without being backed up by direct experience, they may easily regress into religiosity or shift their responsibility for a spiritual future to an established divine force, thereby limiting their own ability to participate in the sacred work of the divine reality. This is expressed by one of Auroville's citizens when the sadhaks are building Auroville as a city, "I don't think it is about finishing the city first, and then the Mother will do what she has to do, which for me is a rather unusual form of collective 'spiritual bypassing'. My interpretation of what Mother said is that it is about developing ourselves and our understanding of this place through the process of building it. The Galaxy (the City Plan) as a destination is an ideal goal, as the Mother foresaw, but the work is in getting there."[38] Those who claim to be in touch with their psychic being may view themselves as higher "evolved," which can alienate them from others and foster an inflated sense of self-worth. In Mother's words, "Because the pitfalls are innumerable and the further you progress in yoga, the more subtle they become, and the more the ego masks itself behind marvellous and saintly appearances. So when somebody says, 'I no longer want to rely on anything but 'Him' is exactly what you want him to be, is the ego.... So, the first thing to do is to pocket your ego-not preserve it, but get rid of it as soon as possible! You can be sure that the God you have created is the God of the ego whenever something in you insists. This is what I feel."[39] The sadhak refuses to look at certain aspects of his own nature, often projecting it to others and offers alternatively a spiritual explanation of what's going on, which veils the real issue.

## Groupthink

Last but not least, could the process of the psychic experience or its realisation be influenced by groupthink, a phenomenon in which the ways of approaching matters and decisions are dealt with by consensus of the group rather than by individuals acting independently? The group members unquestioningly follow the leader's direction, who is unable to remain impartial, and the group fails to listen to those with differing opinions and opposing viewpoints, thereby ignoring important information. Due to a lack of preparation to deal with adverse outcomes, there is a tendency for background challenges to be met with disapproval, which may lead to negative publicity and hinder the project. Shared beliefs and communal reinforcement may lead to the possibility of a self-fulfilling prophecy when expecting certain experiences to be confirmed by other members of the community. As such, these confirmed experiences may lead to groupthink based on confirmation bias. When describing their psychic experience, while disclosing their inner life, they often use in-group jargon. Alternatively, their true understanding of a psychic experience may be coloured by spiritual dogmatism, rather than being an occult event that results in a new perspective on the world, enabling them to experience the Truth.

## Critical Evaluation

The author feels compelled to ask some hard questions about Mother's most essential and often least understood explanations, messages and talks about the development of the psychic being and its function while building Auroville as the city of the future. These questions about what kind of city Aurovilians are building should not be left only to Aurovilians and Mother's disciples, as each of us has a role to play in shaping the future, and we all have a stake in these questions. During the process of psychic transformation, all kinds of outer and inner resistances are awakened, which leads to a battle of opposites. The new approach to spiritual life is often opposed by an endless stream of intellectual questions related to held judgments and values. However, a reversal of attitude may cause the devotee to refuse any interference from the rationalising mind's interpretations, allowing irrational forces to silence any opposition and relapse into blind devotion. It seems both approaches need to be synthesised as one without the other often leads to imbalance.

The Mother, as a guiding power of Spirit, endeavours to awaken the inner potentialities of her disciples and prepare them for a new man and a new world to be born. With her methods, practices and guidance to awaken and nourish the psychic consciousness, she tunes our outer instrument directly or indirectly towards the transmission of the Divine flame. At the beginning of the practice, direct or indirect personal contact is of crucial importance and an indispensable stage on the path. The attempt to mould oneself according to the true likeness of Mother's image may be used to establish a first stepping stone to reach one's goal, causing some initial change. It is for this reason that the devotee often adheres to the image of the Mother and may refer complicated decisions to her. In this initial stage, the sadhaks are encouraged to look more inward and explore their inner depths in order to correct their outgoing attitudes. This inward-looking movement should not be mistaken for an end in itself. Once access is gained to the interior realms, these experiences need to be integrated into the predominantly outward-facing everyday life. Only when the presence of Mother's guidance has become an inner experience does the identification of the devotee with Mother's Force happen on an altogether different plane of existence; otherwise, the devotee lacks the establishment of the relationship which links the inner and higher to the lower parts of one's instrumentation. Suppose this phase of imitation remains on the surface layers and does not penetrate the devotee's inner layers. In that case, the devotee lacks the awakening of an inner living adhesion where the outer instrument is reluctant to undergo further radical change, which restricts spiritual growth. *Continuous dependence on her indicates that her external presence is not sufficiently interiorised, and that the inner adhesion is still not strong enough to receive the direct psychic influence. Once the inner growth develops, it tends to establish immediate and direct contact with the intimate exchange of the psychic consciousness within, independent of the external Guru. This becomes a precondition for a direct transformation of the seeker's inner spiritual guidance.*

So it can be said that the inner presence of the Mother as a human Guru functions as a gateway to the experience of the psychic presence and guidance within us. Once this stage has been reached, exclusive dependence on Mother's presence as a Guru becomes of secondary importance. Is the devotee using Mother's guiding principles as a means for inner intimations, as an inner exploration for further spiritual growth based on practice or is the devotee using her guidance as an end in itself, remaining attached to his outward search and habitual mental reactions, worshipping her as an enlightened being who is teaching us an ideal and promising us an instant means of salvation. On the one hand, there is the development of the inner wellspring of the psychic being, which requires a personal relationship with a genuine Guru to accomplish such a profound undertaking, as there are no shortcuts to reading her books, though this might offer valuable insights and inspiration. It often takes a long time of preparation, practice, dedication and devotion, done with humility and sincerity, though exceptional cases do happen spontaneously. On the other hand, concentrating only on the inner centre all the time and ignoring the difference between the ultimate and the relative may lead to rigid and obsessive patterns. The Mother did not offer the sadhak surviving or conclusive answers, as if the devotee only needs to submit himself without exploring his own progress.

The secret power of the psychic being brings occult mastery over the physical, vital, and neutral parts of the being, and to systematise this occult knowledge and power safely can only be done by a difficult and careful discipline, training, and purification. Without these means, their psychic power would be dangerous to themselves and others. It is something that is hidden in secrecy, and when it manifests itself, not all are able to enter into its secret inner meaning; it needs an occult and spiritual knowledge to know the effects of the latent psychic significance upon the individual's changed character and his actions. Disciples may be bold in their speculation and ingenious in their flight of fancy according to their own light, but this whole process is not always an easy and peaceful march. The traveller on the journey needs to be a tireless toiler who is often encircled by the reigning powers of ignorance, weaknesses and other limitations, which, in their concrete, pragmatic form, need to be expelled and overpowered by inner practice, self-reflection and surrender to Mother's guidance.

According to Sri Aurobindo, "Access to the soul, the psychic being, is less easy because it is covered up with a thick veil of ego, passion and desire. One is apt to be swallowed up in a maze of vital experiences that are not always reliable, the temptation of small siddhis [ yogic powers through sadhana], and the appeal of the powers of darkness to the ego. One has to struggle through these densities to the psychic, being behind and bringing it forward; only then can the sadhana on the vital plane be safe. However, that may be the descent of the sadhana, of the action of the Force into the vital plane of our being, which becomes necessary after some time. The Force does not make a wholesale change of the mental being and nature, still less an integral transformation before it takes this step: if that could be done, the rest of the sadhana would be comparatively secure and easy. But the vital is there and always pressing on the mind and the heart, disturbing and endangering the sadhana, it cannot be left to itself for too long. The ego and the desires of the vital, its disturbances and upheavals have to be dealt with and if not at once dispelled, at least dominated and prepared for a gradual if not rapid modification, change illumination."[40]

A complete union with the Divine is the result of a perfect perfection in all mastery by relentless elimination of the obstacles caused by ignorant desires and attachments. It is usually only the purified parts of the being that surrender to the Divine, whereas the other parts remain influenced by their customary habits and moved by ignorant forces. In due time unsurrendered parts use the progress of the purified parts for their own self-aggrandisement where the idea of self-surrender justifies all one's actions i.e., if the mind is under the influence of the psychic consciousness, but when the influence of the inner light is impervious to the emotional ardours then the total change will take a long time or may not come at all in the present life.

Jugal Kishore Mukherjee, a long-time and close disciple of the Mother, describes the path of spiritual sadhana about the psychic awakening as, "The path of spiritual sadhana has been compared to a razor's edge, *ksurasya dhara*, it is very difficult to tread. At every turn of the way, there is the possibility of an ambush; at every moment of the journey, there arises the dilemma of how to choose the right course of action. ...How is the seeker going to contend with this ceaseless battle of the path and come out successfully of all the deceitful traps and dangerous pits? ... What should the sadhaka do then? If the Guru is present in his physical body, the problem may not arise; but if not? Who will guide the sadhaka then? Here comes the great role played by our psychic being, the luminous representative of the Divine, dwelling in the depths of the heart of every man and sending up its infallible warnings and indications from there. But the difficulty is that this psychic being remains mostly hidden behind the thick veils of the sadhaka's ignorance and is practically inoperative in moulding the daily affairs of the sadhaka's life. But this situation has to be remedied, the psychic being brought to the front and made the constant guide of the sadhaka in all the crises of his sadhana-life."[41] On the slippery path during the journey Sri Aurobindo and the Mother paid over and over again attention to the insidious and seductive forms of the psychic experiment, where the practitioner could use the first results of going inside for one's own advantage, i.e,. inflating rather than transcending the ego. To sincerely aspire for the soul's intervention, the practitioner has to be vigilant that the force to which he opened is the real divine force and not the disguised movement of the lower instrumentation of the ordinary nature.

Could the practice of Integral Yoga to transcend the ego appeal to those disciples who are preoccupied with the investment of their own selfish complacency, whereby they affirm their own egoism, a form of fake egocentric spirituality? A paradox arises where modern Western health culture, which focuses on individual well-being and stress reduction, has little in common with Mother's transformative psychic experience. Next to those who benefit from his psychic experience and who become less egocentric on the journey of the psychic experiment, could it be that others, while descending into the inner realm of being and practising in an exaggerated form with all its pitfalls and competition, become more egocentric when too much focused on personal growth and productivity without a fundamental change in one's dysfunctional character traits? Evoking the Mother in such cases could be contentious when used as an instrument to legitimise personal gains. To overcome this paradox, the sadhak needs proper preparation and guidance with some self-reflection and a skilful attitude where the disciple critically analyses and investigates the effects of the psychic experience and places them in a proper context. This is typically not done in popular workshops, lifestyle blocks, or one-day courses that offer instant psychic gratification in the pursuit of becoming a better person.

Within the inner psychic experience, which requires methodical practice and scrupulous honesty, it is necessary to distinguish between infantile peak experiences and New Age fantasy as spiritual imaginings and the expression of a spiritual reality, such as a power of discernment that can be attained through contemplative practice and verified by experience. Mother's consciousness does not only stand for an individualistic inmost realisation alone, but also for a transformation of one's nature, and which disciples in Auroville feel the need for such a transformation?

In the last part of her life, the Mother received ten-page letters from early Aurovilians "telling her their spiritual experiences-which are completely in the vital. They don't understand a thing. Even in Auroville, they are like that; they don't understand."[42] According to the Mother, "people always think that when they have emotions, feelings, they are entering the psychic. These have nothing to do with the psychic, they are purely vital."[43] "Don't mix up the psychic being with the outer being. The psychic being may be perfect, and the outer being may be idiotic. Don't confuse these two."[44] According to Sri Aurobindo, "there is the true psychic which is always good and there is the psychic opening to the mental, vital and other worlds which contain all kinds of things good, bad and indifferent, true, false and half true, thought-suggestions which are of all kinds. What is needed is not to give yourself impartially to all of them but to develop both a sufficient knowledge and experience and a sufficient discrimination to be able to keep your balance and eliminate falsehood, half-truths and mixtures."[45] One needs to be sincere and only a perfect humility is the condition for all realisations. The Mother is "not speaking of humility as conceived by certain religions, with this God that belittles his creatures... but rather the recognition that one does not know, that one knows nothing... True humility consists in constantly referring oneself to the Lord, in placing before Him. I receive a blow (and there are quite a few of them in my sadhana) my immediate spontaneous reaction, like a spring, is to throw myself before Him."[46]

The psychic being manifests itself rarely spontaneously and mainly through conscious spiritual discipline, and always through successive reincarnations. "The spiritual intrinsic nature of the psychic being always aspires for the good, the true and the beautiful, where there is a constant light of inner guidance and attraction towards higher spiritual values. The deeper, true inner psychic guidance is not misled by outer appearances but is a true guide drawn towards the psychic light of Truth. This guidance opposes everything which is opposed to the divide realisation."[47] Once there is an opening of the sadhak's psychic being towards his psychic center, this psychic center becomes the guiding force and influence in the sadhak's changed life, i.e., an integrating center around which the sadhak organises his life. In Mother's correspondence and talks with her disciples, she endeavoured to awaken the disciples' lethargy regarding the transformation of their imperfect instrument. She considered the Auroville citizens to be instruments for spiritual change, and as a Guru, she offered invisible guidance to all those who opened themselves to her inner divine Force.

The psychic experience does not correspond to the emotions that arise from the lower vital movement; it comes from something that is clearly psychic, full of self-giving and compassion. It is altogether a different kind of emotion, with an extraordinary power, expressing itself in its initial purity. However, it is not like the sadhak who constantly carries within a happy landscape with some idealised mystical images or nostalgic ecstatic moments where he retreats into his dreamland as an escape from reality. This has nothing to do with the intrinsically transcendental experience. In the direct experience of the psychic being, the recipient completely disappears in the experience of total absorption without any interference from outside; however, when explained afterwards in a mere psychological context, this psychic experience needs to be distinguished from the reflective description of the experience, as the psychic experience itself often becomes threatened of being maimed or converted into a dogma. The spiritual quality of the psychic experience itself is not determined by the experience per se, but also by the integral dynamics of the experiencer and the context in which the experience occurs. Although the experience is unimpeachable, its interpretations may be questioned and require critical evaluation and experiential validation. Perhaps the attention should be more focused on the experience itself, rather than the effects related to it. The subjective psychic experience is a state of changed consciousness, but does this mean that this experience is irrational and, therefore, not qualified as a subject for scientific research? Perhaps the psychic experience needs to be studied directly and from within, rather than through the limitations imposed by Mother's written literature. Is the psychic experience only the result of Mother's spontaneous Grace, or can it also be brought about through discipline and Yoga training, independent of religious context or detached from metaphysical doctrines?

It may need a reflective dialogue about the object of the experience, the result of the experience, and the state or condition of the experiencer. Such a study will not offer us a new theory, but will open the way to new channels for the formation of an existing theory and establish a field of research, incorporating some rational methods. Though its experimental data relates to a subjective spiritual force, its specific investigation lacks a testable hypothesis and objective, perceptible, data-driven validation, and remains, therefore, vague. The biased attitude of the disciples is often an obstacle to including a rational investigation in this subjective experience, and while remaining lost in narratives, they overlook the influence of the sadhak's psycho-spiritual behaviour and attitudes. The experience of the psychic being may need some empirical evidence to support sweeping generalisations and a flexibility that encourages the sadhak to revise his views in accord with the evidence of the successful achievements of the community's ideals. In losing his old identity, the disciple is reborn as something different from what he was before.

The Mother has cautioned and advised her spiritual aspirants not to give up morality before attaining the consciousness which is higher than morality. She certainly has respect for sincere social service, but she does not give it the highest status; at the very top, there is union with the Divine. Social service without yogic illumination wages a fight full of subtle, egoistic perversions, and a struggle radiantly guided by the Divine Forces, free from the insidious ego. Without the Divine consciousness, there will always be individual and social suffering, no matter how much we offer social service and philanthropy, because we avoid the manner and form that may harm those whom we serve. The Mother did not ignore or reject pragmatic values that were useful for the prosperity of material life; instead, she integrated them into the actualisation of higher moral, aesthetic, or spiritual values. The higher values should inspire and guide the pragmatic values, casting their refining influence on individuals and collective life. However, exclusively pursuing higher values at the expense of pragmatic ones will not lead to the well-being of the individual or the community.

Once the psychic being is more fully awakened, it becomes influenced by the Divine consciousness, and the psychic being then becomes a living bridge between the Divine and the sadhak's outer nature, serving as a perfect channel for divine manifestation—the inevitable destiny of humanity on earth. This psychic consciousness inflames the sadhak with love for the Divine, where there is no need for moral precepts or humanitarian activities. These beneficial humanitarian activities are helpful for humanity, but they cannot be a substitute for the activities of the psychic, which are guided by the Will and Knowledge of the Divine. Although ethical beliefs and practices, however noble, are merely partial truths when taken as essential and universal, and although built upon a positive foundation for the Mother, they are egoistic hindrances to the Divine plan. Nevertheless, until sufficient sadhaks realise a deeper level of the Divine consciousness, the ethical approach should be treated as a stage in the evolution. Sri Aurobindo, however, gives the ethical practice a purifying function without mentioning the role of the psychic being, as written by him, "And that indeed is the true inmost aim and meaning of ethics, discipline and askesis, to lesson and tame, purify and prepare to be fit instruments of the vital and physical and lower mental life so that they may be transformed into notes of the higher mental and eventually the supramental harmony, but not to mutilate and destroy them."[48] However, elsewhere Sri Aurobindo writes. "This voice of the soul is not what we call conscience- for that is only a mental and often conventional erring substitute; it is a deeper and more seldom heard call; yet to follow it when heard is wisest; even, it is better to wander at the core of one's soul than to go apparently straight with the reason and the outward moral mentor."[49]

In the Mother's vision, divination of the psychic experience makes it a surer guide than reason or even the highest desire, and the voice of the psychic being leads better than the precise intellect and the considering mental judgement. Does this obscure the context of global, moral and social development as the psychic experience is not dependent on outer conditions? Does an overreliance on the psychic being evolve into passivity when the realisation of the psychic being becomes more important than human ethical considerations? The Mother is aware of this dilemma when she says, "Usually those who become conscious of their psychic being expect that it will liberate them from vital and physical attractions and activities; they seek to escape from the world in order to live in the joy and contemplation of the Divine, and in the immutable peace and constant contact with Him. The attitude of those who want to practice Sri Aurobindo's integral yoga is quite different. "[50]

To be a true Aurovilian, the first necessity is the inner discovery in order to know what one truly is behind social, moral, cultural, racial, and hereditary appearances. One lives in Auroville in order to be free from moral and social conventions, but this freedom must not be a new slavery to the ego or its desires and ambitions. Those who are in close contact with the psychic being have the capacity to face difficulties with sufficient inner knowledge, calm, and peace, and they are not troubled. However, when living in the psychic consciousness internally and remaining content with the inner quietude, could this leave the lower external nature unchanged, justifying it by assuming the psychic consciousness is behind it, i.e., as a source of passivity or a blind acquiescence, where the human agency is nullified, "whatever is, is right" attitude? Treating all nature as a sacred whole may turn out empirically false, as this faith in the divine powers may serve as an excuse not to care adequately for analysing disturbing human causes precisely because they are considered to be recovered by the divine's miraculous Powers. Too much emphasis on the inner guidance of the psychic influence may stimulate the sadhak to avoid social disturbances, offering them to the Divine within, thereby escaping the individual's responsibility; this passive "dropping out" may appear fatalistic as it escapes underlying causes. An overemphasis on the psychic experience could lead to the devaluation of the ordinary human experience, potentially causing negligence in the more mundane aspects of life, such as community work, relationships, and other essential elements of human well-being.

What about the obedience of universal social behaviour as determined by international laws and institutions and global standards of justice? Are disciples ignoring the many strengths of these issues and avoiding accountability and responsibility for bypassing secular, international, and universally accepted social norms, laws, and justice? In their psychic level of awareness, they might claim a superior morality over those citizens with a lower level of awareness. Decisions made for the good of all by those who claim to be in contact with their psychic being, assuming what is best for the community through their psychic vision, could lead to paternalistic politics that limit individual freedom and create an oppressive system. Are those sadhaks who claim to be in contact with their psychic being beyond moral or ethical scrutiny? This may lead to spiritual bypassing, where the experiencer ignores his unresolved psychological issues or fails to take responsibility for his own actions because he assumes that he operates from his inmost level of the psychic. Such controversial consequences may lead to alleged abuse of power and exploitation of other community members.

The quest for power may overrule the pursuit of justice. Aurovilians become cruel when, in their self-delusion, they persuade others that they are correct, and the opposition is rooted in ignorance and evil and needs to be silenced and destroyed.

Aurovilians who claim to be in contact with their psychic being would join with others to create an environment in the Township of Auroville that would further their own evolution and prepare the earth's consciousness to move to a higher level of consciousness. But what happens if the spontaneous fusing of the psychic experience fails to materialise to transcend social divisions, when the sadhak is more concerned with the strengthening of his consciousness, rather than assimilating it into the collective consciousness, as the psychic experience does not deal with the source of social conflicts itself even though that source creates an unhealthy life and ignorance. What are the implications of such an image of humanity, where the individual requires long-term experimentation on all levels of their life through spiritual introspection? How will this contribute something useful to the general communal insights? Does it need primarily the power of empathy, brotherhood, engagement in the spirit of fruitful dialogue and ethics of care, where this spirit of universalism unites science, ethics and spirituality, rather than exclusively being involved with the realisation of the psychic experience? Maybe mental analysis and scrutiny offer some insight into these sickening social causes which need to be tackled first, even though these concepts are related to the mere mental level, are relative, not divine and do not transform human nature? To critically look at oneself and one's environment, become conscious of the difficulties without identifying the difficulties as part of one's real spiritual nature and offer them to the Divine, is this mere symptom control while the wound in and outside festers on?

The Mother does not want the sadhak to escape from the activities in the world in order to live in the joy of the Divine. Nevertheless, the moral development of the individual as well as of the community, though a transitory stage, is an indispensable preparation for an ideal social order. The Mother maintains, therefore, that at the human level, the standard of conduct may be temporary yet necessary for its time; the sadhaks who enter the yoga need the human approach at the beginning and long after. In the *initial* stages of sadhana, the development of brotherhood and loyalty supports the seeker's growth process, but ultimately, these qualities have to be transcended as only a spiritual transformation of human nature alone is able to achieve deeper equality, freedom and brotherhood, which is not based on vital needs, ego impulses or reason. Sri Aurobindo says, "In any case, human affection, whatever its value, has its place because through it, the psychic being gets the emotional experiences it needs until it is ready to prefer the true to the apparent, the perfect to the imperfect, the divine to the human."[51] He is aware that there is no shortcut to pass from the mental being to the true spiritual life without having realised the ideal of moral perfection for a certain period.

In their devotion to the temptations of aggrandised power, it may be hard for the spokesmen of the psychic consciousness to resist some of their natural impervious selfishness and their charismatic self-confidence when they fail to transcend their past and remain committed to the limits of their outer parts of the being. These dreamers, with their messianic purposefulness, when put at the utopian centre of Auroville's organisation, may be misled by the deceit of their own heart toward the fulfilment of their own human wishes and momentary trips with little regard for the needs of the community. This upsets and undermines the existing social order, consoling the oppressed with the prospect of milk and honey in a divine paradise, thereby diverting them from the struggle against injustice in the present.

Morality is not essentially an individual inner aspect of self-development, but also adherence to mutually agreed-upon social and legal norms. There is undoubtedly a focus on personal responsibility. Still, those in power can misuse and take advantage of this power when the privileged benefit from a system at the expense of those who are not. It is for this reason that the community needs to establish rules and laws to ensure that those who claim to be in contact with their psychic being care for correcting injustices that other Aurovilians experience every day, even if this care is not in tune with their own virtues. The relative term of practical moral life depends on social relations, and replacing such an attitude with an awakened inner perception of human psychic consciousness does not answer the question related to social injustice. Does it exclude profound experiences of solidarity with others for a common goal? Taking collective care, in which we are responsible for building justice between generations, could be a valuable contribution to post-modernity. To transcend polarisation, how to deal with condemnation of social injustice, human rights violations, violations of international law, or other social issues may be questioned. The emphasis on the transcendence of polarities may lead to a perceived neutrality when these issues are not condemned. However, these controversial issues may need immediate universal concern and organised engagement in urgent calls for justice and action. This serves as a convenient justification for those who benefit from maintaining an unjust status quo. Some situations require immediate moral action for a necessary change. The Mother is not so much concerned with immediate calls for social justice or any other social structural changes, she focuses more on the evolutionary development and transformation of the psychic being first, and there is no consensus on addressing the practical global concerns, such as systematic inequalities and abuse of power, even if these issues may be contrary to the laws of the psychic being.

What happens if the psychic law surpasses the secular law in case the devotee in power defines the Divine law and justifies or ignores his immoral behaviour, regardless of how explorative it might be? According to the Mother, "The soul itself being a portion of the Divine, is above all moral and ethical notion; it bathes in the Divine Light and manifests it, but it can truly govern the whole being only when the ego has been dissolved."[52] The action and influence of the psychic being in the sadhak's life attain their total fulfilment only if they unite with the supramental consciousness. The psychic transformation only makes the descent of the higher spiritual transformation possible and safe for the opening of the supramental transformation. The psychic being, in its intrinsic nature, does not depend on the outer circumstances or stimulations, but can this inner guidance be trusted entirely because its source is a self-existent power within the sadhak? The psychic being comes from the Divine Truth and, as such, functions as an unerring source of the psychic's guidance and wisdom, but is this radiant center of wisdom the sadhak's infallible source of guidance? The psychic experience is not in a position to make a definite truth claim, and although different from the mental and moral guidance determined by all kinds of outer forces, it is still not infallible, as the psychic guidance needs the supramental descent first before it can make any Truth claim. The psychic being, in Mother's view, is a sure judge, and it has to work under the shadow of ignorance with the imperfect human instrument until the supramentalisation of the ordinary consciousness. Hence, the 'sure judge' is not that infallible. Absolute certainty and infallibility can only come with the descent of the Supramental.

The psychic being, as a spark or representative of the Divine consciousness in man, is 'behind' the other gradations of existence and uses them for its growth. The psychic experience is an ecstatic, transcendental experience with direct contact or reflection with the Divine. Discussing the psychic experience is like trying to capture it and limit it. As soon as it tries to express itself in words, it becomes mentalised. A sophisticated discussion about the nature of the psychic experience has little use for those with a more practical outlook on life who use reason as a guard against the pitfalls of this experience. Many irrational emotions can parade under the guise of this psychic experience. Sri Aurobindo advised his disciples that it is desirable to discuss their spiritual experiences only with sadhaks from the Ashram, "it is not desirable to discuss them and publish to outsiders or the general public."

There remains a distinction between earthly reality, the realm of exaggerations and imagination, and spiritual insight. Factual accuracy may often be less important than the pursuit of spiritual truth. Sadhak's own interpretation of his psychic experience as a mystical concept may not necessarily be correct for the ordinary mind. It may lead the sadak towards anti-rationalism, away from critical reflection. If sadhaks involve themselves in these spiritual experiences without the availability of direct perceptible data and any evidence for such intuitive experience, they must include incalculable limitations. The psychic being is not an experience of the pleasure of emotions and sensations; it is an experience of delight that is independent of objects. Actually, the psychic experience is almost incommunicable; its range of expression is so vast, and there are so many accounts of it that it becomes difficult to locate the boundaries between the spurious forms and genuine occurrences. To have a psychic experience, could there be a possibility that during and after the experience, the sadhak is deceived in the description of the plethora of accounts? Moreover, are the disciples, in their interpretation of the psychic experience, trained to question interior revelations of truth, as the psychic encounter is a subjective inner personal experience and may be subject to error or its interpretation guided by speculation? The description of the effects of the psychic experience and the sadhak's interpretation is often interpreted in terms of concepts with which one is familiar, and these confirm their pre-existing ideology and beliefs. Mental constructions afterwards, when considered as true, are often used as a rational examination and understanding of the sacredness of the psychic experience. In Sri Aurobindo's opinion, "in the psychical and other middle domains there is a very large room for the possibility of misleading and often captivating error, and here even a certain amount of positive scepticism has its use... in the integral Yoga psychical experience, especially of the kind associated with what is often called occultism and savours of the miraculous, should be all together subordinated to the spiritual truth and wait upon that for its own interpretation, illumination and sanction. But even in the purely spiritual domain, there are experiences which are partial and, however attractive, only receive their full validity, significance and right application when we can advance to a fuller experience".[53] Moreover, the experience of the psychic being may also be the result of, or be influenced by assumptions or auto-suggestive, imaginary or speculative aspects. Do they play an essential role in the psychic experience?

As a transcendental experience, descriptions even in mystical metaphysical language can be given, but does this mean that any of these descriptions can be deciphered, and do they make sense of the original experience itself? Overreliance on the sadhak's subjective interpretation and possible misjudgment may lead to reinforcing the disciple's own blind spots. When the inner force enters an impure instrument, it becomes a force of greed, doubt, fear, or whatever. The sadhak who has a psychic experience and claims this experience as real, does it follow that the content of such an experience must be real in itself? How can the content of this typically experienced phenomenon of Divine Consciousness be articulated when the infinite experience is limited to a particular context and becomes finite? It is one thing to describe some of the effects of the psychic experience, but it is something entirely different when this experience is degraded by or combined with the so-called New Age spiritualism, producing a kind of postmodern hedonistic spiritualism. Is the psychic experience merely based on faith or belief in Mother's teachings, or is it more rooted in direct experience, a potential inner stage of humanity's evolutionary journey? Simplification of complex concepts without the deep metaphysical framework found in Sri Aurobindo's and Mother's vision, when removing from these experiences the spiritual context, it loses much of its meaning. When decontextualised and oversimplified, the psychic experience overlooks more specific and challenging elements, thereby focusing too much on personal growth and individualism, with a lack of engagement in the full richness of Mother's vision.

Not many disciples discuss the potential pitfalls and the possible harmful side effects of the psychic experience, instead focusing primarily on the positive effects without challenging various claims. Ego dissolution and self-transcendence may cause all sorts of psychological disturbances, and this is more likely to occur in spiritual practitioners who do not have a sufficient background in Mother's spiritual teachings and lack a theoretical and practical framework. Transcending the self may cause unintended and disruptive side effects; often, the ego's dissolution of its adaptive function and the deconstruction of the self as a social construct may not lead to the desirable outcome. The psychic experiment is experientially accessible, but this experience is not a simple access route to an unambiguous reality; on the contrary, the psychic experience is highly ambiguous and dependent on background assumptions underlying the claims of Mother's spiritual yogic insights and is also influenced by her explanation about the effects of the psychic experience. According to the Mother, "It is a long and minute work which must be undertaken with an increasing sincerity, ever more scrupulous and integral. The easy paths generally lead nowhere."[54]

There have been a few Aurovilians who attempted to organise a group of Aurovilians, some of whom claimed to have had contact with or been under the influence of a psychic being or felt its presence. One investigator selected sixty persons with a psychic sweetness with whom he had discussions, but not in an organised interview. Unfortunately, in his research paper, the survey lacks a methodological approach and analysis; in the context of the present work, it appears more like a superficial form of New Age reductionism. Recently, a small group of Aurovilians, known as the 'Inner Being Team', invited fellow Aurovilians to share their experiential journey of exploring contact with or feeling the presence of their inner being. More than fifty Aurovilians responded and spoke as honestly as possible from their hearts about their experiences, while they were asked to avoid quoting Mother and refrain from giving lectures. The interviews about their experiences seeking their inner being can be viewed on the YouTube channel. Although the interviews are more personal than the previous investigations, this author finds them to be a mostly loose, often confused variation of descriptions of the psychic experience. The team members aim to demystify the psychic experience and share with the community that it is not something out of reach, but rather an experience that can be had at any moment of the day. They "hope through this project to normalise discussion about this topic in all areas of the community, because this will bring a lot more energy to the inner work." One of the team members assessed that "if this inner quest receives more attention, little by little, it will have a contiguous effect upon the larger community."[55] In Mother's emphasis on the experimentation of the subjective psychic experience, there is a glorification of man's metaphysical longings and his exploration of the wide range of human potentialities in the search for meaning and purpose in life, and to justify one's actions. However, the noble initiative of the 'Inner Being Team' may not fit well with the purpose of community life. The emphasis on the individual's subjective experience does not often provide a stable basis for experiments in communal solidarity, and it may be questioned whether any of these selected interviewees, with their claims, have been able to contribute something constructive to the solution of today's polarising crisis within the community.

Open and sharp questions stimulate the sadhak to critically look at and investigate his own statements, which may bring him to the place where he actually wants to be, rather than a plethora of narratives as a reaction to the question. The seeker can claim to feel the presence of the psychic consciousness or its influence or to be in contact with it, but which experiences support such claims, and what does that show, or how does it express itself and give meaning to one's changed behaviour? How does the paradigm shift translate itself into looking at the world from a new perspective? Such and other questions invite an answer of the sadhak and not the answer that the questioner thinks or expects he would like to hear. (Groupthink). Real answers come from the field of action, and this requires the united participation of citizens themselves. Unless these sadhaks unite together, where their shared efforts permeate the collective consciousness of Auroville, the same challenges will not be solved.

With all the various obstacles and pitfalls on the path towards the psychic influence, psychic contact or psychic realisation as described before, is there a need to investigate the psychic experiment in a different way through dialogue with a need for some form of practical objective verification or some empirical evidence to support the sweeping generalisations? Testing the results of their experiences, not merely in qualitative verbal research but more in the realm of action and uncovering self-deceptions from those who confuse the surface vital pseudo-psychic experience with the inner genuine psychic consciousness. This may revise our concept about the psychic process with some evidence. Perhaps they can share with each other that over-reliance on Mother's sacred Truth may discourage them from gaining insight into self-defeating behaviour, or that passive surrender often proves to be a form of self-deception, inviting an influx of ignorant forces, impure actions, or egoistic claims. Yogic research combines the requirements of spiritual practice with the strict conditions of scientific discipline. In one of his letters, Sri Aurobindo writes," We know well what is the difference between a subjective experience and a dynamic outward-going and realising Force. So, although we have faith (and whoever did anything great in the world without having faith in his mission or the Truth at work behind him?), we do not found ourselves on faith alone, but on a great ground of knowledge which we have been developing and testing all our lives. I think I can say that I have been testing day and night for years upon years more scrupulously than any scientist his theory or his method on the physical plane."[56]

Though this kind of research is not academic and is not directed to produce rapid external results, it is essentially an inner work, an exploration of the unknown hidden psychological ranges of the sadhak's inner and higher consciousness. This inner research does not need a withdrawal from external life but can be pursued amid daily activities. In this research work, the discoveries and advancements in deeper self-knowledge and power must be fruitfully applied to practical and concrete results in external life. When the disciple opens himself to the center of the soul's interiority, this interior power is expressed in the exteriority of the experiencer. For the Mother, "this interior power as essentially psychic virtues need to be expressed in its original purity as compassion and gratitude, without mixing compassion with any trace of condescension or gratitude with any sense of inferiority.[57]

## Notes

1.) Sri Aurobindo; *Essays Human and Divine*, p 359

2.) Peter Heehs; *The lives of Sri Aurobindo*, p 357

3.) The Mother; *Mother's Agenda*, 19-6-67

4.) Ibid., 5-11-68

5.) Sri Aurobindo; *Letters on Yoga*, p 233

6.) Ibid., 265

7.) Ibid., 268

8.) Sri Aurobindo; *The Life Divine*, p 539-540

9.) Ibid., p 226

10.) Ibid., p 893

11.) The Mother, *Collected Works of the Mother*, Vol 7 p 263-264

12.) Ibid., Vol 6 p 33

13.) Ibid., Vol 6 p 365

14.) Ibid., Vol 7 p 423

15.) Sri Aurobindo; *The Synthesis of Yoga*, p 145

16.) The Mother; *Collected Works of the Mother,* Vol 6 p 249-250

17.) Ibid., Vol 8 p 172

18.) Sri Aurobindo; *Letters on Yoga*, p 1099

19.) Ibid., p 1069

20.) Ibid., p 1093

21.) Sri Aurobindo; *The Life Divine*, p 907-908

22.) Sri Aurobindo; *The Synthesis of Yoga,* p 169-170

23.) Ibid., p 69

24.) Sri Aurobindo; *The Life Divine*, p 970

25.) Sri Aurobindo; *Letters on Yoga*, p 1025-1026

26.) Sri Aurobindo; *The Life Divine*, p 914

27.) Ibid., 905-906

28.) Ibid., p 894

29.) Ibid., p 895

30.) Sri Aurobindo; *Letters on Yoga*, p 1099

31.) The Mother; *Collected Works of the Mother*, Vol 8 p 192

32.) *Auroville Today*, February 2017

33.) Sri Aurobindo; *The Life Divine*, p 543

34.) Ibid., p 909

35.) Ibid., p 356

36.) The Mother, *Mother's Agenda*, 1-7-1953

37.) Sri Aurobindo; *The Life Divine*, p 436

38.) *Auroville Today*, September 2022

39.) The Mother; *Mother's Agenda*, 16-5-60

40.) Sri Aurobindo; *Letters on Yoga* part IV p 690-691

41.) Kishore Mukherjee; *The Practice of Integral Yoga,* p 256

42.) The Mother; *Mother's Agenda*, 6-3-71

43.) The Mother; *Collective Works of the Mother*, Vol 7 p 253

44.) Ibid., Vol 7 p 20

45.) Sri Aurobindo; *Letters on Yoga*, p 1047

46.) The Mother; *Mother's Agenda*, 21-12-57

47.) Sri Aurobindo; *The Life Divine*, p 907-908

48.) Ibid., p 714-715

49.) Sri Aurobindo; *The Synthesis of Yoga*, p 145

50.) The Mother; *Collective Works of the Mother*, Vol 12 p 45

51.) Sri Aurobindo; *Letters on Yoga*, Part IV p 296

52.) The Mother; *Collective Works of the Mother*, Vol 6 p 249

53.) Sri Aurobindo; *The Life Divine*, p 229-230

54.) The Mother; *Mother's Agenda*, 28-7-60

55.) *Auroville Today*, January 2024

56.) Sri Aurobindo; *On Himself and the Ashram*, p 468-469

57.) The Mother; *Collective Works of the Mother*, Vol 15, p 277

*CHAPTER EIGHT*

# CRITICAL REFLECTION

The author would like to offer some reflective comments and a supplemental wrap-up of the various chapters, as previously discussed, before drawing his conclusion. The many questions hopefully offer some renewed insight and serve as a final reflection upon the complicated events of Auroville's present crisis.

## Mother's Role as a Guru

The creative Conscious Force, as the Divine Mother, in her transcendent poise, has created the whole universe. This Divine creative Force takes direct ground in the workings of the world. Through individual forms, she manifests some rays of herself, and when the hour is ripe, she descends, and a full individual embodiment can come forth. The Mother is such an embodiment, visible through her role as the Divine Shakti on earth. It is this Mother who is related to the Divine Shakti in all its forms, the Universal and Transcendental Force which the sadhak has to call into all his being and life. She emphasised the development of the disciple's divine potentialities within us, as an inner guide to whatever obstacles lie in the course of their unfoldment. These obstacles have to be looked at as something wrong in the machinery of human nature, which has to be observed and changed; this needs one's own efforts in a steady, quiet rejection of defects, keeping oneself open to the Force.

For that, the sadhak must be conscious of the divine presence in himself. According to the Mother, "To find the psychic one must conquer the desires of the vital, silence the mind and then make a sincere submission to the Divine of whom the psychic is the instrument in man." [1] Consciously observing faults and failures can lead to depression and discourage faith.

Though the true Guru is able to share with the disciple the removal of obstacles on the spiritual path to the divine, will her protection be effective in the present polemical atmosphere? Lack of unity, where various groups pursue their own plans of action, is the primary cause of all the difficulties. Is Mother's vision infallible, and has Auroville's struggle anything to do with some form of the fanaticism of those disciples who are not able to understand the essence of Mother's vision and assume to be the illuminated ones? Are some citizens able to overcome the inconsistencies in Mother's spiritual vision related to contemporary developments and new knowledge? Her early messages to the first Aurovilians about goodwill and human unity may have been rather general, but when she discovered the widening gap between her vision and reality, her messages became more closely related to the unique purpose of Auroville. Is the Mother, as a means for further growth, offering us a practical way and spiritual method of reaching the Divine within, or are we worshipping a perfect spiritual Master who is searching for a spiritual ideal, and we mould ourselves according to the image of the teacher without a radical change? Does she ask the sadhak to support her in her metaphysical vision, or does she prefer the sadhak to have faith in the spiritual meaning of her integral sadhana with the support of her integral method during the practice on the slippery path?

Her guidance on the path is intended as a tool, not a dogmatic doctrine. Did the Mother have the intention of becoming a traditional Guru, encouraging dependency on her legacy, or did she encourage her disciples to use their own spiritual resources and find their own true guidance within, of whom the human Guru is but an external representation? The external human Guru is helpful in the earliest stages of the practice, but unless the Guru is installed within, the process of yoga can only really make headway.

Regarding the Mother as the Guru, Sri Aurobindo says," There will always be doubts and confusion of the vital and the mind, so long as the vital approaches the Mother from the wrong standpoint, -e.g. if it insists on judging her by her response to its demands and ideas of what she ought to give it. Sadhana's true attitude is not to impose one's mind and vital will on the Divine but to receive the Divine's Will and follow it. Not to say, 'This is my right, want, claim, need, requirement, why do I not get it?' but to give oneself, to surrender and to receive with joy whatever the Divine gives, not grieving or revolting, is the right way. Then what one receives will be the right thing for one"[2] When at a certain stage in the Yoga, the mind is sufficiently quiet, the vital steadied and physical altered and removed its inertia, the inmost being long hidden within can come forward and take up the lead of the sadhana.

The Mother, as a guide, has offered us an opportunity to follow certain signposts on the road of the inner and outer journey so that the traveller may know which direction to follow. With her signposts, she encourages us as we build and walk the road while travelling. Mother's road is like a pilgrimage in which the discovery and development of the soul is the pivot of the whole process. The signposts should be used as a means for sadhana, as an opening to get in contact with the inner soul of man and his higher consciousness. In embarking on a complex spiritual journey to discover the Divine within, the sadhak often encounters previously unexplored and uncharted paths of transformation.

Mother's signposts on the roadmap indicate the direction to take for the next step in its realisation. Initially, it requires the sadhak's conscious choice, consecration, aspiration, and effort to join hands with faith in the efficacy of her method and the practice of her teachings, so that transformation becomes possible. The journey on the proper path does not follow a straight line, and it is the practice that forms the foundation of sadhana. This secret Force behind the sadhana guides the seeker during future practice.

Though as a spiritual guide, the Mother is in the initial stages a virtual necessity on the road, however, when the sadhak has sufficiently travelled part of the road, the psychic being as true guidance comes forward and starts performing the function of the inner Guru and at that moment her authority gradually diminishes; sadhaks need no longer bind themselves on her predicted future vision of Auroville's development. It is the growth of this inner teacher which marks the individual's level of spiritual evolution.

It's not always easy to understand Mother's messages, and that's why it's easy to read her words in a dogmatic context, treating her guidelines as a set of dogma. She is afraid that people make dogmas with the creation of Auroville. Are those Aurovilians who are parroting Mother's words without the necessary need to walk the road themselves and follow her signposts useful for the progress of Auroville? Taken out of its context Mother's words may be easily misunderstood when Aurovilians confuse their difficulties related to the indulgence of their undesirable and ingrained character defects that come to the surface (fear, ambition, power) with the psychological challenges Aurovilians encounter while in contact with the psychic consciousness where the psychic is in front, i.e., when difficulties are caused due to psychological resistances of the vital/mental parts during the process of psychic transformation. To feel the Divine presence, the sadhak must do everything from within; a quiet occupation and quiet contact enables him to be in contact with it. Using her words again and again, clinging to forms without a living content and taking it out of their context, may turn her vision into a sectarian religion or may create a personality cult, rather than being receptive of her Force and interpreting her words as guidelines for the practice of sadhana and using her future vision of Auroville as a flexible rhythm of spiritual development where nothing is fixed. In the initial, challenging stage of the practice, the influence of the Guru is invaluable, and one can imagine that if implementing integral sadhana was difficult with the benefit of Sri Aurobindo's and the Mother's constant guidance, it is significantly more difficult in their physical absence. Mother's prophetic perspectives need piecemeal engineering through trial and error; there is no shortcut to perfection. Although Divine Grace is essential for the success of the sadhana, its constant presence is achieved through practice, as it is the practice that prepares the descent of the Grace. For this, the sadhak must learn to go inward, quiet the mind, and become aware of the Mother's working in him.

Mother's words are guidelines and frameworks for understanding the purpose of building the city, not as the destination itself. Her map can serve as a springboard to explore one's own experience, an invitation to look inward into the realm of the inner and inmost consciousness. She offers us some instructions to explore these inner regions and the depth of our being. She does not offer a belief in her metaphysical vision but invites her disciples on an adventure of self-discovery. Before entering the path, Aurovilians need to understand the map before walking the territory, and before they can know 'how' to walk the territory. The fundamental call of life is the struggle on the journey to the Divine, and it is the sleeping Divine within the disciple that must be stirred. In the map, the Mother offers several paths or methods to direct the Aurovilians' gaze inwards.

## The Role of the Psychic Being

A more or less prolonged period of purification and preparation of the instrument is recommended so that the nature is ready to make good use of the descending spiritual forces. Actually, "suddhi [purification] is the most difficult part of the whole yoga; it is the condition of all the rest... to prevent suddhi, the lower nature in you and around you will exhaust all its efforts and even when it cannot prevent it will try to retard....When you have once found calm, peace of mind, firm faith, equality, and be able to live in it for some time, then and only then, you may be sure that suddhi is founded; but you must not think it will not be disturbed. It will be so long as your heart and Prana are still capable of responding to the old movements. The one thing necessary when the renewed trouble comes, is to stand back in your mind and will from it, refuse it the sanction of your higher being even when it is raging in lower nature."[3] In the ordinary consciousness of the Aurovilians, there may be aspiration, sincerity, faith and some form of self-surrender, but a lack of knowledge of the precise nature of the sadhak's goal and the obstacles on the path will not guarantee immunity for the errors on the journey. From the start a certain amount of knowledge about the practice of Integral Yoga is essential, as without such knowledge, and only by sheer strength of one's will or the desire for 'doing good', the journey may end in a disastrous fall from the path. The difficulty lies in the transformation of these lower parts, as explained by Sri Aurobindo; "The real difficulty even for those who have progressed is with the external man, even among those who followed the old ideal, the external man of the Sadhak remains almost the same even after they have attained to something. The inner being gets free, the outer follows still its fixed nature. Our Yoga can succeed only if the external man too changes, but that is the most difficult of all things.... The internal being of most of the Sadhaks here, however imperfect still, is still different from that of the ordinary man, but the external still clings to its old ways, manners, and habits. Many do not seem even to have awakened to the necessity of a change."[4]

The average human being who lives in the waking surface psychological existence appears fairly simple, but as soon as seekers go deep within themselves, they discover that their being is "a roughly constituted chaos, surrounded by a whole complex world into which we have to introduce the principle of a divine order." During sadhana, the sadhak becomes aware of the different parts of the being-physical, vital, and mental-each of which has a separate individuality. Through sadhana they can be separated from one another and gradually experienced as independent entities. When the seeker gets beyond the ordinary surface consciousness, he discovers their distinctiveness and separate forces. Their division or conflict is the cause of most of the more acute difficulties during the practice of sadhana. The forces of the lower mental, vital, and physical nature, which stand in the way of sadhana, can do as they please by simulating experiences and creating unreal formations. If these things are not eliminated, and the higher powers begin to descend, the lower may come across and cover up the descent, and the stimulation it gives is misused for the purpose of the lower nature. It is mainly due to this reason that many sadhaks fall into a state of magnified ego, upheavals, exaggerated sex or other vital passions after having higher spiritual experiences. The outer instruments of human nature have no force to carry the sadhak through the severe ardour of the spiritual journey. As long as the lower nature is active, personal effort in the form of aspiration, rejection and surrender remains necessary. In the words of Sri Aurobindo," For this penetration into the luminous crypt of the soul one has to get through all the intervening vital stuff to the psychic center within us, however long, tedious or difficult may be the process. The method of detachment from the insistence of all mental and vital and physical claims and calls and impulsions, concentration in the heart, austerity, self-purification and rejection of the old mind-movements and life-movements, rejection of the ego of desire, rejection of false needs and false habits, are all useful aids through this difficult passage: but the strongest, most central way is to found all such or other methods on a self-offering and surrender of ourselves and of our parts of nature to the Divine Being. A strict obedience to the wise and intuitive leading of a Guide is also normal and necessary for all but a few gifted seekers."[5]

Could it be that there are Aurovilians who are unable to advance on their journey because they open the vital plane before the mental and psychic planes are ready, or after some initial, true spiritual experiences on the mental plane, there is a premature descent into the vital plane, which causes confusion and disturbance? Still more worrisome, if the vital desire-soul opens to experience before the psychic experience has touched the mind. It often happens that the surface desire-soul is misinterpreted as the psychic being, mixing an egocentric infantilism with a transcendental, ecstatic outburst, and an illuminative, self-actualising experience of psychic consciousness. Where genuine love is mixed up with blind passion, where the psychic consciousness is captured for the enlargement of the lower instrument, which ends up in erroneous results, what is in itself pure in action.

The psychic experience is an intrinsic experience that is not the result of an ego reaction or an expression of something external. The psychic light gets diminished by the surface disability of the lower instrument, which needs therefore to be purified by the psychic influence to become a fit instrument for the descent of the Divine. However, without a metaphysical and psychological background of the psychic experience and its difference from the pseudo-psychic experience [the ego], psychic influence, psychic contact, psychic vision and psychic realisation, the sadhak is not encouraged to find answers related to the effects, difficulties and pitfalls before, during and after the experience. Indirectly related is the role and influence of autosuggestion, imagination, and expectation in clarifying the psychic experience. Do they create room for errors and misleading interpretations?

The results of the psychic experience can be rather contradictory. The Mother, again and again, paid attention to the insidious and seductive forms of the psychic experiment, i.e., taking the first results for one's own advancement, ego-inflation rather than ego transcendence. What about those Aurovilians who take egoistic advantage of the psychic influence and try to capture the psychic power for their own interest and degrade it into an aggrandised lower instrumentation for desire and ego, i.e,. using the psychic experiences for selfish motives, which confirms their egoism?

Can increased capacity of psychic insight be misused to control and manipulate, when there is no concrete virtual contact with the higher universal realm and when the psychic consciousness is not at the same time accompanied by the inner truth; suggestions of the vital desire-soul are misinterpreted for the psychic being where the pure action of the psychic being gets mixed up with mental ideas, vital instincts and desires? The sadhak may be quite advanced in terms of his psychic experience, but what happens when he lacks human compassion for or service to others, or when some of his powerful, disturbed character traits emerge on the spiritual path and intensify with further practice? In such cases, the psychic experience becomes like a bundle of straw. When living in the inner quietude, could the sadhak remain passive, assuming that the Divine consciousness is behind it, a blind quiescence where the human agency is nullified? Such an attitude may easily lead to avoiding social disturbances by offering them to the Divine, thereby escaping individual responsibility and the underlying causes, i.e., moral indifference.

It is not so difficult to assess the material construction of the city, but it is much more challenging to determine the deeper spiritual levels of transformation within the Auroville community, the invisible subjective aspects of Auroville to form a new society based on human unity in diversity. Are the Aurovilians, in their aspiration, able to confront their shadow? This confrontation of their shadow is the transformation Auroville needs. Auroville's present circumstances, while being encountered by dark forces from within and without, do they allow the psychic to act visibly? If some Aurovilians claim to be in touch with their psychic being, why are they unable to effectively address these dark forces? Will something different emerge out of this dark passage when a few Aurovilians are receptive to the true nature of their psychic consciousness within and can act from the psychic demand for the betterment of the community?

Could it be that one of the flaws in the community's crisis lies in the failure to reconcile the citizen's search for the psychic experiment with the ideal of group harmony? In Mother's vision of a spiritual experimental community, she emphasised the initial spiritual growth of the individual. Therefore, focusing on their development within a supporting group would enable the particular citizen to become one of the active leaders of the future city. Those Aurovilians who are endowed with superior psychic talents for social leadership could guide the rest of the community into a more spiritual mode of existence. However, it turned out that those individuals who are on their own path to realising the psychic experiment and who pursue their own development are unable to form organic groups willing to make commitments to each other and transcend the values that motivate change. As mentioned earlier, the results of the psychic experience can be somewhat contradictory; without proper knowledge and guidance, the applicability of psychic experiments may lead to unwanted psychological issues. The psychic experience needs no evidence based on proof, but are Aurovilians aware of and concerned about questionable consequences? This question may lead to controversy and might hurt the sentiments of the Aurovilians.

## The Role of Social Change

In Sri Aurobindo's view, the principle of social compulsion has not always been used properly, as it is a law of man's imperfection, imperfect in its methods and results. Only until man has grown out of the causes of his necessity, a growth out of the subjection to the needs and laws of social life, he cannot be really ready to draw to his true and natural perfection, unless the outer law is replaced by the inner law. Developing rational social ideas overlooks the fact that men in human life strive for higher perfection and strive to go farther. Only a spiritual inner freedom can alone create a perfect human order, and this needs an inner change. If this change is too difficult to be ever effected by a few, if this is not certain, "if this is not the solution, if this is not the way, then there is no way for humankind. Then the terrestrial evolution must pass beyond man as it has passed beyond the animal and a greater race must come that will be capable of the spiritual change, a form of life must be born that is nearer to the divine."[6] Integral Yoga accomplishes the preliminary steps for societal change, i.e., it changes the essence of men's inmost nature. All other attempts fail because, "Human, social and political endeavour turns always in a circle and leads nowhere; ...Altruism, philanthropy and service, Christian love or Buddhist compassion have not made the world a whit happier, they only give infinitesimal bits of momentary relief here and there, threw drops on the fire of the world's suffering. All aims are at the end transitory and futile, all achievements unsatisfying or evanescent; all works are so much labour of effort and success and failure which consummate nothing definite; whatever changes are made in human life are of the form only and these forms pursue each other in a futile circle; for the essence of life, its general character remains the same forever."[7] But what about virtues, which are constructions of the mind? When in touch with the psychic being, the seeker acts not autonomously but as an instrument of the Divine; can such consciousness ignore virtue ethics as a guide of action, and what are the consequences of such vision for the devotees?

The unity of an ideal human society needs more than a mere search for individual and collective freedom or to live for the individual or collective ego, it needs a spiritual aspiration and awakening to give shape to a new and ideal social order where every man is motivated by the force of spiritual consciousness to become perfect in action. In Mother's spiritual humanism, with all its diverse cultures, each individual can reach their highest ideal only if their fellow human beings can reach the same. This spiritual motive force for social transformation cannot be supplied by institutional support or religious movements, but needs to be realised from the inner Truth to the outer forms. To walk this challenging path is reserved for a few enlightened human beings who are in touch with the inner and higher parts of their being and who will, at times, strengthen the spiritually more gifted soul-searchers. The other, less gifted members of mankind are obliged to follow mechanical and institutional means. Actually, the issue need not be phrased as the group versus the individual. The question is more related to the future, specifically, how to promote individual growth within the context of community organisation. A few enlightened individuals in the unenlightened mass of humanity must act from their inner light for the benefit of mankind in preparation for a better future. However, establishing a separate community, forming a group with a separate collective life with its own rules of living like other-worldly soul-seekers in a monastic life to realise in themselves the spiritual reality, such attempts are for the Mother always confronted with the ignorance of the human vital nature and fails by its own imperfection or the imperfection from the outside world.

When the Mother was asked the question "Why does one live in Auroville she mentioned in the first paragraph of 'being a true Aurovilian'; "we come to Auroville to escape social and moral rules that are artificially practised everywhere, but it is not to live in the licentiousness of the satisfaction of every desire; it is to rise above desires in a truer consciousness." [8] For the Mother, social laws offer only momentary relief and only throw drops on the fire in the world's suffering. They are necessary and temporary, helpful, and of immense significance in the unfolding of the soul, but beyond mental development, social laws stagnate. At the beginning of yoga practice, a human approach is necessary, but gradually these social laws become purified and perfected through the divine intervention of a spiritual force.

The dynamics and new challenges of the present society require constant change in all aspects of life, including culturally, economically, socially, and religiously, which in turn changes human nature. If Aurovilians accept these changes, they lose their faith in the perfectibility of human nature and the creation of a perfect new social environment. At the same time, Aurovilians cannot achieve long-lasting self-sufficiency in an interdependent changing world by excluding these changes and new innovations and withdrawing into their experimental laboratory. In their new way of living within a self-governing community, did the Mother expect too much from her disciples who joined her? In the absence of introspective spiritual practice or the devaluation of the search for spiritual meaning, could a more temporary concentration on the outward-looking style of social reform provide a satisfactory alternative to the present chaotic formal organisation with its bureaucratic instruments? Is the disciple's faith in Mother's Grace freed from the constraints of moral law? Even though morality is in the end only relative and arbitrary, and though her Force is beyond all morality, does this provide a solid base for a communal life with its rigorous demands for the citizens' common good, brotherhood and recognition of each other's rights and freedom? Though the survival of Auroville's community depends on instituting its own authoritative system, does such a system ignore the dangers of moral tyranny in the community of those who rule by forced conformity?

The Mother warned the citizens to see a utopian future as more than a fantasy and to avoid the pitfalls of a spiritual ideology that promises to create a utopia in a relatively short time through societal transformation, which may ultimately lead to prolonged difficulties. Could it be that, for this reason, her planning may have to depart significantly from her predictions, and new ideas must be implemented to build a truly human world? The era of transition towards the transformation of human society and psychology is a never-ending process that requires unity in diversity on a rugged path.

Auroville's laboratory of social change. How will it be applicable to mainstream societies? Does the intended perfection have a connection with reality, i.e., mediation between the development of ideal aspiration and present conditions? How does social injustice express itself in the context of the psychic experiment? To critically look at oneself, become conscious of the difficulty without identifying the difficulty as part of one's real nature, and offer it to the Divine, is this mere symptom relief while the wound festers on?

The organic unity of society is, for Sri Aurobindo, the primary characteristic of the external self of society; it often overlooks the deeper psycho-spiritual aspects, where there is an inner change along external judgment. What is the role of social moral laws and their function in a future just world order within Auroville's community? Does it *initially* need to include the objective structure of social reality and its organic interdependence between rational human ideas and social reality? Is Auroville's spiritual society in tune with a society more based on social efficiency in the context of present-day reform movements? For the Mother, social standards as empirical means are too narrow, complex, confused and uncertain as they have no vision of the cause and origin of the malady it attempts to cure. In Mother's idea of spiritual progress, she does not aim to solve human problems on a mental basis; she would like to create a new foundation of our being and our life. She admits that external changes can at least prepare favourable conditions for more substantial improvements, but as Auroville intends to hasten the advent of the supramental reality upon earth, she expects the Aurovilians to dissociate themselves from the old world and work for a new and better world ready to be born. Nevertheless, are social laws not necessary as an *indispensable* preparation for an ideal social order, and is unpreparedness not the chief stumbling block of spiritual change? In the initial stages of sadhana, social laws are not destroyed but purified, and the development of brotherhood, loyalty and self-discipline are essential supports during the preparatory stages and the sadhak's growth process.

For Sri Aurobindo, the actualisation of social laws requires a metaphysical basis, but are social laws ineffective means of changing human life because they lack the human power to transform the human race? Does this contradict the various views of those who aim at psycho-social change, where the actualisation of social laws brings about a desired change within oneself and the world? Could altruistic social service lead to an expansion of consciousness, and does society express itself solely in terms of a metaphysical or transcendental process? Is the collective struggle for a harmonious social world order not able to develop some form of inner transformation? The rules of social laws need to be continually reinforced to sustain them, otherwise they get lost. Do human and social deficiencies demand a more honest critical investigation of Auroville's collective self-reflection? Could solidarity with other Aurovilians for a common goal, and taking collective care in which we are responsible for building justice between Aurovilians, be a valuable contribution to the outside world? Does the successful assimilation of various positive aspects of new knowledge in social sciences depend on some form of *mastery first*, rather than taking a shortcut before overcoming all the weaknesses of the outer nature, which may create all kinds of indulgence for so-called freedom? Mother's vision postulates inevitable progress ending in perfect freedom. The law of any freedom, free from egoistic motives, obeys the compulsion of the Divine Being within us, for it is that subjection which is the condition of our freedom. But every solution creates a new situation with its own problems, needs and demands. She could not have precisely anticipated the unintended consequences of her ideal plan because the process of social change, once set in motion, can seldom be directed with the precision she desired. There is always a disparity between the real and the ideal when it comes to a complex society. This contradiction in the complex interplay between social organisation and spiritual faith requires a kind of reconciliation that serves to strengthen commitments.

Concerning the outside world, allegiance and identification are profoundly based on social, cultural, and political relationships, and to maintain this, it needs the capacity to sustain internal diversity and constant renewal through consent. Do Aurovilians, in their spiritual ideal society, take significant *initial* consideration in the practical aspects of complex social problems and the actions that are needed to solve these problems critically? The idea of Auroville as a social spiritual utopia, could it create certain dangerous situations when its citizens call for certain drastic changes with potentially unknowable consequences? Auroville's assumption of the utopian quest becomes hazardous in the hands of ruthless ideologues, where the bureaucratic organisation has the power to control, which often destroys the community. The devaluation of social and moral laws and their replacement with highly mystical insights that can be practised only by a few could create a spiritual vacuum. Does it devalue the personal human power of the individual? In exploring new ways beyond moral and social conventions, are Aurovilians with their high spiritual ideals throwing the baby out of the bathwater when they don't take sufficient advancement of approved external means of new knowledge used in the humanities and social sciences, i.e., present-day practical achievements in human and social sciences that are universally accepted and appreciated, though relative yet extremely useful?

The domains of the scholar and the believer are different, like the realms of competence between the practitioner of Integral Yoga and the person who writes about Integral Yoga. However, the non-expert is open to new facts, accumulated techniques, methods of investigation and data of sociology in general, whereas the practitioner tends to present sociological knowledge in highly abstract and speculative terms, which rarely produces concrete results.

The Mother enunciated a transcendental humanism, where her Integral Yoga of perfection involves a comprehensive development of the human being through the psychic being. As a realisable utopianism, the Mother examined humanity's inner potentialities and higher aspirations. What must be achieved for our human destiny is the spiritualisation of the sociology of human behaviour; as for the Mother, humanitarianism is not the ideal solution because it only glorifies the sentimental idealism of empirical man. Only a radical change of inner consciousness offers a perfect solution. However, the practice of ethics is the first step towards the liberation of all human bondages and is initially supportive of the individual's quest for inner progress. Before reaching the stage of a collective psychic consciousness of its citizens could it be helpful to remove first rigid boundaries around the city and make also an engagement with social injustice in the outside world, such as recommended by the Universal Rights platform, as without this engagement the festering of Auroville's collective neglected misery may continue, even though this engagement is only related to a relative solution.

To be too eager to change the world, could it overlook the fact that it is essential to understand the world first? Moreover, does a new world need, initially, not to erase but to reform the old, not aiming at ultimate perfection but at an initial improvement first? The old social structure, which has its universal benefits, such as the end of slavery, the rise of the social welfare state, the emancipation of women, and the partial removal of inequality, ultimately led to cohesive social change over time. In the challenging process of societal transformation, it may not always be necessary to discard old and beneficial aspects of social laws, but rather to reform them and utilise them in a more purposeful manner.

A new and greater perfection includes the possibilities of the achieved lower perfect organisation of earthly life, or whatever perfection has already been attained. Values and virtues, such as love for one's fellow seekers, for one's work, sincerity, discipline, and friendship, along with arts, justice, equality and technical achievements, are they not more practical in determining the quality of Auroville's development? Is selfless behaviour always egoistic? Could it be that research which centres on eternal human values and virtues, which have formed us in history and form the building blocks of present-day society, proves that these eternal universal values and virtues also have a transcendental value?

## The Role of Secularism

Is Auroville, as a contemporary ideal, a practical and intentional community still a growing experiment in attempting to build a new life on earth, or has Mother's grand Utopia of the past been replaced by those utopians who are pressing their own communal self-interest and sharing their secular ideals and modest values with like-minded seekers? Mindlessly adhering to past traditions and static repetition as a means of adoration, regardless of changed circumstances and new requirements, opposes a reinterpretation of Mother's creative spiritual vision for Auroville's future development. Although Mother's spiritual vision of Auroville is an article of faith with some grounding in facts, is this enough to convince those disciples who joined Auroville with all their goodwill, but don't dismiss all evidence that indicates some aspects of her spiritual illuminations are not practical for the final foundation of the city? It might end in an inadequate experiment being swallowed up by all sorts of devoted disciples when, in their experimental enthusiasm and their faith in Mother's guidelines, they ignore a more realistic approach related to the present situation. It appears that Auroville's younger generation and various newcomers are increasingly disregarding the values of the original members, as they are more secular-minded and may attempt to transform the utopian experiments into a commercial enterprise. For those people, it may seem that Auroville is disconnected from its complexity, and perhaps the project should adopt a more modest and realistic approach to the challenges of the 21st century in order to navigate through the uncertainties of the present crisis.

Are there signals of the completion of Auroville's spiritual experiment? Does the present situation become a ripe one for interested exploitation in matters of the spirit? The population continues to grow gradually, but it is far from reaching the peak size Mother had imagined. Is there a tendency towards gradual contraction, or are there tendencies towards revival where the emphasis shifts gradually from a more social secular utopian society in the spirit of devotion to the common good, to more spiritual principles? Conflicts arose when working towards an abstract notion of the common good gradually evaporated, and overcoming this difficulty demands a more fundamental return to the basics of Mother's spiritual principles. Are the Aurovilians as a group still a utopian community fulfilling Mother's dreams if the guidance of the administrative people of the Governing Board gradually takes it over? Is the new Secretary sufficiently concerned about the incremental inner progress of the Aurovilians or is she more interested in a model city for the future that will inspire thousands of daily visitors but will certainly not trigger their vision about Auroville as a spiritual city of the future, as an experiment for a new society, a new man with a new consciousness? If the government manages to build the city and establish a viable social organisation, once their utopia is attained, then the citizens hope they can promote and return to mysticism, and the governmental authorities will value their faith and unquestionably accept the future citizens with more intellectual analysis.

In this context, it may be helpful to mention A. Maslow's naturalistic mysticism and his 'democratisation of the soul', in which he attempted to integrate science and spirituality. Maslow acknowledged man's innate yearning for ultimate values and virtues as principles of man's higher nature, originating inside the individual and the possibility for the realisation of these potentials. Maslow's inborn higher instinctive 'metaneeds' for personal development and strengthening of character is a life-long process of transcending needs. These 'metaneeds' or 'becoming divine' are part of human nature and, for Maslow, a natural human characteristic. Could aspects of the transcendental reality also be found in the intimacy of pure mutual love, in the metaphors of art, or the powers of literature or music, rather than only in the muddy journey of the psychic being within? In Maslow's transcendental values, a secularised world humanises the Divine rather than divinising the human; this offers us transcendental values within a secular world where the sacred has a human face. The sacred is a dimension within our existence; it exists in our deepest pain and our highest joy, in the beauty of life. In this humanitarian utopia, love, the profane, has a human face which represents something sacred. The inherent divinity of human beings and the cultivation of these humanising impulses require no faith in a transcendental divine order, but rather a human pull. One is most spiritual when one is most human. Maslow's humanisation of spirituality represents spiritual phenomena in terms of human potential, and his naturalistic mysticism is based on the complete fulfilment of human nature through the gratification of metaneeds. Failure to achieve one's metaneeds may cause spiritual illness that is characterised by a lack of higher and more deep-rooted needs. More future research on Maslow's naturalistic mysticism and his attempt to humanise spirituality may be highly valuable and offer a useful contribution to Auroville's chaotic situation within the community.

Auroville's future progress stems from the initiatives of a few self-advancing seekers who are aware that it may first acquire an intermediate society, a temporary secularised world where transcendental values humanise the Divine, serving as a transition from the old to the new world. The question of how many citizens should inhabit the perfect society has always been a concern for utopians. Does Auroville need to grow to 50,000 citizens, or would a small, less ambitious spiritual society trigger a new and perfect existence that aims to manifest a transformed society and nature?

Once Auroville has fulfilled Mother's dream and the city is built and inhabited by 50,000 people who are all oriented toward their spiritual ideology, what will be the character of her destiny: spiritual or secular? According to E.M Cioran," When an ideology's moment has come, everything contributes to its success, even its enemies; neither polemics nor police can check its expansion or delay its success; but the better it succeeds, the greater risk it runs of exhausting itself; once established, it will be drained of its ideal content, will extenuate its resources, compromising the promises of salvation it possessed, only to degenerate into a bugbear or humbug."[9]

We don't know where Mother's path may ultimately lead because nobody has been there yet, but as a place for the psychic being's soul, it is the condition of the Spirit. In their dynamic speculations, are the citizens able to judge Mother's vision, considering all the anomalies inherent in the practical realisation of building the city? Infinite progress, where the Aurovilians offer their efforts to build a perfect city for the future. Ultimately, such an approach may be a grandiose venture, but will such a noble attempt ever be realised? It requires an honest faith when the devotee is tormented by the frenzy of the intellect. One needs to be a 'true hero' to reconcile Mother's utopia, a new earth, with the aspects of dystopia, where the latter interpenetrates and forms a third, nationalistic genre that may threaten its present citizens. However, the justification of Auroville as a utopia need not be merely empirical; its transcendental character avoids a premature rejection of its existence, although it may require some necessary demythologisation. Mother's presence comes by practice, learning to go inward and gradually cease to live only in the external world, and though success in the sadhana certainly needs the Divine Grace, it is the practice that prepares for the descent of the Grace in the purifying process of the development of one's psychic being.

## Notes

1.) The Mother; *Collective Works of the Mother*, Vol 13, 5-4-72

2.) Sri Aurobindo; *The Mother*, p 46

3.) Sri Aurobindo; *The Hour of God*, p 155-156

4.) Sri Aurobindo; *On Himself and the Ashram*, p 140

5.) Sri Aurobindo; *The Life Divine*, p 967

6.) Sri Aurobindo; *The Human Cycle*, p 207

7.) Sri Aurobindo; *The Life Divine*, p 416-417

8.) The Mother, *Collective Works of the Mother*, Vol 13, 3-6-70

9.) E.M Cioran; *History and Utopia*, p 95

*CHAPTER NINE*

# CONCLUSION

When Sri Aurobindo anticipated the evolutionary need for a utopian community, he foresaw many of the problems that Auroville currently faces. In the words of Sri Aurobindo, " At a certain stage it might be necessary to follow the age-long device of the separate community, but with a double purpose, first to provide a secure atmosphere, a place and life apart, in which the consciousness of the individual might concentrate on its evolution in surroundings where all was turned and centred towards the one endeavour and, next, when things were ready, to formulate and develop the new life in those surroundings and in this prepared spiritual atmosphere... for each seeker, carrying in himself the possibilities but also the imperfections of a world that has to be transformed, would bring in not only his capacities but his difficulties and the oppositions of the old nature and, mixed together in the restricted circle of a small and close common life, these might assume a considerably enhanced force of obstruction which would tend to counterbalance the enhanced power and concentration of the forces making for evolution."[1] As Auroville prospered and grew larger, the organisation increased in complexity, which gradually created a distance between its citizens. This has become subject to influences pulling away from Mother's dream. The larger size of the population necessitated an increased emphasis on an efficient organisation, which developed a rather bureaucratic system that became detrimental to the community's structure and violated many of their utopian ideals.

In due time, conflicts arose, related to ideological differences with the original ideals, organisational and financial problems, individualism, impatience, competition, power, and various other issues that are common in society outside Auroville. Conflicts increased when working towards an abstract notion of the common good gradually evaporated, which demanded a purifying return to the essence of Mother's spiritual principles. At the time of Auroville's crisis, a bureaucratic framework became one of the obstacles when the city needed innovations and improvisation, and where things were supposed to be done differently, without a paternalistic approach from outside governance. Bureaucracies rarely remain neutral; they invariably end up giving the authorities unlimited personal power and producing complex rules, while departures from the bureaucratic principle are interpreted as abuses. Once bureaucratisation has established itself, it is almost impossible to get rid of it and becomes indispensable to those trying to wield power.

Currently, the community is somewhat fractured, as citizens tend to rely on their imperfect mental constructions of the past, unable to replace their mental consciousness with a new psychic consciousness. However, this situation offers the inhabitants an opportunity and a challenge to explore their inner levels of being. Some individuals may have tapped into their psychic consciousness, but their efforts have not yet permeated the collective consciousness. A dispersed force of numerous people engaging in numerous discussions may have easily necessitated the top-down intervention of the government's management system.

The primary aim of Mother's Future City is not only the realisation of her ideology but also the work of building the city. A loose conglomeration of individuals cannot solve difficulties related to work and construction, but requires a more collective effort to succeed. Disputes, conflicting interests and differences in character and culture will never be abolished by themselves, but their roots and real causes need to be uncovered through cooperation by forming a united brotherhood, for these are rooted in the very essence of Auroville's future society. Individualistic tendencies and emphasis on fulfilment and other personal desires often undermine this unity in communal living. Opposite parties need to unite and be aware that this is more important than concentrating on filling holes in issues such as building the crown road or other side issues. It requires the unity of citizens to address a significant danger, a government that challenges the fundamental values of Mother's spiritual heritage.

One of the main issues that challenges the community at this moment is the polarisation between those who aim to create utopians while building the city and those who prefer building the city first without simultaneously creating utopian citizens, focusing on the city first, and spiritual utopians later. A way beyond theorising utopia requires karmic action where the subjective spirit of the soul meets the objective structure of the utopian city. The process of building a utopia is probably as important as the finished product, for it allows citizens to explore the implications of their ideals and their endeavour to convince themselves, during the process, that these ideals address the real requirements of the divine nature of man, which is accessible to all. No outside reformer can rigorously mould the citizens into a perfect pattern, as their road to physical manifestation has not been previously mapped in detail; it is left to those people who dedicate their lives to Auroville's experiment. The city to be built serves as a material tool to evolve the citizens' consciousness, guided by her Grace on the path, with the ultimate aim of being a willing servant of the Divine consciousness.

In building the city the Mother emphasised the creation of a new society based on a series of precepts given by her; "A Dream", "The Auroville Charter", and "To Be A True Aurovilian" At the end of her life it seemed that she did not want to have a city of 50,000 people," Twelve good men would be better than hundreds of stupid persons. Auroville is not for comfort but for the servants of the Divine."[2] Her planned city of 50,000 people might be too big to allow bonds of care and friendship to exist between their members in a well-organised society which provides for all their needs and where all matters are settled by the inner authority of their goodwill. This requires an atmosphere of freedom that pervades the entire community.

Will the community thrive in a glorious future, as envisioned in the collective imagination of Auroville's citizens? In Utopia, it is the size which makes all the difference. The present stage of Auroville's small-scale and grand ambitions may offer a clear insight into the practical cultivation of their psycho-social and spiritual experimentations. This cannot be implemented in a short time, as if human nature can be transformed overnight. It may take generations, as it is a well-known fact within utopian communities that premature declarations of victory are often made.

According to George van Vreckem, a well-known author and long-term Aurovilian, "Suppose that financially it suddenly becomes possible to build the city, would that, in this early stage of its growth, be the Auroville that

Mother envisioned? It might resemble a resort of the Club Mediteranee, but what about the spiritual content which is the real rationale of Auroville's existence? Auroville lives in the hearts of the simple Aurovilians, the quiet and patient ones who, in surrender, keep working in good times and bad times. Buildings have to be constructed; creations have to come about in beauty and harmony; but most important of all is the work on oneself, the inner unfolding, starting from very little (the ordinary human being all of us are) to go towards very much (beyond man). All else has been done before, it is this that is new. And it will automatically externalise itself into a visible city...Auroville's material growth can only be the outcome of its spiritual growth, and it is at the moment not yet ripe for a material development of such dimensions. The real Auroville exists- in the hearts of the Aurovilians; it is there that it has to develop fully before a complete outward shape makes any sense. At present, there is little more than the embryo of a city. But the fact that Auroville still exists after 25 years is, by itself, considering its purpose and circumstances of its beginnings, a miracle."[3]

Man is a self-exceeding creature who aims to make progress while discovering new secrets of the physical world and the life world; however, it may be questioned whether all types of progress are good and welcome. Yearning for a better and nobler form of life is an integral part of human nature itself, and the realisation of Mother's spiritual utopia is to be the fulfilment of a promise from our inmost being, even when this utopian realisation is described in a mystical, metaphysical language and therefore not easy to decipher. In Auroville, as a spiritual utopian project, Aurovilians have struggled to bring about lasting harmony within their community; its achievements have brought mixed blessings, not always for the better. The citizens' consumer mentality and self-centeredness often reflect a declining confidence in faith and a lack of appreciation for Mother's vision. However, criticism should mediate between naivety and cynicism, between the utopian ideal of perfection and the practical affirmation of an existing society as the best of all possible worlds. Is Auroville's utopian vision still concrete enough to be applied to the real world, i.e., intending to integrate their achievements into the real world in order to try to change it? In Sri Aurobindo's Utopia, "the experiment of human life on earth is not now for the first time enacted. It has been conducted a million times before and the long drama will again be repeated a million times. In all that we can do now, our dreams, our discoveries, our swift or difficult attainments we profit subconsciously by the experience of innumerable precursors and our labour will be fecund in planets unknown to us and in worlds yet uncreated. The plan, the peripheries, the denouement differ continually yet are always governed by the conventions of an eternal Art. God, Man and Nature are the three perpetual symbols."[4]

The Mother envisioned Auroville as a collective evolutionary experiment in embodying a spiritual society, one that could not be anticipated but instead would have to be progressively elaborated through experimentation and applied spirituality. As an experimental laboratory for the evolution of consciousness, Auroville aims to transform earthly life into a divine life. The Mother offered Aurovilians a method to practice in order to accelerate its manifestation, but how it would manifest, or its duration, was not always clearly provided by the Mother; instead, it was left to the Aurovilians themselves. Only when they gradually move inwards, towards an area of inner reflection and growth within, are they able to realise the present external circumstances of Auroville's reality from a different perspective. The Mother created Auroville as a social experiment in human unity, a communitarian society influenced by the psychic being through the practice of Integral Yoga, a place that provides the freedom for the collective growth of consciousness, thereby developing the conditions for a divine life. Unlike any other spiritual or religious community Auroville does not reject the earthly life to create favourable conditions for the citizen's development of an inner life, on the contrary, Aurovilians embrace the world to be relevant to it, and the purpose of Auroville is to bring forward the divine center, the psychic being of each of its members and uniting it with all its other members. The Mother knows it is not easy," it's not easy, I would like people to feel that coming to Auroville does not mean coming to an easy life- it means coming to a gigantic effort for progress. And those who don't want to keep up with it should leave. That's how things stand. I wish it were so strong-the need for progress, for the divinisation of the being, so intense-that those who are unable (unable or unwilling) to adjust to it would leave by themselves."[5]

The citizens may offer various practical explanations for finding a solution to the present problems, but this has not resulted in a resolution of the conflicts because the real problem lies deeper. In the realisation of their own basic and inner/higher needs, the citizens are confronted with the gap between aspiration and reality in their endeavours. The Aurovilians may be on their way to realisation, but they often don't tolerate any criticism. The members feel continuously aggrieved in their personal freedom, which they experience as a personal possession, rather than as an individual responsibility for the collective good. Their frustration lies in increased resistance to what they perceive as an infringement on their individual freedom. They are longing for a leadership who rigorously abolishes all restrictions related to their personal freedom. The Mother did emphasise freedom; the citizens should be given the freedom to succeed as well as err, and only in this way can Auroville grow. However, not a freedom 'we do as we like' but freedom in a self-disciplined manner without falling into licentiousness. Such freedom implies and complements responsibility, which requires that the individual is himself established in that freedom inwardly before giving freedom to others.

The absence of laws in Auroville is not an excuse to live out the citizens' egoistic desires; on the contrary, for the Mother to unite with the Divine, it is the duty of every good Aurovilian to conquer the very possibility of desire and rise above desires into a truer consciousness. According to the Mother, "Since we have set aside all conventions, immediately everybody thinks; Ah!, nice place to satisfy our desires and they nearly all come with that intention.... And they turn freedom into license, they use it to satisfy their desires. And all the things that we have truly worked all our lives to master, they indulge in a dissipation. I am absolutely disgusted."[6] In March 1971, Mother wrote, "Oh, they are all quarrelling among themselves! And some even disobey deliberately, they refuse to recognise any authority."[7] A few days later on the 4th of April she said, "instead of taking an active position of 'Go away' (which for many reasons is very difficult), if we put them under an authority they don't accept, they will be forced to leave. They will protest at first, but we must remain firm: 'This is how it is.' We must find the people capable of doing this, with the required strength of character, and once we find them, they can be given the authority, and if the others don't like it, they'll have to leave!"[8]

Initially, in Mother's future vision, she did not want any outside interference, nor did she want any religion or government. The citizens should proceed through their free development from within and help others do the same. She was aware that, at the beginning, only a few individuals used Auroville as a field for the realisation of their psychic being and incorporating the eternal, divine values into their everyday lives, beyond the practical use of utilitarian ethics. Those Aurovilians who were not incorporating even the practical use of utilitarian ethics have been warned several times by the previous secretaries of the Auroville Foundation, who expressed their views on some of the issues that confront today's Auroville.

In one of Mother's last messages to Auroville, she wrote, "Auroville is created to realise the ideal of Sri Aurobindo who taught us the Karma Yoga. Auroville is for those who want to do the Yoga of work. To live in Auroville means to do the Yoga of work. So all Aurovilians must take up work and do it as Yoga."[9] All the different types of activities undertaken by the sadhaks are a part of their yogic endeavour. Each activity must be pursued in the true spirit and with the right attitude, i.e., the activities are pursued with a spirit of sincere dedication and with a sole motive of making them fit means of manifesting Divine Truth in life. This process needs to be developed gradually, it takes time to grow from the lower forces and open oneself to the higher Divine force. The work done in Auroville is not intended to showcase one's capacities, but rather as an opportunity for Karma Yoga. It is a process of learning to work in the true yogic way through practical selflessness, discipline, order, patience, and becoming an instrument of the Divine. The work is of value only when it is done as a field for spiritual progress and self-perfection and offered as a service to the

Divine. The sadhak works according to his essential nature and law of being in tune with the Divine Will. Gradually, the sadhak becomes aware of the Divine Force supporting him in his work with the right energy and right intuition. When the truth perception grows due to the influence of the psychic, the sadhak gets tuned to the Divine Force, and he gradually realises that all works are initiated by the Divine and that he is only an instrument in the hands of the Divine.

The building of the town through the current Master Plan, with its emphasis on circular roads and large stretches of concrete buildings outlining the shape of the Galaxy model, looks like a mechanical placing of bricks upon bricks, but if it is a form of Karma Yoga, then it becomes a means to develop another higher consciousness. The act itself is not the truth, it is only a consequence, but it is the intention behind the act. However, mere credulity and faith in her vision is not a reason to escape the necessary practical aspects of her vision. When difficulties arise at work, they are often related to something amiss in the sadhak's inner attitude, such as egoism, ambition or vanity. To correct this disharmony, the Mother advised her disciples to look for the cause of the difficulties within themselves rather than in others or the circumstances of the situation. The external situation could be an extension of one's inner consciousness expressed in the outer world. Could it be that one of the difficulties in Auroville is related to those sadhaks who want to work according to their own personal ideas and plans and expect that these are to be sanctioned by all the citizens?

There are not only the difficulties and obstacles with the development of the psychic being during the practice of Integral Yoga, but any form of spirituality has its harmful occurrences, such as dogmatism, fanaticism, escapism, exploitation of disciples, neglect of practical concerns, self-centeredness, psychopathology, regression to infantile states, or power games. It needs critical and reflective awareness on the part of the spiritual seeker to avoid such pitfalls.

Auroville, as an exceptional community, is not being built like any ordinary city. Currently, it seems that for many Aurovilians, the primary emphasis lies more on creating a new society rather than only building a town, as envisioned by Mother more than 55 years ago. This appears to be based on a series of precepts given by her before the inauguration of the city, including "The Dream," "To Be a True Aurovilian," and "The Auroville Charter." Building Auroville as an open spiritual society is a never-ending process, not a ready-made product; it involves instability and requires space for the development of new ideas that are not contrary to the latest accepted universal insights. In building the utopian city within a certain time limit, material abundance may easily become associated with selfishness and greed. In such a world system of passive consumption within a well-ordered society, citizens may struggle to transcend themselves into a changing new society. Are one of the project's present disturbances due to the pressure to deliver immediate results while addressing immediate concerns? Does this lead to short-term reactions and fragmented decision-making, which undermine the requirements of a long-term, holistic and integral approach? The new society of the utopian future requires not only a radical vision but also a radical practice and a commitment from its citizens, as well as their personal engagement within a collective effort. Each individual's particular contributions are parts of an overall effort involving many types of Aurovilians.

Life in Auroville is not without its challenges that hamper the development of the ever-evolving experiment. As a dream coming into action, the project has its shadow sides. Although Auroville, in its manifestation of a better world, has achieved various unique and substantial successes, it has also faced some serious obstacles and insurmountable setbacks. Each individual comes to Auroville for a reason, representing something for humanity, and participating in the life of Auroville means living with a wide range of difficulties. Once the obstacles and resistances to the new creation come to the surface, they need to be encountered first in order to surrender them and ask Mother's guidance. However, the idealism of Aurovilians, which sustains them, can also be a convenient form of escape, to refuse to deal with the world as it is or with oneself. Auroville is undoubtedly not a place on earth where human success is achieved, inhabited by an exemplary superhumanity equipped with all the latest technological and digital developments. To come to Auroville in search of a peaceful retreat or any form of escapism is not the sadhana as elaborated by the Mother, on the contrary, she emphasised Karma Yoga, the Yoga of work.

Auroville's project profiles itself as an intentional community of more than sixty nationalities that aims to live together with nature, humanity, and equality in this kingdom of world citizens for everyone with goodwill. This makes the project staggering, and the hardened native citizens will not surrender their dream to the area of darkness. Will Auroville, as a universal Township, survive, and will it continue to remain a vital force for offering practical solutions and alternatives to the shortcomings of the materialistic world? Is Mother's prevailing spiritual ideology of her time, with her practical collective utopian experiment, still relevant in the present changed reality, considering the dangers and advantages of all new ideas, experiments, and revolutionary advancements in technological, digital, and artificial intelligence? Which part of Mother's spiritual vision, which was useful at her time, and when adjusted to the latest modern developments, is able to penetrate the present Auroville community gradually? Mindlessly sticking to past traditions and static repetition, regardless of changed circumstances and new requirements, does this attitude oppose a reinterpretation of Mother's creative spiritual vision about Auroville's future development, and does communication through Mother's direct one-liners offer solutions for the present-day social dormant discomfort of the citizens? For the Mother, action is more important than the loftiest adoration of her metaphysical insight, and the first step following the Divine life is Karma Yoga. The Mother employed the practical program of Integral Yoga as an experiment in dynamic community life, aiming to realise a new man in a new society.

Now that the whole of Mother's utopian project is under pressure and is encountering serious problems, this time due to the centralisation of power by the government and the ideals of a dogmatic ideology, it seems that Auroville is again at the crossroads where old forces of the lower nature are still besieging the city since its inauguration. Auroville's negative publicity and factional infighting make Auroville a different community, where consensual decisions are no longer made by majority rule, and where court cases and lawyers are involved, which hurts the feelings of many members.

Man is a hopeful being, and if people lose hope, then there is indeed no more hope; that's why we cannot live without hope. Is there still something to hope for in Auroville's complicated situation, where all its citizens aim at changing the world for a better future, i.e,. to change the world in such a way that the psychic consciousness becomes the guiding principle in human life? If we discuss hope, we discuss the ultimate aim in life, a personal belief in the future goal of Auroville, in which each of its citizens has a psychological need to participate in a wider collective narrative and a more universal truth with which they can identify. Mother's hope for the future lies within man himself, as man carries within, deep beneath the surface mind, life and body, the divine element or the psychic being. Once the psychic being comes forward and becomes the leader of our path, then man becomes master of himself. Similarly, the collective, represented by the nation, also has a soul, although most people are not aware of this. Hope is not only an emotion, but it is akin to optimism, which concerns the future. As long as we keep hope, we will continue to move forward. This suggests that hope motivates action with the expectation that things will turn out best when we work for it as our moral duty. It is this hope that functions as a stimulating force, the oxygen of the soul. Though hope always relates to an uncertain future, when it also refers to something unquestionable, then it is not hope but an illusion. Critical thinking without hope is cynicism, but hope without critical thinking is naivety. It needs courage to move beyond facts, to believe a wish may not be fulfilled as probable, but at least it may be possible.

The magnitude of the present problems Auroville encounters forces the citizens to reflect on new possibilities for their realisation in the future. They are mixed with hope as well as fears. Does the hope of Aurovilians need to be primarily dependent on the development of an endless growth of the psychic consciousness throughout the journey, or will the notion of an indomitable human spirit survive without divine intervention? It may be necessary to implement some of the developments in a truly global society, though they should be put in perspective with the aim of Auroville's future. What should be done now that government officials are more in control and have the authority to issue directives and regulate the city's activities? There should be hope that the government will gradually return Auroville to a more appropriate body that can better consider the spiritual participation of all citizens without being concerned with the immediate results of its own policies and prudence, making long-term decisions based on its expected long-term benefits. This is the hope for the future in a life of unity, mutuality, and harmony, which can replace the imperfect mental constructions of the past; it is the driving force for change in the direction of achieving a better world. In whatever direction Auroville is moving, in the citizens' hope, there are better times, not just ahead of them but more within their souls.

*Maybe some of the citizens are still enriched by Mother's force, but could it be that another force of greed, fear, power or doubt has encircled the community and is this one of the reasons that the citizens are confronted with the unlimited growing encroachments of the Foundation authorities into the activities of most Aurovilians?* Is the ineptness of Mother's immediate followers and their insufficient ethical dynamic one of the reasons why Aurovilians are unable to carry forward her utopian work?

Now that her experiment has been confronted by a mixture of her ideal dream and shrewd realism, what can Auroville teach us about the future? As a model community that aims to create a new social order and a better condition for all mankind, is it able to inspire imitation? May it become more like a total institution, where power resides at the top, rather than a spiritual community where citizens live in a free society and their movements are not restricted by external forces within the community, even though a certain order and structure are necessary for sustained social life? There remains a paradox in any utopia regarding the balance between freedom and control: to gain a sense of mastery over one's own future destiny and, at the same time, dependence on one's own autocratic system. Reality often modifies the dream.

Are its citizens functioning as pioneers of ideas that could inspire and improve new universal social experiments, or is it merely an abstract set of ideas in contrast to a much messier reality? As long as Aurovilians are encapsulated in their idealistic utopianism, which lacks any sense of reality, could it bring about its own destruction, where everything that has been established from inside the community may be demolished by outside forces? It seems for some citizens that their grand vision of the past is gradually taken over by experts, developers, and city planners from the outside world. There is a sense of urgency to reach a form of agreement, but how can this be achieved? Do we need some other kind of leaders, as Mother predicted, or the pressure of court cases? Does this have a significant impact on today's problems? Nobody wants the relationship between the inhabitants of Auroville's project and the government to collapse into chaos in the future. Does Auroville's future need a renewed evaluation of Mother's traditional ideals in the context of concrete results in today's Auroville's existence? Only sincere devotion may imperceptibly evolve into religious devotion. The Mother was more concerned about the need for harmony and work in the spirit of collaboration rather than today's anti-institutional extremism. Both groups need leaders who support Mother's ideal, not their own well-intended vision. To solve this problem, there needs to be more space for a sense of urgency to come to some form of agreement and more space for negotiation, which does not seem very bright now; it can certainly happen, but not at this time.

Auroville has its limitations; the citizens face a set of forces that appear to grow in magnitude and are the cause that erodes the commitment to hold Auroville together as a successful community. The comprehensive spiritual ideology legitimates the demands on its citizens by reference to higher principles, a transcendent divine social order. However, it seems that the sadhak's superficial happiness is the new law of nature, scattering the Aurovilians as if they are back in their selfish world from which they came. The identification of material abundance and passive consumption with greed, selfishness, and even exploitation, how to overcome the side-effects of this productive surplus meant for the well-being of all humanity? Could more severe self-discipline and control of all forms of indulgence as a moral asceticism function as a more favourable condition rather than a condition to transcend?

Aurovilians do not merely aim for pragmatic results; they do not measure worldly success as a mature criterion of their effort. Nevertheless, the contesting citizens have to agree and specify where they want to go and how to get there. In the words of the Mother, "To be practical you must first have a clear vision of your goal, of where you are going... There is a long way to go between what we are and what we must be. And for that, we must be very flexible, never losing sight of the goal, but knowing that we cannot reach it at one bound and that we must find it. Well, that is much more difficult, even more difficult than to make the inner discovery. Truly speaking, that should have been made before coming here.... To have a life that wants to grow and perfect itself, that is what the collective ideal of Auroville shall be: A life that wants to grow and perfect itself, and above all, not in the same way for everyone, each one in his own way. Well, now there are 30 of you, it is difficult, isn't it? When there are 30 thousand of you, it will be easier because naturally there will be many more possibilities. You are pioneers, you have the most difficult task, but I feel it is the most interesting one. Because you must establish in a concrete, durable and growing way the attitude that is needed to truly be an Aurovilian." [10]

Though being overpowered by its immense bureaucratic organisation that has the power to control the community and the tendency that many of its citizens pursue their own private interests without much regard to the needs of the community and other unanticipated consequences of the actions of the citizens, such failures have not deteriorated the Aurovilians in their faith in the perfectibility of human nature and they continue to attempt to create a new social-spiritual environment for the betterment of man and society. Mistakes and failures in the Auroville experiment, where citizens work out the details of their growth toward the manifestation of the Divine, serve as helpful aids for general progress and lessons learned the hard way. Each failure indicates an inherent weakness and stimulates the striving mind towards a more sound attempt; as such, failures can be the gateway to new opportunities and may function as a catalyst for change. Sri Aurobindo describes failures as, "Failures must be originally numerous in everything great and difficult, but the time comes when the experience of past failures can be profitably used and the gate that so long resisted opens. In this, as in all great human aspirations and endeavours, a prior declaration of impossibility is a sign of ignorance and weakness.... The thing to be done is as large as human life, and therefore the individuals who lead the way will take all human life for their province. These pioneers will consider nothing as alien through them, nothing as outside their scope."[11] Each difficulty observed in the right spirit is a challenge and helps the sadhak to grow by overcoming the challenge. Auroville's experiment is a failure only if nothing useful is learned from it; its failures may lead to a necessary change and new opportunities. An attitude that Auroville fails is doomed to fail.

Faith, as a fundamental principle and a dynamic, intuitive conviction in Integral Yoga, must be free from attachment to the forms of the disciple's endeavour and the successive stages of their realisation. It is not a crude mental belief but the knowledge of the soul to the divine guide within, unlike belief as an aspect of the mind and intellect, which is more related to the cognitive contents of a religious belief. In contrast to the blind faith of inert passivity, dynamic faith needs the cultivation of personal effort in refusing doubt and scepticism. Doubt has its utility and necessity only in the lower knowledge to get out of an ignorant belief and to be able to escape from its errors. Perfect faith is an assent of the whole being to the truth seen by it, and its central working is the faith of the soul in its own will. The Mother did not ask for indiscriminate faith; all she asks is fundamental faith by quiet discrimination, a faith in the soul's witness to something not yet manifested, achieved or realised but which the Knower within us feels to be true. This faith in spiritual things is not an ignorant, blind faith called by the sceptical intellect because it refuses to be guided by outer appearances or seeming facts and does not walk on the crutches of proof, but it is an intuition which looks for the truth behind and leads the sadhak towards knowledge and experience.

For the Mother, faith is indispensable to man; he needs it to proceed forward in his journey through the unknown. However, does this mean that the practice of Integral Yoga and full faith in her total spiritual vision determine Auroville's success or failure? Suppose the sadhak's faith is rooted in emotional attachment rather than an assessment of evidence. In that case, a critical rational mind, uninitiated in the subject, will not contribute much to a fruitful debate about the flaws and hypocrisies in their integral practice. For an analyst, faith is often pitted against reason and entails periods of questioning about the distinction between belief and doubt, as well as resistance and surrender. Too much faith can be rather dangerous and can have disastrous consequences, as it may blur one's judgment and may end in fanaticism. The inadequacies of Aurovillians' professed faith in the perfectibility of man's nature, could this be traced by the errors committed in the hands of those who misused their faith, which has led to many absurdities?

This may not be a time to dream, but citizens have to deal with a kind of general exposure that is no longer deniable. After the denial stage is accepted, a new direction is possible in which it becomes a moral duty to transcend one's boundaries. The present problems of the lower nature and the city's past history are overwhelming it again. These difficulties can be faced or encountered in the accustomed way, with new expectations that may succeed or fail, but most likely will end in disillusionment again. What remains is a conservative, accustomed, non-renewed attitude that emphasises old memories and self-commiseration and celebrates what was. But the manner of approaching conflicts in this traditional way may not work any longer, and it is for this reason that Aurovilians have to try something different, not going around in fixed circles but moving to the centre of the city and then looking at roads outward and choose the way, i.e., incorporating the accumulated insights of the community and developing ways of dealing with conflicts in a renewed approach of consciousness-raising.

In the author's detailed analysis, he attempted to approach Auroville's crisis with a magnifying glass, and although his analysis may know a great deal about the conditions 'how' conflicts arise, he may know nothing about the inner situation of the Aurovilians when their values are shattered and how to find themselves again in a meaningful goal of their life. While being confronted by so many internal and external threats, would it not be unwise to busy Aurovilians, at this junction in Auroville's history, with something as vague as the psychic and supramental consciousness? As mentioned before, is only sustained practice without proper guidance able to overcome all kinds of habitual reactions of the confused parts of the lower nature? Though the Aurovilian end is driven by divine supramental ambitions, which keeps the devotee on the slippery path of spiritual practice, could it be that this firmness of purpose degenerates into obstinacy when errors in the practice of the devotees are not recognised, reconsidered and redressed? Are Aurovilians not opening their difficulties and pitfalls in the inner explorations of sadhana to outside evidence because it does not fit their prevailing convictions and belief system? Could the results of sympathetic outside investigations stimulate self-questioning regarding the practice of their sadhana, and could it affect transformation by bringing confronting results to the surface? A moment of truth arises when conclusions and bold positions may not be particularly pleasing to many Aurovilians.

From times immortal man has attempted scientific, social, psychological, political, religious, economic and moral reforms without exploring the heart of the Divine, leaving the instruments—mind, life and body—of the divine activity on earth to their imperfection, seeking to cure symptoms but not touching the roots of the diseased matters. Even though it is necessary to tackle these mundane matters first, these reformers don't dig deep enough, as the critical issue confronting mankind does not lie in outer conditions but in man's inner and higher consciousness. In challenging times, a turning point often arises when policy and opinions create space for a decisive change that would otherwise be impossible to implement. Auroville, as an intentional experimental community, is not a realised spiritual utopia but an experiment in progress to realise a new way of life. In the best-planned community, things go wrong, and it seems Auroville is not yet able to develop an effective system for resolving the polemic conflicts within the community. Auroville, as a laboratory envisioned by the Mother where Aurovilians could develop solutions to humanity's challenges, may require the recovery of citizens' true participation in a collective experimental field of evolution for humanity. One of the solutions Mother advises the Aurovilians is , "Each one has good reasons to support their own opinion, and I am not an expert to judge between them. But from the spiritual point of view, I know that with true goodwill, all opinions can be harmonised in a more comprehensive and truer solution. This is what I expect from the workers of Auroville. Not that some give way to others but that, on the contrary, all should combine their efforts to achieve a more comprehensive and perfect result.[12]

## Notes

1.) Sri Aurobindo; *The Life Divine*, p 1062

2.) Shyam Sundar Jhunjhunwala, *Message from the Mother*, 9 6-1971

3.) George van Vreckem; *Beyond Man*, p 418-420.

4.) Sri Aurobindo; *Essays Human and Divine*, p 149

5.) The Mother; *Collective Works of the Mother*, Vol 13, April 4

6.) The Mother; *Mother's Agenda*, p 354

7.) The Mother; *Collective Works of the Mother,* Vol 13, March 30

8.) Ibid., Vol 13 April 4

9.) The Mother; *Collective Works of the Mother*, Vol 13, p 227

10.) The Mother; The Mother on Auroville, p 91-92

11.) Sri Aurobindo; *The Human Cycle,* p 266

12.) The Mother; *Collective Works of the Mother*, Vol 13, p 221

# BIBLIOGRAPHY


Sri Aurobindo; Essays *Divine and Human*. Sri Aurobindo Ashram Publ, Pondicherry 1994.

Sri Aurobindo; *Essays in Philosophy and Yoga*. Sri Aurobindo Ashram Publ, Pondicherry, 2020.

Sri Aurobindo; *The Human Cycle*. Sri Aurobindo Ashram Publ, Pondicherry, 1992.

Sri Aurobindo; *The Life Divine*. Sri Aurobindo Publ. Pondicherry, 1970.

Sri Aurobindo; *The Synthesis of Yoga*. Sri Aurobindo Publ, Pondicherry, 1992.

Sri Aurobindo; *The Mother*. Sri Aurobindo Publ. Pondicherry, 2012.

Sri Aurobindo; *Letters on Yoga* Part I, II, and III, Sri Aurobindo Publ, Pondicherry. 1988.

Sri Aurobindo; *Letters on Yoga* Part IV. Sri Aurobindo Publ, Pondicherry 2015.

Sri Aurobindo; *Letters on Himself and the Ashram*. Sri Aurobindo Ashram Publ, Pondicherry 2011.

Sri Aurobindo; *The Hour of God*. Sri Aurobindo Ashram Publ, Pondicherry 1972.

Sri Aurobindo; *The Supramental Manifestation*. Sri Aurobindo Publication, Pondicherry, 1989.

Amrit; *Children of Change*; Prisma Publ, Auroville 2018.

Andre Beteille; *Anti-Utopia*. Oxford University Press, New Delhi, 2011.

Marie Louise Berneri; *Journey through Utopia*. Freedom Press, London, 1982.

Alfred Braunthal; *Salvation and the Perfect Society. The Eternal Quest*. The University of Massachusetts Press. Amherst, 1979.

Susan Love Brown; *Intentional community. An Anthropological Perspective*. State University of New York Press, New York, 2002.

G Bradford Delong; *Slouching towards Utopia. An Economic History of the 20th Century*, Basic Books, 2022.

Martin Buber; *Paths in Utopia*. Syracuse University Press, New York, 1996.

Nicolas Carr; *Utopia is creepy and other Provocations*. Northon and Company, New York, 2016.

D.P. Chattopadhyaya; *Sri Aurobindo and Karl Marx. Integral Sociology and Dialectical Sociology*. Motilal Banarsidass Publications, New Delhi, 1991.

E.M. Cioran; *History and Utopia*. Arcade Publ, New York, 1987.

Gregory Claes; *Utopianism for a Dying Planet. Life after consumerism*. Princeton University Press, New Jersey, 2022.

Dan Chodorkoff; *An Anthropology of Utopia: on social ecology and community development*. New Compass Press 2014

Nell Eurich; *Science in Utopia. A Mighty Design*. Harvard University Press, Cambridge, Massachusetts, 1967.

A Grandcolas: *Experience of the Psychic Being and its growth*. Prisma Auroville, 2017.

David Greaber; *The Utopia of Rules. On Technology, Stupidity and the Secret Joys of Bureaucracy.* Melville House Publication, New York, 2015.

Gilles Guigan; *Auroville in Mother's words Part I and II*. Auroville Publ press, Auroville 2018.

Elisabeth Hansot; *Perfection and Progress*. The M.I.T Press, Cambridge 1974.

Peter Heehs; *The Many Lives of Sri Aurobindo*. Columbia University Press, New York, 2008.

Russell Jacobi; *Picture Imperfect. Utopian Thought for an Ant-Utopian Age*, Columbia University Press, New York, 2005.

Chris Jennings, *Paradise Now. The Story of American Utopianism*. Random House, New York, 2017.

S. S Jhunjhunwala, *Down Memory Lane*, Shri Aurobindo Ashram Press, Pondicherry, 1966.

Clint Jones/ Cameron, Ellis, *The Individual and Utopia. A multi-disciplinary Study of Humanity and Perfection*. Routledge Publ. New York, 2020.

Rosabeth Moss Kanter; *Commitment and Community, communes and Utopias in Sociological perspective,* Harvard University Press, Cambridge, 1972.

Akash Kapur, *Auroville, Dream and Reality: An Anthology,* Penguin Random House, Gurgaon, 2018.

Akash Kapur; *Better to Have Gone; Auroville Love, Death and the quest for Utopia a review*. Laugh Das and the Quest for Utopia. Scribner, London, 2021.

Krishan Kumar; *Utopianism,* Open University Press, Buckingham, 1991.

Krishan Kumar; *Utopia and anti-utopia in modern times.* Blackwell publication, Oxford, 1987.

Melvine. J. Lasky. *Utopia and Revolution. On the origins of a Metaphor.* Routledge. Oxfordshire. 2004.

Ruth Levitas*; The Concept of Utopia*. Phillip Allen Publishers. Hertfordshire, 1990.

Karl Mannheim; *Ideology and Utopia. An Introduction to the Sociology of Knowledge*. Routledge and Kegan Paul. Reprinted London 1968.

Anna Meina; *The Utopians*, Picador, London 2021.

Jessica Namakkal; *Unsettling Utopia; The making and unmaking of French India*. Columbia University Press, New York, 2021.

Anu Majumdar*; Auroville; a City of the Future.* Harper Collins, India, 2017.

A Maslow; *The Farther Reaches of Human Nature.* The Viking Press. New York, 1968.

William McCord; *Voyages to Utopia; From Monastery to Commune-the search for the perfect society in modern times.* Northon and Company, New York, 1989.

Robert Minor*; The Religious, The Spiritual and the Secular.* Sunny Press, New York, 1999.

Tom Moylan; *Demand the Impossible; Science Fiction and Utopian Imagination*, Peter Lang Publications, Bern, 2012.

The Mother; *Collective Works of the Mother, Volume 13*. Sri Aurobindo Trust, Pondicherry. 1972.

The Mother; *Notes on the Way,* Sri Aurobindo Publications. Pondicherry, 2020.

The Mother on Auroville; Sri Aurobindo Ashram, Pondicherry 1999.

Jugal, Kishore Mukherjee; *The Practice of Integral Yoga*. Sri Aurobindo Trust, Pondicherry 2003.

Timothy Miller, *The Sixties Communes, Hippies and Beyond*. Syracuse University Press, New York, 1999.

Lewis, Mumford; *The Story of Utopias*. Pinnacle Press, Hayward, 2017.

Satprem; *The Mother's Agenda volume 1 to 13*. Mira Aditi Centre, Mysore (English Edition) 2000.

Lucy Sargisson and Layman T. Sargent, *Living Utopia,* Routledge Publication, New York, 2016.

L.Tower Sargent/ Gregory Claes; *Utopian Reader*, New York University Press, New York, 1999.

L. Tower Sargeant. *Utopianism. A Very Short Introduction*. Oxford University Press, New York, 2010.

Rebecca Solnit: *A Paradise Built in Hell*. Penguin Books India, New Delhi, 2009.

Anthony Storr; *Feet of Clay: A Study of Gurus*. Harper and Collins. London, 1996.

Fritz Staal; *Exploring Mysticism*. Penguin Books. Middlesex, 1975.

Joseph Vrinte, *The Perennial Quest for a Psychology with a Soul. An inquiry into the relevance of Sri Aurobindo's Metaphysical Yoga Psychology and Ken Wilber's Integral Psychology*, Motilal Banarsidass Publication, New Delhi, 2002.

Joseph Vrinte; *Reflections upon Psycho-spiritual Obstacles in Sri Aurobindo's Integral Yoga*, Motilal Banarsidass, New Delhi, 2022

George van Vreckem; *The Mother:* The Story of her Life, Rupa Publications, New Delhi, 2004.

George van Vreckem; *Beyond Man*: The Life and Work of Shri Aurobindo and the Mother, Harper and Collins, New Delhi. 1997.

David Yount*; America's spiritual utopias: The quest for Heaven on Earth*. Praeger Publ, London, 2008.

# INDEX